Additional Praise for *The End of Ethics*

"Ted Malloch and Jordan Mamorsky have astutely zeroed in on the critical importance of virtue in the marketplace and its opposite, economic vice. Those companies whose management teams are intentionally 'values-driven' retain a significant, long-term advantage over their peers. As one successful company wisely stated, 'Integrity—in every sense of the word—defines how we take on the world's challenges. It is the reason for our success.' Thank you, Ted and Jordan, for your inspired and insightful treatise on business ethics."

—Carter LeCraw, CEO, American Values Investments

"Messrs. Malloch and Mamorsky have looked into the abyss of the dark side of man and paint a picture of hope that this wakeup call is for real! Denial, complacency, and fear have to be conquered and it is well overdue that the good guys stand up and shout to be heard against the global disaster of greed and self-interest. The book lays out the battle between good and evil that results from man having a choice on how to behave. The challenge is who and how many will stand to be counted?"

—Stephen Clark, former Chief Executive, Gerard Asset Management

"*The End of Ethics* is the most important book to come out this year. With potential global financial collapse on the horizon this book is a wakeup call to examine the root of the problem and to take action in ways that are in alignment with what is most virtuous in humanity. Malloch and Mamorsky know what they are talking about and this book provides the inspiration to take action, and offers specifics on what needs to be done."

—Judi Neal, PhD, Director, Tyson Center, Sam M. Walton
College of Business, University of Arkansas

"This is a courageous book that needed to be written and deserves to be widely read. The authors set forth a compelling indictment of abuses that nearly led to financial catastrophe. Not only do they thoroughly document the problem, they show us a solution: the conscientious road to future prosperity."

—Theodore Becker, JD, PhD, National Trial Attorney
peer-rated AV Preeminent by Martindale Hubbell

"Morality in the market is often marginalized or ignored but this book uses compelling real-life examples to move it center stage. Read it with close attention to detail!"

—*Peter S. Heslam, MA, BA, DPhil, FRSA, Director,*
Transforming Business, University of Cambridge, UK

"Many people are looking for the lessons to be learned from the financial crisis. However, before we turn to the lessons learned, we need to explore what went wrong in the first place. This is exactly what Malloch does in *The End of Ethics* by peeling off—layer for layer—the dark side of the financial sector. This results in a most detailed and insightful overview of financial cases of obvious fraud, gambling with other people's money, and governance failures. Based on these insights, they propose important, concrete measures on the organizational and systemic level to restore ethics as an integral part of the business. A must read for everyone who wants to understand what happened in the recent financial crisis."

—*André Nijhof, PhD, Professor, European Institute for Business Ethics,*
Nyenrode Business Universiteit, The Netherlands

"*The End of Ethics and a Way Back* provides an in-depth discussion of the causes of the present state of audits and disgust with governments and their agencies, public interest, and even uprisings, grass-roots political movements, and reforms throughout the world. Ted Malloch and Jordan Mamorsky, the authors, have captured the root cause of these occurrences—the end of ethics and a decline in the spiritual foundation—through documented examples and real cases. The book concludes with a useful fiduciary audit."

—*Robert D. Hisrich, PhD, Garvin Professor of Global Entrepreneurship;*
Director, Walker Center for Global Entrepreneurship,
Thunderbird School of Global Management, Arizona

"Dr. Malloch and Mr. Mamorsky address the fundamental issue at the core of our economic and corporate malaise: the end of ethics. We know that an economy is ultimately the sum of the qualities of its people. An individual, company or economy that lacks values or virtue will produce little of lasting value and in fact over time destroy wealth, as pointed out in this book. Malloch's recommendations, given our predicament, provide a viable way forward because they focus on the reality that we should and cannot expect an economic renewal, without a deeper renewal. This rebirth must start with each of us and then permeate into all of life."

—*Jonathan M. Wellum, CEO, ROCKLINC Investment Partners, Canada*

"*The End of Ethics* provides an urgent, timely message about the consequences of pervasive self-interest and reckless decision-making within the global financial system. Above all, it reminds us that future wealth creation must be aligned with a better understanding of societal purpose, not profit maximization alone if we are to avoid a repeat of the financial calamity of 2008."

—*Simon Pickard, Secretary General, Academy of Business in Society, Brussels*

"Ted Malloch describes the ethics dilemma of vices *versus* virtues which always has existed from time memorial. As the global stakeholders get smarter, 'A Way Back' seems to describe the 'Harmonious Society' that balances the best of both and leads us to a brighter future."

—*Sam Yoonsuk Lee, CEO, InnoCSR, Shanghai, China*

"The pursuit of liberty and profit may not ignore the crucial importance of moral foundations without great damage to society as this volume so ably demonstrates from a rich acquaintance with historical and contemporary sources."

—*Luder G. Whitlock, Jr., President, Excelsis Foundation, Florida*

"For decades, the message prevailed that in modern times 'moral sentiments' are to be replaced by government regulations, compliance management, and incentive schemes: It's the institutions, stupid! Malloch's *The End of Ethics* in a lively fashion shows where we got with such an approach. By delegating ethics to 'social engineers' we destroyed self-regulating civic forces including their esteem for virtues and practical wisdom. Let's revamp the corporate culture so that the tears resulting from that cultural experiment are not shed in vain!"

—*Prof. André Habisch, Catholic University Business School, Ingolstadt; regularly works for the German Bundestag.*

"Malloch and Mamorsky paint a vivid picture of traditionally prudent companies and markets overrun by inflated egos and greed and characterized by a web of conflicts of interest that undermine internal controls, accurate ratings, and regulatory oversight. Beyond describing a cast of characters who are exemplars of vice, they offer hope by providing compelling suggestions for restoring virtue to companies and the markets."

—*Mitchell J. Neubert, PhD, Chavanne Chair of Christian Ethics in Business; Associate Professor of Management and Entrepreneurship, Hankamer School of Business, Baylor University, Texas*

"The overriding message of *The End of Ethics* is this—good ethics is foundational to good business and bad ethics is the polar opposite. Unethical business behavior inevitably results in a failure of governance and to the financial demise of an individual, a company, or even the entire financial system. This extremely readable book is a 'must read' for anyone considering or involved in a career in business."

—*Gerald D. Facciani, former President, American Society of Pension Actuaries*

"*The End of Ethics and a Way Back* is a tightly written account of the recent ethical foibles in finance. It's also a clarion call to college and business school educators to equip our students with an enduring moral compass—or else they too will fall to the vices of greed, avarice, and corruption."

—*Dr. Arthur Schwartz, Executive Director, Oskin Leadership Institute, Widener University*

The End of Ethics
and a Way Back

The End of Ethics

and a Way Back

How to Fix a Fundamentally Broken Global Financial System

Theodore Roosevelt Malloch
Jordan D. Mamorsky

WILEY

Other Wiley Editorial Offices
John Wiley & Sons, 111 River Street, Hoboken, NJ 07030, USA
John Wiley & Sons, The Atrium, Southern Gate, Chichester, West Sussex, P019 8SQ,
    United Kingdom
John Wiley & Sons (Canada) Ltd., 5353 Dundas Street West, Suite 400, Toronto, Ontario,
    M9B 6HB, Canada
John Wiley & Sons Australia Ltd., 42 McDougall Street, Milton, Queensland 4064, Australia
    Wiley-VCH, Boschstrasse 12, D-69469 Weinheim, Germany

ISBN 978-1-118-55017-5 (Cloth)
ISBN 978-1-118-55022-9 (ePDF)
ISBN 978-1-118-55026-7 (Mobi)
ISBN 978-1-118-55027-4 (ePub)

Typeset in 11.5/14 pt. Bembo by MPS Limited, Chennai, India
Printed in Singapore by Ho Printing Singapore Pte Ltd

10 9 8 7 6 5 4 3 2 1

Contents

Foreword

First delivered as a speech by Sir John Marks Templeton[1]

E very economic system is built on a spiritual foundation. This foundation can be found in the personal ethics of the people that make up the economy. And it can be found in the economic system itself, which is an outgrowth of personal values.

As we know, the economy is about trading material goods and services. Yet trade is made possible only by agreement on what is mine and what is thine. These are essentially ethical concerns.

To even talk about the economy, there must be agreement about the rules of play. To get those rules, we must have some sense of fair dealing.

Where does this sense of fair play come from? It comes through reference to an ethical order outside of ourselves and beyond our own times. In short, by reference to the transcendent. The transcendent is the beginning of economics.

---

[1]The Religious Foundation of Liberty and Enterprise, Buena Vista College, March 1993.

In the same way, a spiritual and religious system requires a material context in order to have full meaning. Although the choice of poverty can be virtuous, when poverty is imposed by a brutal regime it distracts from spiritual pursuits.

The ethics that govern an economy must be secure and meaningful, and they must match our highest spiritual aspirations if we want our economy to meet society's needs. If people cannot see meaning beyond material accumulation, even a prosperous and efficient economy lacks an ultimate purpose.

Most people agree today that society has lost much of its spiritual moorings. We no longer have enough collective sense of our responsibilities to each other. Not surprisingly, such problems are reflected in the behavior of consumers, businessmen, policy makers, and the economy at large.

What, then, are the vices and virtues of our modern economy, as judged by the standards set for us by religious faiths? There are many valid opinions on this vital subject.

We would like to present five of the most conspicuous economic vices and virtues and we'll begin with the vices. When these vices proliferate in private life and are institutionalized in society, they can cause social disarray. Until they are addressed, amounts of technical changes are not going to help.

The first economic vice I will discuss is *envy*. Envy has been a concern of philosophers and theologians from the ancients to the present. It has always existed. And it has been a personal and social menace wherever it has appeared.

Cicero defined envy as "sadness caused at the happiness of others, and a certain joy . . . at the misery of others." He thought envy could be a feeling of pleasure when bad things happen to others. Or it can be a feeling of pain when good things happen to others. In its worst form, it can be a desire to destroy what another has gained simply because he has gained it.

Plato said, "to feel oneself overpowered by envy, whether or not it causes damage to others, is . . . unjust." St. Augustine condemned envy as "hate at the happiness of others."

Dante, in his poem of the afterlife, places the envious in the second circle of Purgatory, where the condemned say: "I was happier with the pain of another than with my own happiness."

Clement, a father of the early Church, tells us that envy is the root of many evils in history. Because of envy, he said, Cain killed his brother Abel, Jacob had to take flight, Joseph was sent into slavery, Moses had to leave his people, Aaron was set aside, Dathoan and Abiron were condemned, and Saul and David were at war. Envy, he said, fueled the persecutions of the Apostles, the suffering of St. Peter, and the death of martyrs.

Envy has existed in all societies and in all times. On the personal level, it is a corrosive force that is at odds with the goal of sanctification. To feel joy when others suffer leads to indecencies, which morally compromise us. When institutionalized in government, it can dramatically change the way we save, invest, and earn our livelihoods.

Ironically, the temptation toward envy is intensified in a society with a great deal of freedom. Under an older system of rigid class distinctions, people might tend to blame an unfortunate plight on forces outside their control. In a democratic market society, with more personal responsibility and more individual obligations, personal shortcomings are more evident and envy an even greater temptation.

We must guard against it, in part, because envy can blur the boundaries of private property. When the boundaries of private property are gone, so too go many of the moral rules of society. The social conscience is affected and vice becomes more generally practiced.

For example, economic redistribution for its own sake can represent an outgrowth of envy. Society has a responsibility to the poor, but remember that envy often disguises itself as charity or justice. Helping the poor, not harming the rich, should be the true intention of any such program. Furthermore, if a government program fails to live up to its stated aims, and creates big bureaucracies instead of rising prosperity, then it should be reevaluated. Politicians should be keeping envy at bay and not fueling it through ill-advised rhetoric.

We all know about the concept of the *evil eye*, that hateful and drilling look given to another. It is often considered a curse of sorts. We may laugh at it today, but medieval theologians took the issue very seriously. St. Thomas said the evil eye's "poisonous and harmful look" was the physical manifestation of envy. The evil eye and envy are linked linguistically. They both derive from the Latin word meaning to see ["videre" (to see) and "invidere" (envy)]. Unfortunately, the "evil eye" can persist even in many enlightened people.

A culture of envy is incompatible with civilized behavior. We should take joy in others' joy and never take pleasure in another's suffering. And we should never wish harm on those who achieve. No economy can thrive and serve people so long as it is encouraged by a social ethics and social policy that is based on envy.

A related economic vice is greed. Because of greed, the modern form of capitalism is often too hedonistic and unethical, and too far removed from traditional values. This meaning of the term *greed* is more vague than envy. At the very least, it suggests an inordinate longing for material wealth.

It is not the acquisition of material wealth itself that constitutes greed. The desire for wealth becomes inordinate when it leads to value wealth accumulation above all else.

This can be done in our private lives. We can make a new car a priority over spending time with our young children or our elderly parents. Instead of helping a neighbor in need, we may choose to buy something entirely frivolous. These choices are the consequences of greed.

Let me make myself clear. It is not wrong to better our lot. In a theological context, greed occurs when the desire for material acquisition clouds our vision of spiritual matters that should reign supreme.

In ancient literature, greed is often, and rightly, used as a synonym for covetousness. The feeling of covetousness is the longing for things lawfully owned by others. The biblical commandment (do not covet) speaks not of material desire but in the abstract, but covetousness of a neighbor's property. The concept of greed is bound up with our behavior toward our neighbors.

The economic vice of covetousness is not to want more than you already own; instead, it is the desire for property that is not properly yours. Biblical commentators suggest that the sin of covetousness is not only an inner impulse. It is also an action that attempts to attach something to oneself illegally. It means to desire and to take.

This economic vice is a source of many crimes, public and private. It can also turn up in bad personal habits, like accumulating too much debt or going on buying sprees to improve self-image. If our image of ourselves is tied to what we own, that can be a symptom of greed.

It is not wrong to desire property that you intend to acquire peacefully through exchange. In any voluntary economic exchange, both parties benefit. Covetousness and greed are wrong because they express a desire for property that cannot and should not be yours. It is to desire and to seek what is forbidden.

To be sure, the sin of greed or covetousness is not only personal. It can be institutional. Government can be and often is as guilty of greed as individuals are. It can desire ever more of the people's property when it should not. If too much is taken, an economy cannot function efficiently or effectively. Government greed can lead to taking away the authorities of church and family, which are the mediating institutions of society.

An additional economic vice is *pride*. Every businessperson who has to work in an economy knows this temptation. It often occurs on the occasion of business success. The economy is up, and so is the firm's public profile. Profits are up and investors are on your side. It seems that nothing can go wrong—and yet it eventually does. The market economy has a way of punishing the economic vice of pride.

Every successful entrepreneur is a servant. He must be oriented to matters outside of himself. He has to look to consumers and their needs. He must rely on their voluntary patronage to bring about his goals. That is service.

But pride is something different. It is inward looking. It forgets about serving others and becomes selfish. Pride is not the key to success under free enterprise. When the business owner becomes too internal, she loses her customer base and ceases to anticipate the future. She loses profits and, if wise, learns a valuable lesson at the same time.

As Proverbs chapter 13, verse 11, says, "Wealth gotten by vanity shall be diminished: but he that gathereth by labor shall increase."

The vice of pride has deep roots. It is the belief that men can fully and successfully control the world without the aid of God. Just as the business can forget whom it is serving, people can forget about their need to serve God.

There was a time in the 1930s when many American economists came to believe they could entirely plan the economy. Working out of an office in Washington, they could determine what would be produced, when it would be produced, who would consume it, the price of everything, and the cost of everything.

This theory said the economy could be made "rational," but it was really just the sin of pride applied to economic policy. The belief that these individuals' decisions can be fully planned by government is folly.

When the vice of pride becomes entrenched in government, we find the government assuming functions that is not capable of doing well.

The first economic virtue is the ability to cooperate. That simply means getting along with others.

Cooperation is not a word we tend to associate with capitalism. Since at least the turn of the century, we have tended to associate capitalism with dog-eat-dog competition. That is a grave error, for the overwhelming amount of activity of capitalism is people cooperating with other people.

Think about our daily activities. Consumers cooperate with producers at every economic exchange, from the local fruit stand to the trading floor at Wall Street. Each person involved in the exchange is giving up something for something of great value. When I spend two dollars for a carton of milk, both the grocer and I come out ahead. That is the virtue of cooperation.

Employees cooperate with employers. They come together to make a deal, and the terms of the agreement are expressed in a wage or a salary. Each is using his or her respective talents in a way that fits the desires of others.

Cooperation is a virtue essential to every economy. Through it, the baker is not concerned with plowing land, sowing seeds, weeding the ground, or cutting, threshing, and milling the wheat. The baker comes together with others who do that. He need only bake and to offer it to others.

We tend to think of capitalism as being solely competitive because we treat capitalism as if it is a modern invention. But capitalism did not begin with Protestant Reformation or the Industrial Revolution. While these events had great effect on economic development over the centuries, the capitalist institutions of property, trade, and cooperation have always been with us.

Cooperation occurs not only in enterprise. It also occurs in our voluntary associations where no monetary profit is involved. These are what Tocqueville saw long ago as America's greatest strength, but his point applies everywhere. These associations make life more pleasing, help us care for others in need, and help to form common bonds of culture and values.

It is one of the virtues of capitalism that it insists on cooperation. If we become more aware of this and become better at getting along with others, we create a better and more productive economy.

The second economic virtue is that of *creativity*. This is another word for entrepreneurship. It is the ability to imagine possibilities that have yet to come into existence.

Long before business owners realize a profit, they must take a risk in an uncertain future. They put their own resources on the line. They pay wages before they get any personal benefit. They must have the capacity to discern the unmet needs of others and attempt to meet them.

From the economic point of view, the virtue of creativity is the most important cause of wealth in society. It introduces new goods and services. It helps us to use our resources more effectively. It creates jobs and raises our living standards. It is the key to bringing the world from poverty to prosperity.

Of course, creativity demands the freedom to act. Wherever people are left free to exercise their creative capacities, the wealth of societies will grow.

Millions of new businesses appear every year. But where enterprise is hindered, both prosperity and human liberty suffer. The society will stagnate. People will not be able to fulfill the biggest potential.

In the book *Ethics*, Aristotle saw the need for allowing for creativity. He also added a related virtue of *emulation*. This is the ability to learn from others' ability to create. Emulation, says Aristotle, is a "good feeling felt by good persons . . . . Emulation makes us take steps to secure the good things in question," whereas he says, "Envy makes us take steps to stop our neighbor from having them."

Economic progress is in part driven by both the virtue of creativity and the related virtue of emulation. Success in a market economy comes from improving the degree of efficiency in the way goods, services, and labor are used. And others' success at this can induce us toward right ambition. It leads us to seek entrepreneurial gain and to find better ways of doing things, making us better and more productive members of society.

The third economic virtue is *charity*. Profit and exchange alone are not enough to sustain the good in society. We need to care for those in society who cannot care for themselves. At a minimum, that means giving attention to children and the aged who cannot care for themselves.

It is one of the tragedies of modern life that this is often forgotten. Some young people no longer feel the need to return the charity of their parents by caring for them in later years. This is a direct violation of God's commandment to honor our mothers and fathers.

We cannot help but be encouraged by the extraordinary generosity that leads American people to contribute billions to charitable causes every year. The most generous societies that have ever existed are also the freest. Why? A free economy fosters the wealth and the sense of responsibility that leads to charity. The Bible says (Luke 6:38), "Give and it will be given unto you."

This has been recognized at least since Aristotle, who said in the Politics that: "The abolition of private property will mean that no man will be seen to be liberal and no man will ever so any act liberality; for it is in the use of articles of property that liberality is practiced."

We see evidence of this in the societies that experimented with the abolition of private property. Collective ownership fostered nothing but mutual suspicion and greed. Visitors from the old East Bloc routinely comment on how generous and charitable people from capitalist countries are. This, needless to say, contradicts what socialist leaders told them about the West.

The virtue of charity recognizes that none of us are the ultimate owners of private property, for God is the ultimate owner and master of all our resources. We are merely stewards of it. It is by being obedient stewards that we can best practice the economic virtue of charity.

Just as there are many ways to be charitable, there are many ways people can contribute to society. That is why we need to be able to understand the fast pace at which society changes, to roll with the punches, be willing to change, and understand the fourth economic virtue: the virtue of *adaptability*.

The state of the world is never static and never homogenous. Every day is unique and requires a unique response from all of us. Entrepreneurs respond to this uniqueness by always evaluating investments and current concerns. They are ready and eager to meet changing circumstances.

The consumer, too, must be eager and adjust to modern realities. Laborers need to understand that they cannot always get the kind of salaries they want or the particular job they want.

Most of us, at some point in our lives, will suffer disappointments, get fired from a job, have our wages cut, or be asked to make undesirable career moves. We may be called to change our occupations or undergo some kind of retraining. We must learn to adapt. New challenges help us to grow.

The world is a world of endless diversity, and therein lies its essential beauty. There is no need to long for what has passed. Rather, we must welcome progress and attempt to make the world the best place it can be.

In confronting our economy, we must strike the right balance between the arrogant desire to mold everyone that surrounds us to our own image and the equal and oppose error of fatalism and resignation.

Businesses must learn to hire and promote new and different types of people to serve new kinds of clientele, to look at new and different ways of doing things. It's a virtue to learn to welcome progress and turn the occasion into a blessing.

People with an extraordinary amount of ambition will always have special difficulties with the virtue of adaptability. Why? Because there will always be someone out there with more talent, more drive, and even more ambition. If these people can learn to welcome this and adapt, they can lead better and more satisfied lives.

How can we do all this? How can we learn to practice the virtue of adaptability? We must learn to celebrate changes, differences, surprises, and diversity as attributes of beauty.

Ridding ourselves of the economic vices and adopting the economic virtue of adaptability, we should strive to see the complex world as a place of increasing beauty and opportunity. George Santayana described it this way in his book *The Life of Reason*:

Variety in the world is an unmixed blessing so long as each distinct function can be exercised without hindrance to any other. For it is the presence of variety, and a nearer approach somewhere to just and ideal achievement, that gives men perspective in their judgment and opens vistas from the dull foreground of their lives to sea, mountain and stars.

The final economic virtue is the most important: it is integrity. In the Old Testament, we find many references to the uses of property. Most deal with the ethics of its use. And the rules all come down to personal integrity. Pay your debts. Don't cheat your neighbor. Don't use false weights and measures. Keep your financial commitments.

Not paying one's debts is a form of stealing. The creditor who extends a service is making a contract. Not paying that creditor on the agreed terms is a violation of contract. It takes another's property without rightly restoring it in the agreed upon time.

Similarly, laborers should practice diligence in their work habits. Goofing off, too, is a form of theft, just as hard work is the practice of exercising integrity.

St. Paul enjoins us to "render therefore to all their dues: tribute to whom tribute is due, custom to whom custom, fear to whom fear, honor to whom honor" (Romans 13:7).

An individual who makes too many promises and cannot keep them all is not acting with integrity. But a person who keeps commitments and deals honestly with others is practicing this fifth economic virtue of integrity.

The market economy depends for its survival on the personal integrity of those acting within it. People that don't act with integrity are also punished by the mechanism of the market. Credit will not be extended, for example.

Governments, too, can practice the virtue of integrity. We have gotten used to governments that run high deficits. Every day we hear about politicians that do not tell the truth about the state of the nation's finances. Inflating the currency away through unsound political practices is a form of changing weights and measures.

An economically virtuous government will not do these things. Instead, it will insist on practicing the kind of integrity that religious faith expects from individuals.

Nothing can kill economic liberty like a widespread lack of personal integrity. Over time, people stop trusting others. When you cannot trust your neighbor, you cannot trade with your neighbor. Enterprise comes to a halt.

But when people do what they say they will do, and deal honestly, then you have a moral foundation for economic growth. The society can then flourish economically and morally.

That concludes our list of economic vices and virtues. Though they reflect ancient standards, standards most religions throughout history have agreed upon, no society has ever perfectly put them into practice. That is because we live in an imperfect world, and we always will. Still, it is the social purpose of religion to point us to higher values, just as it is the private purposes of religion to improve our souls.

Just because economics and religion are controversial areas does not mean we should not talk about them. As we undertake the enormous human enterprise of commerce and distribution and the necessary exercise of foresight, honesty, and diligence, let us never forget the attitudes and conduct required by our being children of God.

If we do our very best, our Lord can say to each of us, "Well done, thou good and faithful servant." Then we will witness also the flowering of our economy and civilization.

Sir John Marks Templeton

Acknowledgments

When Daniel Bell penned *The Cultural Contradictions of Capitalism* in 1976 he was on to something. He wrote:

> When the Protestant ethic was sundered from bourgeois society, only the hedonism remained, and the capitalist system lost its transcendental ethic . . . While the business corporation wants its employees to work hard, pursue a career, and delay gratification, at the same time its products and advertisements promote the vision of pleasure, instant joy, relaxing, and letting go. One is to be "straight" by day and a "swinger" by night. This is self-fulfillment and self-realization.

Evagrius Ponticus, a fourth-century Christian monk and ascetic, drafted the *logismoi*, a thoughtful primer on eight evil temptations that have the potential to transform a virtuous man into a sinner.

The *logismoi* was intended to instruct. Ponticus wanted to ensure that people were aware of temptation, vice, and identification of their fallibility. With similar intentions, in 590 A.D. Pope Gregory the Great refined the *logismoi* to a list of seven. From then on, the seven deadly sins were formally established.

Fast-forward to today and we have a postmodern culture, where the public vocabulary no longer is keenly aware of the teachings of the *logismoi*. On a worldwide cultural level, we lack the urgency to maintain consistent standards of virtue and ethics.

Our MBA students, some of the best and brightest on the planet, actually ask in courses on business ethics, "What is virtue?" They seem to know the vices a bit better, thanks to trashy TV shows, debauched films, and the damage of everyday life. They generally, however, do still see something slightly wrong with fraud, Ponzi schemes, theft, and cheating but they can't quite put their finger on why.

As recent surveys show, students (even at top Ivy League schools) and people everywhere don't mind a little lying or stealing. It is accepted in order to get ahead, since nearly everyone does it, anyway.

This book is about how we have lost virtue in our society, why it matters, and what the arc of trust provides in markets. It takes a close look at the worst of the worst cases of economic vice.

But it is not about just a glass that is half empty. It is about refilling the glass—that is the core of this book. Without all of our diligent efforts at the personal, corporate, cultural, and societal levels, we will fall further into the abyss. It is about restoring the radius of trust, overcoming the Bell thesis, and regaining what Wilhelm Ropke argued in his seminal work on *The Humane Economy*; namely, the fact that without honesty and trust the market degenerates and our economy (now global in nature) will spin out of control.[1]

This book grew out of a lifetime of thinking and work experiences. We both witnessed what appeared at first to be the misdeeds of a "few rotten apples" but in the last decade spawned a devastating global credit crisis. The problem is now systemic. That troubles us, deeply.

We need to thank all who taught us along the way, and especially Yale University, where one of us is a research professor and the other was a hard-working legal scholar and postdoctoral research fellow. We also would like to thank Stefan Skeen and Gerry Dfacciani for their most helpful edits in writing this book. Any errors are ours.

The Spiritual Capital Initiative at Yale has been our home, and the John Templeton Foundation has graciously supported our efforts in case writing, public speaking, and research over the past three years. Jack Templeton, MD, Barnaby Marsh, and Kimon Sargeant, our grant program officer, have been most helpful in their time and support, and we thank them profusely. It was, truth be known, Sir John Templeton himself, the great twentieth century investor and philanthropist, who engaged me over 15 years ago at his home on Lyford Cay, the Bahamas, and challenged me to take up this task.

   This work is fully dedicated to our loving parents. Ted and Dorothy, now deceased, were truly great exemplars of virtue, that anyone would be fortunate to copy, and Jeffrey and Debra, who teach us to reach for the stars and follow our passions with deep conviction, love and grace.

New Haven, Connecticut
2013

Note

1. Wilhelm Ropke, "A Humane Economy, The Social Framework of the Free Market," October 1, 2008, Intercollegiate Studies Institute.

Introduction

In the aftermath of the worst financial crisis since the Great Depression, there has not been a work that comprehensively addresses the systemic root causes of a global recession that has had a profound domino effect, including worldwide public unrest, grassroots political movements, Dodd–Frank reforms, government agency audits, and general disgust with Wall Street corporate excess.

The groundswell of public anger against the perceived evils on Wall Street and the financial markets has been extraordinary. Not since the Vietnam War has the United States rapidly mobilized behind a cause in such a passionate manner. Between the conservative Tea Party movement and the left-leaning Occupy Wall Street protests, "Main Street" has found a convenient scapegoat for all that ails the US economy and society as a whole.

Is it really right to blame only those Wall Street "criminals?" What is structurally wrong with our entire system, culture, and ethical notions as a society? Has it lost its original moorings and morphed into managerial or crony capitalism where managers can routinely loot their firms without reprisal or prosecution?

Defects in our societal moral fabric have produced financial swindlers, perhaps more evident than ever before. For example, Bernie Madoff and Tom Petters stole billions of dollars from everyday Americans as if it was standard business process to do so.

CEOs such as Jon Corzine, Jimmy Cayne, and Dick Fuld presided over the demise of proud international banking institutions. They allowed druglike addictions to boom or bust synthetic derivatives to marginalize risk management procedures and ultimately result in a massive overdose: the very destruction of their companies.

Others such as Tyco CEO Dennis Kozlowski and WorldCom CEO Bernie Ebbers were so tragically obsessed with retaining power and keeping their gravy train of profits moving that they lied to their investors and markets with inflated financial statements.

These collapses, scandals, and crimes demonstrate an ethical decay never seen before in global history.

"Main Street" expects its CEOs, Fortune 500 companies, and private equity firms to hit "home runs" on a daily basis. Unfortunately, no matter how much quantitative acumen and market awareness an investment manager may retain, no Wall Street all-star can consistently hit the ball over the fence for investors and shareholders. Sometimes, they strike out. Inevitable losses are part and parcel of a capitalist economy.

However, to appease investors and shareholders, executives have turned to the proverbial performance-enhancing drugs: what we will call *economic vice*. Economic vice produces artificial home runs for shareholders and creates unrealistic market expectations.

The saturation of economic vice in our culture is why this book is titled *The End of Ethics*. On a systemic level, the allure of vice has captured the human spirit. On Wall Street, traders concoct complex structured credit derivative products with the sole goal of making excess cash to increase the short-term bottom line. On Main Street, investors clamor for enhanced returns to fuel a continuing addiction to real and personal credit.

Prior to the real estate bubble, there was not a Tea Party movement nor an Occupy Wall Street protest capturing the eye of cable and network news—only homeowners who signed mortgages they could not afford. The failure of citizens and investors to demonstrate accountability through their own due diligence has only intensified recent financial calamities. Ponzi schemes victimize new and old investors alike because investors do not raise red flags when they see consistent unrealistic returns they are glad to stuff into their wallets.

On the other hand, overwhelming pressure is placed on modern-day corporations. Heroics are expected in quarterly conference calls announcing earnings. Cable news talking heads dissect every stock movement, every executive business judgment and movement. Without warning, a company's reputation on the "street" can take a nose-dive. Counterparty liquidity can evaporate in seconds. Reputations must be delicately cultivated and protected. In order to do so, more and more corporations turn to economic vice.

As a result, we are witnessing the end of ethics.

Firms have not only shifted or lost their sense of judgment but have dramatically lost their way like no other time in the post–industrial era. The entire landscape has changed. Companies and employees may know right from wrong and may have an ethical compass. Yet, because of the temptations of various economic vices and diseased corporate cultures, they often fall into deadly habits, which inevitably lead to their own demise.

Corporations often lose valuable capital in the process, increase leverage to unsustainable levels, reduce staffing, and suffer damages to their growth potential and industry reputation. The costs of unethical business are huge for everyone in the downstream value chain.

Business and personal ethics are no longer an integral part of global corporate cultures. The reality is that ethics has been dumbed down to mean compliance. Compliance is generally seen as a "back office," ineffectual division of a corporation or investment bank. Managers simply don't want to know of ethical dilemmas or failures. The new normal is to simply know just enough to stay out of courtrooms and, potentially, jail. Best practices, doing the right thing, or building lasting bonds of trust have become reduced to an idealistic goal, not the actual reality.

For modern-day executives, the devil is in the details. Leaders are increasingly driven to various forms of corruption. Corrosive and systemic, governance failures drive companies and markets with out-of-control demands, unbridled ambition, and corrupt practices. In the

xxxvi   I N T R O D U C T I O N

process, the very corporate modality as we know it has the potential to take down the entire global economy.

Like Olympic and cycling doping scandals, or steroids in professional baseball, the counterintuitive analogy holds that you should do anything to win, even if in the long run you are found out and suffer the consequences. Lance Armstrong is a quintessential example of this tragic quest for glory and fame.

Maybe you won't get caught? The prior formal sets of ethics and important business virtues no longer hold sway. Today's corporate culture and CEOs increasingly encourage nearly any behavior that produces short-term results, supposedly satisfying shareholders and boosting the stock price in the process.

This short-termism is the very root of the problem, causing the end of ethics as we know it. It is a mania and a mantra. Leaders focus on results now, without regards to the consequences and any lingering ethical qualms. CEOs ignore "how they got here" and, instead, focus on short-term performance and reward, concentrating solely on this quarter, not the next ten.

This mantra abandons any real sense of risk management, reputation, or durable and sustainable reward. It throws responsibility and character under the bus. Companies have become willing and ready to forsake any moral compass or ethical rudder for bumps in stock price and industry *perception*.

One of the reasons doping and steroid use is so rampant in many professional sports and international competitions is the constant pressure to be super-human and to perform ever better in order to garner recognition and enormous, immediate reward. This does not excuse the use of so-called performance-enhancing drugs, but it may explain why athletes, even famous and accomplished ones, take them. The payoff almost requires it, which makes the breach of ethics that much easier for them. Everyone is doing it, so why not us, too?

In the last decade, more companies have come to operate in much the same way. This is outlined in William D. Cohan's Prologue of this book. Vice has overtaken Wall Street and the human spirit.

Moreover, demands from shareholders and international markets have become so tremendous because a premium is placed on rapid, short-term results. Accordingly, the personalities and vices of Jon

Corzine, Bernie Madoff, Tom Petters, Jimmy Cayne, Bernie Ebbers, Dennis Kozlowski, and Kenneth Lay have flourished. Many executives now feel the only way to meet profitability and performance standards, quarter to quarter, is to breach established ethical codes and norms.

This is why the end of ethics has overtaken us. This is why governance, risk management, and business virtue are no longer much of a priority for corporations and their top leaders. Sadly, resorting to economic vice is now viewed as a necessity for survival.

Prologue

On Wall Street, when the lines of fear and greed cross, big things tend to happen.

For instance, during the Ides of March 2008, when the board of directors of Bear Stearns, the venerable 85-year-old investment bank, realized it had little choice but to sell the company over the weekend or file for bankruptcy on Monday morning, at first it held out for a high price. The company's stock closed on Friday afternoon at $30 per share, and it was not unreasonable for the board and management to expect that a buyer would pay a premium. That's the way deals normally get done.

But Bear Stearns was in serious financial distress. The previous day, the Federal Reserve Bank of New York had arranged with JPMorgan Chase to provide Bear with a $30 billion line of credit so that it could open for business on Friday morning. Bear's management thought the $30 billion would be available for 30 days. As the market realized throughout Friday just how desperate the straits were at Bear Stearns, its stock dropped 40 percent in the first half hour of trading.

Then the government dropped the hammer on the firm. That Friday afternoon, Treasury Secretary Hank Paulson called Alan Schwartz, Bear

Stearns's short-tenured CEO, as he was heading home to Greenwich after not sleeping the night before. The credit line had been pulled, Paulson told Schwartz, setting off a weekend scramble to find a buyer. Panic set in quickly.

The only serious buyer for Bear Stearns turned out to be JPMorgan Chase, which coveted Bear's clearing business, its prime-brokerage business, and—most of all—its luxurious new $1.5 billion skyscraper on Madison Avenue, right next to JPMorgan Chase's headquarters. On Saturday, subject to additional due diligence, JPMorgan Chase offered between $8 and $12 per share for Bear Stearns. The Bear board found the offer insulting, given how far below it was Friday's closing price, and asked for a higher price.

Instead, on Sunday morning, the clever negotiators at JPMorgan Chase, confident the bank was the only game in town, told Bear Stearns' management, there would be no bid at all for the company. JPMorgan Chase was out. Suddenly, Bear Stearns faced the prospect that it would not be able to open for business on Monday morning and would have no choice but to file for bankruptcy. Forget $30 per share for shareholders, or even $10 a share—in a bankruptcy filing, share-holders would end up with nothing. Creditors, too, would take it on the chin and receive recoveries of pennies on the dollar.

The lines of fear and greed were crossing. Later on Sunday, when JPMorgan Chase returned to the negotiating table with an offer for Bear of *$2 per share* plus an agreement from the New York Federal Reserve Bank to take $30 billion of toxic assets from Bear that JPMorgan Chase did not want, the Bear Stearns board of directors quickly—albeit unhappily—capitulated to the deal.

When the news crossed the tape hours later, most people thought the price was a typo. It wasn't. Faced with the stark choice of a bankruptcy filing or a piddling offer for the equity that also gave Bear's creditors 100 cents on the dollar, the Bear board of directors overcame its greed and calculated that the JPMorgan Chase deal was far better than the alternative. Something that was impossible to conceive of 48 hours earlier had happened. That's the way things work on Wall Street. (As a reminder, the tables were turned a bit a week later when a mistake in the merger agreement forced JPMorgan Chase back to the negotiating table. JPMorgan Chase ended up paying $10 a share in its stock for Bear Stearns.)

The same Kabuki theater played out six months later in boardrooms across Wall Street at AIG, Merrill Lynch, Wachovia, Washington Mutual, and, most infamously, Lehman Brothers. In the wake of the near meltdown of capitalism, there was only one inescapable conclusion. The very architecture of Wall Street was flawed. No longer did it make sense to borrow money in the overnight repo markets secured by squirrelly mortgage-backed securities.

That formula—which had worked for decades—turned out to be a recipe for disaster since it gave Wall Street's short-term creditors a vote every night about whether to continue to do business with it the next day. In nearly every case—Bear Stearns, Merrill Lynch, and Lehman Brothers—the short-term creditors decided that they no longer wanted the collateral being offered in exchange for the overnight loan. The risk of not getting paid back was not worth the reward of the small fees being paid.

The financial crisis also revealed a flawed compensation system on Wall Street that rewarded bankers, traders, and executives with huge million-dollar-plus bonuses for taking risks with other people's money. The bankers underwriting the mortgage-backed securities that were chock full of mortgages that should never have been issued in the first place were rewarded handsomely for packaging up the faulty mortgages into securities and selling them off as investments around the world. Why in the world would they stop selling these securities when continuing to do so made them fabulously rich and without any accountability?

The traders at Goldman Sachs, who, in 2007, made a massive proprietary bet with their shareholders' money against the mortgage market—correctly, as it turned out—were paid tens of millions of dollars in return for a gamble that made Goldman $4 billion in profit and kept them far from the danger that brought down Bear Stearns, Merrill Lynch, and Lehman Brothers. Why in the world would the traders not swing for those fences when home runs rewarded them with a nice slice of the profits and strikeouts (losses), if any, were reserved for their shareholders, or for the American public?

Come to think of it, why does anyone invest in the publicly traded Wall Street firms, where some 50 cents—or more—of every dollar of revenue goes to vastly overpaying the people who work there? If anything has become obvious, it's that Wall Street firms exist for the benefit of their high-level employees, not their shareholders or creditors.

You would think such an obviously dysfunctional and corrupt system—that some have compared to La Cosa Nostra, without the murder—would be desperately in need of reform. But it hasn't happened. After pumping trillions of dollars back into Wall Street banks—both through bailouts and Federal Reserve monetary easing—Washington was eager to re-regulate Wall Street. However, in July 2010 came the passage of the 2,300-page Dodd–Frank Act, which, by design, was meant to obfuscate and confuse, and to restore the status quo on Wall Street as quickly as possible.

As of this moment, the new rules and regulations that Dodd–Frank mandated—for instance, about how and when financial instruments such as credit-default swaps will be traded on an exchange—are still being thrashed out in Washington, with plenty of help from Wall Street lawyers and executives. Yet, the truth is that nothing much has changed on Wall Street, despite the new regulations. By comparison, the last great effort to reform Wall Street—the Banking Act of 1933, also known as Glass–Steagall—was 37 pages long, and its requirements were few and straightforward: In a year's time, Wall Street banks had to choose between investment banking and commercial banking. Period.

Plenty of people have noticed, too. "People feel like the system is rigged against them," Elizabeth Warren, recently elected senator from Massachusetts, told the 2012 Democratic National Convention, in Charlotte. "And here's the painful part: they're right. The system is rigged. Look around. Oil companies guzzle down billions in profits. Billionaires pay lower taxes than their secretaries. And Wall Street CEOs—the same ones who wrecked our economy and destroyed millions of jobs—still strut around Congress, no shame, demanding favors, and acting like we should thank them."

Warren, one of the architects of what became the Consumer Financial Protection Bureau (now part of the Federal Reserve), had hoped things would have changed after the events of 2008. "It's not a story of one side wants government and the other side doesn't," she told the *New Yorker* magazine in September 2012. "This is a story about how government gets used. Government gets used to protect those who have already made it. That becomes the game. And so we had the Big Crash, and I thought, O.K.! We tested the alternative theory. Cut taxes, reduce regulations [on] financial services, and see what happens to the economy. We ran a thirty-year test on that, and it was a disaster."[1]

The truth is, it's still a disaster. Nothing material has changed on Wall Street. And the evidence of this fact abounds—and is the subject of much of this book—in the plethora of financial scandals that have been uncovered *since* the passage of Dodd–Frank, the law that was supposed to curtail the bad behavior on Wall Street.

There was the "London Whale," the name given to the trader in JPMorgan Chase's London office who lost nearly $6 billion gambling with depositors' money in the late spring of 2012 by making an obscure, proprietary bet on an esoteric debt index, hoping that interest rates in Europe would rise as the economies continued to collapse under too much debt without regulators doing anything to fix them. That this bet was made in a dark corner of the bank—the so-called Chief Investment Office—that housed the $350 billion of depositors' cash that had not yet been lent out merely added to the intrigue. How could Jamie Dimon, the famously hard-driving, detail-oriented CEO of JPMorgan Chase, have missed this bet, as he claimed he did? And what possessed the trader, Bruno Iksil, to make the trade in the first place, just to get a few more basis points of yield on a huge portfolio? Why did Iksil's boss, Ina Drew—who was paid $15 million a year—not monitor Iksil's trade more carefully?

The only logical explanation for their collective bad behavior is that Iksil was swinging for the fences, hoping for a big bonus, while both Drew and Dimon had become cocky and complacent, having pocketed tens of millions of dollars (in Drew's case) and hundreds of millions of dollars (in Dimon's case) for taking risks with other people's money, with little personal accountability when things go wrong. As happens frequently on Wall Street, Dimon had become an imperial CEO, living in his bubble, surrounded by his court of well-paid sycophants.

The case of the collapse of MF Global, in October 2011, is equally illustrative of how little has changed on Wall Street in the wake of the financial crisis and how warped incentives drive bad behavior. One of the largest individual investors in MF Global was Chris Flowers, a former Goldman Sachs partner and one of the most respected M&A bankers doing deals in the financial services industry.

He was a close business and personal friend of Jon Corzine, the former Goldman Sachs senior partner. Both Flowers and Corzine were allied at Goldman against Hank Paulson, Corzine's deputy (and the future secretary of the treasury). One thing led to another at Goldman in 1998 and 1999, when the firm was on the cusp of its long-awaited IPO, and Paulson succeeded in orchestrating a coup d'état that forced both Corzine and Flowers from the firm.

The two men dusted themselves off and started again. Flowers founded an eponymous private-equity firm focused on the financial services industry. One of his very first deals—the purchase of a distressed bank in Japan—netted him and his financial partner a billion-dollar fortune and a form of redemption he was desperately seeking. The successful bank deal also reinforced in Flowers's mind his own fabulousness. Corzine, too, recovered quickly from his humiliating departure from Goldman. He ran for a vacant US Senate seat in his adopted home state of New Jersey, and his gregariousness proved politically appealing. (He also poured tens of millions of dollars of his Goldman fortune into the campaign.) In 2006, Corzine decided to run for governor of the state. He won that race, too. But his political luck ran out in 2010, after one term and a near-fatal car accident—he wasn't wearing a seatbelt as his chauffeur barreled down the Garden State Parkway at more than 90 miles per hour—and he lost his reelection campaign to Chris Christie.

In the aftermath of the election, Flowers contacted Corzine and persuaded him to join the struggling MF Global as its CEO and also be a partner in his private-equity firm. They agreed that Corzine would be paid a relatively small annual salary—$3 million in cash—and a boatload of out-of-the-money stock options.

The incentive was obvious: Turn MF Global into a serious Wall Street firm, increase its profitability, and raise the stock price. In the aftermath of the financial crisis that had eliminated Bear Stearns and Lehman Brothers as competitors and defanged both Merrill Lynch and Morgan Stanley, the idea of transforming MF Global into another Goldman Sachs—as Corzine said repeatedly was his ambition—was not illogical, especially with a former head of Goldman Sachs as the new CEO of MF Global.

In short order, after announcing that he intended to take advantage of the dearth of competition in the market and try to remake MF Global in Goldman Sachs's image, Corzine fired many of the existing MF Global employees and brought in more aggressive salesmen and traders from around Wall Street. He moved the company into new, sleek offices in midtown Manhattan. Corzine, a former government-bond trader at Goldman, also decided to make a $6.3 billion proprietary bet with his shareholders' money on the direction of distressed European sovereign debt. Had the bet paid off, MF Global would have made a small fortune and, more than likely, its stock price would have gone up, increasing the value of Corzine's stock options. The stock option incentive encouraged him to swing for the fence, and that's exactly what he did.

But it was a bad bet, not because he was wrong about how the bonds would trade (he was mostly correct about that) but because he completely misjudged the market's reaction to his decision to make such a huge gamble that was beyond the scope of its business as a futures broker. When news of the trade first began to leak to the market, the reaction from investors and short-term creditors was swift and exacting. They fled in droves.

On Halloween 2011, MF Global filed for bankruptcy protection and was eventually liquidated. (Still being debated is what happened to some $1.6 billion in customer funds that disappeared in the days leading up to the bankruptcy filing and most likely were used to repay short-term creditors in a failed last-ditch effort to keep the firm from collapsing.) As a result of Corzine's reckless behavior, MF Global's shareholders and creditors lost billions; it remains unclear if its customers will get back 100 percent of their money. Somehow, Corzine has avoided criminal prosecution for his actions. (For more on MF Global, see Chapter 2.)

Warped incentives also played a role in the still-unfolding scandal in which banks in Europe and the United States manipulated the London Interbank Borrowing Rate, known as Libor. As discussed in Chapter 1, Libor is used to set the price of millions of loans issued worldwide, and its manipulation meant that hundreds of thousands of borrowers probably paid higher interest rates on the money they borrowed than they otherwise would have.

The manipulation was shameful and widespread. Other scandals revealed during the summer of 2012 involved money laundering at HSBC, Standard Chartered PLC's bookkeeping shenanigans to help Iran, and Nomura Holding Inc.'s insider-trading scandal. These happened after the financial crisis laid bare a corrupt Wall Street culture.

Why has there been so little change on Wall Street, even though individual bankers, traders, and executives seem to be falling over themselves to sort of accept blame for what went wrong? The most recent example came in September 2012 from Anshu Jain, one of two new leaders of Deutsche Bank, who laid out a plan for an internal change of culture with the admission that "tremendous mistakes have been made. We can see times have changed and we need to change and change rapidly."[2]

Part of the answer, perhaps, is that Wall Street behavior merely reflects the latest acceptable norms in society as a whole, which sadly has seen a steady decline in ethics, morality, compliance, and leadership in the last generation. Wall Street has taught Main Street the wonders of stock options, "golden parachutes," and excessive executive compensation, among other things, all of which are designed to enrich the few at the top with a minimal amount of accountability for their behavior.

It all adds up to a steady stream of messages that amount to an imitation of Gordon Gekko (the character played by Michael Douglas) in the classic movie *Wall Street*. If the financial crisis and its aftermath have taught us anything, though, it is that greed is not always good. Not even close. If I were a Wall Street CEO hauling in tens of millions of dollars a year, I would be embarrassed to call myself a leader while perpetuating a compensation system that continues to reward bad behavior at my firm.

Once upon a time, Wall Street was composed of small, private partnerships where partners supplied the firm's capital and were liable for losses the firm incurred, up to their entire net worth. While this structure tended to make Wall Street firm's undercapitalized, it also made the partners of Wall Street firms highly risk-averse and finely attuned to the behavior of their partners. (It also made many of them wealthy.) The idea that one poorly conceived trade or underwritten stock offering could jeopardize the firm and everything the partners had worked their entire lives to achieve was a powerful force guiding behavior on Wall Street.

What was the point of allowing a partner to swing for the fence on a risky trade when it could mean the loss of everything—including Fifth Avenue apartments and houses in the Hamptons—that partners had worked so hard to earn? The partnership structure on Wall Street forced partners to become prudent risk takers and to monitor closely what each other was doing.

That ethic began to change—and not for the better—beginning in 1970 when the highly respected and profitable investment-banking firm Donaldson, Lufkin & Jenrette stunned the rest of the Wall Street partnerships by announcing its decision to go public in an IPO. DLJ's successful offering made the partners wealthy, gave it access to seemingly unlimited sources of cheap financing, and allowed for older partners to exit gracefully in favor of the next generation. The logic for the IPO was impeccable; the rest of Wall Street quickly emulated it.

By May 1999, when Goldman Sachs went public, nearly every major Wall Street firm had followed DLJ's lead and sold part of itself to the public. Partners got wealthy, capital flowed in, and succession planning was made easier. By 2005, even smaller Wall Street partnerships, such as Lazard, Evercare, and Greenhill—focused almost exclusively on M&A and asset management—could not resist the clarion call of the IPO and the opportunity for huge wealth.

But renouncing the partnership culture on Wall Street was not without its consequences. By replacing a culture focused on prudent risk taking and pretax profits with a culture that rewarded taking risks with other people's money in order to get huge, multimillion dollar bonuses, a whole generation of bankers, traders, and executives forgot the lessons of partnership accountability and reverted to their animalistic pursuit of personal wealth. Even better, great wealth could be accomplished without taking any personal financial risk.

Greed had utterly replaced fear on Wall Street. No surprise—big things happened. What remains shocking, though, is that the lessons of the 2008 financial crisis remain unlearned. Until Wall Street's leaders again have their full net worth on the line every day—as they did two generations ago when Wall Street was a series of small, private partnerships—the idea of real change on Wall Street remains an unfunny joke.

William Cohan

Notes

1. Jeffrey Toobin, "Elizabeth Warren's Long Journey Into Politics, *New Yorker*, September 17, 2012.
2. Jack Ewing, "Deutsche Bank Chiefs Outline Overhaul Plan," *The New York Times*, DealBook, September 11, 2012, http://dealbook.nytimes.com/2012/09/11/deutsche-bank-chiefs-outline-overhaul/.

Part One

ECONOMIC VICE

*P*art One illustrates the most egregious manifestations of vice in the global economy. Ranging from the Libor rate manipulation to credit rating agency "games" to the bankruptcy of MF Global, these troubling cases provide powerful reasons to believe we have lost our ethical compass and that a way back is required.

Chapter 1

The Selfish Betrayal of the Global Investor: Libor and Its Consequences

Virtue itself turns vice, being misapplied,
And vice sometimes by action dignified.
—*William Shakespeare*

In the post–credit-crisis market climate, international promises of financial governance and reform have too often fallen by the proverbial wayside. The allure of depravity, corruption, and market manipulation prove to be powerful motives that continue to harness virtues deeply seeded in the human spirit.

The voracious personal desire to assemble profit by illicit means is the most traditional of economic vices, and the most obvious. Yet, perhaps like never before, on a systemic level, the recent Libor crisis demonstrates how greed can push governance out of the way for maximum profit and personal gain for the few with great costs to many.

Unlike most financial scandals, the Libor fraud did not originate with one man, pervasively toxify one company, or rest on one financial product aimed to deceive. The Libor scheme defined the way that a cartel of large, "too big to fail" international banks conducted daily business.[1]

Widespread manipulation of Libor for short-term proprietary reasons is only another intense warning sign that economic vice has become part and parcel of the way institutions, governments, individuals and entire societies conduct their affairs.

Enhancing governance and lassoing out-of-control risk is essential for any banking institution considering long-term, sustainable growth, rather than a short-term profit boom. For example, in the case of Libor, a July 2012 report by Macquarie Research estimated that banks face $176 billion in legal liability because of the scandal.[2]

Can any short-term profit be worth $176 billion in potential losses?

What about other liabilities created by the fraud—such as share price nosedives, investor confidence failures, and a firm's own reputational crisis? It is hard to believe that any fraudulent scheme has such value for interested parties. So why do it?

Unfortunately, as will be demonstrated throughout Part I of this book, the end game is never fully considered.

Vice becomes the new normal. A never ending hunt for profit, envy of others, and perverse lust for power, money, and fame blinds financial swindlers to the obvious wrongs of their actions. Simply put, they not only believe they can get away with it, but they do get away with it, for years.

Tragically, Barclays, the company at the heart of the Libor scandal, was viewed as an exemplary ethical company prior to its fall from grace and an outlier from other big banks.

In 2009, Barclays was rated "Retained Platinum" in business in the Community's Corporate Responsibility Index. Barclays was selected as a company that demonstrated "continued broad level commitment to CR" (corporate responsibility).[3]

Barclays even published a "citizenship report" in which governance, controls, and sustainability in its daily operations and company affiliations were emphasized. With a vaulted history going back to its Quaker origins, Barclays was a good bank with a long history going back centuries, and it had the reputation to prove it.

In the corporate governance world, Barclays was the A student that got caught stealing answers to the exams.

Despite the public perception, Barclays manipulated the Libor rate for years without consequence or reprisal. This enabled the bank to make money on their Libor-related products for years without any downturns. Through cheating the Libor system, Barclays had all the answers so it would never fail.

In addition to Barclays, seven other banks were allegedly involved in the Libor-rigging process. UBS and RBS have also been the subject of government investigations and regulatory fines. However, these reactionary investigations should have occurred years before, when international regulators knew about the fraud and did little if nothing to blunt the effects of the rate manipulation.

At a time when global trust in markets is at a tipping point, big-bank sham governance has once again corrupted our faith in efficient markets, best practices, and ethical corporate culture.

If Dodd–Frank legislation, European Union reforms, and lessons from the credit crisis (that nearly destroyed the world economy) were evidence that we have approached the end of out-of-control risk, speculation, and corruption, the Libor scandal provides even more reason to believe that we have approached the *end of ethics* as we know it.

The Calculation of Libor

The London Inter-Bank Offered Rate (Libor) is a global interest rate benchmark used to set payments and distributions of more than $800 trillion worth of financial instruments.

Because Libor determines interest, generally, the most important metric in the heart of finance, tiny fluctuations in the Libor rate can swing pension plans up and down, reduce or increase profits for Fortune 500 companies, change simple mortgage payments, and destroy small business liquidity.

Libor has immense value to the market. Yet, over the last ten years, traders treated the benchmark like their own neighborhood jungle gym, disregarding market ripple effects for their own personal gain.

Libor was published on behalf of the British Bankers' Association (BBA). The BBA selected the banks that were to become part of their association to create the Libor index. Each bank member submitted subjective daily quotes of what it deemed the current cost of lending money was.

The Libor definition published by the BBA was: "The rate at which an individual contributor panel bank could borrow funds were it to do so by asking for and then accepting interbank offers in reasonable market size . . . "[4]

This definition was then put into action through well-established procedures. BBA members submitted their estimated interest rate they would need to pay in order to borrow money on that specific day. In turn, Thomson Reuters collected their responses. Reuters removed the four highest and four lowest submissions to calculate an average rate.

Libor is not just one interest rate. It encompasses different rates calculated in over 15 currencies for loans of 10 different maturities, ranging from overnight liquidity deals to 12-month contracts. In fact, there are 150 Libor interest rates calculated on a daily basis spanning 10 different currencies.

Thomson Reuters did not fact check or research the Libor rates submitted. Instead, the role of Thomson Reuters was limited to copying the rate distributed—not to ascertain if the rate itself was accurate.[5]

Libor setting began each morning between 11:00 A.M. and 11:10 A.M. (London Time) when a person in one of the designated Libor banks entered a number into Thomson Reuters software indicating the borrowing rate in a "reasonable market size" prior to 11:00 A.M. of that day.[6] Typos were frequent, so clerks often checked to ensure that submitted rates were indeed accurate. Other bank Libor rates were never divulged.[7]

Thomson Reuters employed a "calculation engine" that ranked the bank rates in descending order and trimmed off the highest and lowest 25 percent of Libor submissions. The middle 50 percent were averaged, producing rates that are published at 11:30 A.M. daily.[8] Thomson Reuters then published the separate submission of each panel bank.

This highly subjective process—beholden to the brains or lack thereof of a group of traders and computer errors—was estimated to create the value of global financial instruments controlled by the Libor rate.

In addition to Libor's importance in ascertaining value, Libor is also a critical barometer of market risk. A higher Libor rate means it is riskier to lend money, and a bank will ask for a higher interest rate to insulate itself.

Trends of higher-than-normal Libor rates are tools that investors, highly paid analysts, mortgage bankers, and others use to monitor markets for appropriate decision making.

Although Libor is an integral part of global markets, it was lightly regulated if at all. And, unfortunately, the smidgen of regulation of Libor that did take place was entirely toothless. Libor has operated for years in the absence of any independent or governmental regulation.

Worse, persons with immense conflict of interests governed the Libor interest rate. On July 2, 2012, former Barclays Chairman Marcus Agius resigned. Agius quit not only from Barclays but also as Chairman of the BBA, the organization, which was responsible for overseeing the Libor process. For years, Agius, as chairman of the BBA and Barclays, maintained the authority to use Libor as an arm of the firm.

"The BBA represents the interests of the big banks," said Andrew Hilton, director of the Center for the Study of Financial Innovation, to *The New York Times.* "It does not represent the interests of borrowers or the financial system at large."[9]

Within the BBA, a subdivision committee called the Foreign Exchange and Money Markets Committee (FEMMC) was responsible for overseeing Libor. The FEMMC was overwhelmed with conflict of interests. For example, its members included BBA member CFOs, treasurers, and money managers from the banks responsible for setting the Libor rate.

Because of this intense conflict of interest, Barclays and other banks were left unpoliced to submit whatever Libor numbers they deemed fit, based on market happenings. During the financial crisis, banks felt the need to underreport Libor to show they were more fiscally solvent than their books showed.

The Libor fraud, if nothing else, demonstrated why self-regulation with existing perverse incentives is ineffective. FEMMC had great power over selecting the banks eligible to contribute Libor rates. Every six months and on a rolling basis, FEMMC had the authority to determine if a member bank was setting Libor in a manner satisfactory to the organization. If not, the BBA through the FEMMC subdivision, could have precluded that institution from further setting Libor rates.[10] Despite the known market manipulation of Libor rates, FEMMC stood idly by.

In September 2012, the BBA was stripped of its authority to oversee the Libor setting process because of this gigantic failure of self-regulation.

The Rise and Fall of the World's Financial Benchmark

Libor began with honest, virtuous intentions. Spawned by Cretian banker Minos Zombanakis in 1969, the interest rate benchmark exponentially grew over time. Zombanakis, at that time running the London Branch of Manufacturers Hanover (now JP Morgan), needed a benchmark interest rate for an $80 million loan for the Shah of Iran.[11]

"We had to fix a rate, so I called up all the banks and asked them to send to me by 11:00 A.M. their cost of money," he said. "We got the rates, I made an average of them all and I named it the London interbank offer rate," Zombanakis said.[12]

According to Zombanakis, the early success of Libor was due to the interlocking sense of responsibility and trust between banks that drove to the heart of the system's value.[13]

While the BBA took off with the Libor concept in 1985, the interbank rate in London first became a significant global benchmark with bankers like Zombankis in the 1960s. Because of the Bretton Woods system of fixed exchange rates, US policy makers sought to restrict international bank lending originating within the United States.[14] Therefore, many bankers decided to originate deals from London because of a more favorable lending climate.

With the plethora of deals originating overseas, standardization became critical to withstand interest rate fluctuations. Zombanakis and others used Libor as a common benchmark that deal participants could rely on because of the increasing intertwined nature of complex syndicated lending agreements.

When the BBA established the standard rate terms on interest rate swap products in 1984, they were implementing a metric that was already in use among most bankers doing international business. The shining moment came in 1986 when the BBA first introduced Libor to standardize rate terms on a wide variety of securities, including syndicated loans, futures contracts, and forward rate agreements.[15]

At this time, the BBA recognized the importance of navigating the liberalization of interest rate markets, which had created new products, swaps, and derivatives. In this new climate, the goal of the BBA was to create a reliable, trustworthy benchmark to fill the need for standardization and fairness in growing worldwide markets.

The first Libor rates were published in January 1986, initially in US dollars, Japanese yen, and British sterling.[16] From then, Libor took off as one of the most common interest rate benchmarks in the world.

In fact, it became THE benchmark for many types of loans associated with all aspects of American and international business, including student loans, credit cards, bank loans, floating rate corporate bonds, municipal contracts, and mortgages.[17] Today, the Federal Reserve of Cleveland estimates that Libor rates control 45 percent of adjustable rate mortgages.

Libor succeeded over time because of the perceived virtue and responsibility of its members. People trusted that Libor rates were accurate and the BBA was effectively monitoring its members to ensure that the rates were reasonable. This faith enabled Libor to surpass the popularity of other competing interest rates such as the prime rate and the Fed funds rate because of the perception that each suffered from "more market manipulation than Libor."[18]

In the modern era of free-floating exchange rates and interest rates, Libor provided a usable benchmark to produce the comfort of trust—trust embedded in the belief that the BBA was a reliable steward. This was the secret to the success of Libor. Persons all over the world, whether hot-shot banker, CFO, or an average person taking out a mortgage, have all believed that the benchmark was fair, equitable, and honest.

Libor's history of market faith and respect makes the breach of trust even more enormous. In 2008, the BBA proudly announced on its website that "Libor is the primary benchmark for short-term interest rates globally."[19]

The effects of Libor manipulation are dramatic. The Libor fraud was not in any way restricted to one deal, one person, or one company.

It was a betrayal of the very system in which institutions, government, small businesses, and everyday people interacted, trusted, and structured deals for over 25 years.

Although Libor has traditionally operated as the most critical financial benchmark in the world, it was treated casually, like an interest rate piñata. Incredibly, traders used the index to make money exponentially without regard for the macroeconomic consequences.

The Libor trouble first began to break on May 29, 2008. *The Wall Street Journal* reported then that several global banks were reporting questionably low borrowing costs in submitting their Libor rates.[20] *The Wall Street Journal* hypothesized that banks were reporting lower borrowing rates to avoid looking desperate for cash.[21]

On June 2, 2008, the *Financial Times* also hinted that the Libor rates reported were inaccurate: "The rate of borrowing in Libor has lagged behind other market-based measures of unsecured funding used by the vast majority of financial institutions. This has aroused suspicions that the small group of banks which supply the BBA with Libor quotes have understated true borrowing rates so as not to fan fears [that] they have funding problems."[22]

In the summer of 2008, the BBA and its members accused financial journalists such as the *Financial Times*, Gillian Tett, as "scaremongers" who were not presenting accurate information.[23] In the midst of a scheme of deceit that had gone on for many years, the reaction to the initial uncovering of the fraud was strong, dismissive, and defensive.

Even throughout the summer of 2012, when the Libor fraud finally was uncovered, many in the financial community sought to convince the world that the problem with Libor was the lone acts of a handful of traders that did not have a wider effect on global economics.

Tett explained: "No doubt some financiers would like to dismiss this as the work of a few rogue traders. And, in line with usual banking practice, the more junior authors of the incriminating e-mails have already been fired. But the wider symbolic significance of these revelations cannot be overstated; for they expose a big conceit at the very heart of the modern banking world."[24]

The market deceit was massive. As former Barclays Chief Executive Bob Diamond pleaded to British Parliament on July 4, 2012, "It's difficult for Barclays . . . to be isolated on this."[25] With this comment,

Diamond ominously hinted that the Libor fraud was systemic and tragically widespread.

Libor rigging was not a new problem; it was a well-kept secret in close-lipped financial circles. "Fifteen years ago, the word was that Libor was being rigged," said one industry veteran to the *Economist* magazine. "It was one of those well-kept secrets, but the regulator was asleep, the Bank of England didn't care . . . [the banks participating were] happy with the reference prices."[26]

Worse than uncovering the black heart of finance during the summer of 2012 were the cavalier attitudes of banking professionals and regulators prior to the public explosion of the Libor crisis.

The vice-ridden motivation for Libor manipulation boiled down to profit and deceit—profit in the respect that if Libor rates were manipulated even so slightly, interest rate derivative products could widely fluctuate in value.

For example, the role of greed in manipulating interest rate swaps in the Libor scandal was massive. An interest rate swap is merely an exchange of interest rate payments between two parties, one a fixed interest rate stream of payments and one a variable rate, tied to Libor.

Since Libor controls the profits for the party receiving the variable-rate side of the deal, small changes in Libor could be worth millions or more. An excessively high Libor submission could skew the daily Libor rate to such an extent that it has a massively profound effect on the interest rate swap market. In the case of Barclays, the Commodity Futures Trading Commission (CFTC) found that interest rate traders drove all Libor submissions to meet their own bottom lines.[27]

The CFTC identified these e-mails from 2005 to 2008 as hard evidence of manipulation of Libor to avoid short-term losses in the interest rate derivative swap market:

1. "WE HAVE TO GET KICKED OUT OF THE FIXINGS TOMORROW!! We need a 4.17 fix in 1m (low fix) We need a 4.41 fix in 3m (high fix)" (November 22, 2005, Senior Trader in New York to Trader in London).
2. "You need to take a close look at the reset ladder. We need 3M to stay low for the next 3 sets and then I think that we will be completely out of our 3M positions. Thenits on. [Submitter] has to

go crazy with raising 3M Libor" (February 1, 2006, Traderin New York to Trader in London).

3. "Your annoying colleague again . . . Would love to get a high 1m also if poss a low 3m . . . if poss . . . thanks" (February 3, 2006, Trader in London to Submitter).

4. "This is the [book's] risk. We need low 1M and 3M libor. PIs ask [submitter] to get 1M set to 82. That would help a lot" (March 27, 2006, Trader in New York to Trader in London).

5. "We have another big fixing tom[orrow] and with the market move I was hoping we could set the 1M and 3M Libors as high as possible" (May 31, 2006, Trader in New York to Submitter).

6. "Hi Guys, We got a big position in 3m libor for the next 3 days. Can we please keep the lib or fixing at 5.39 for the next few days. It would really help. We do not want it to fix any higher than that. Tks a lot" (September 13, 2006, Senior Trader in New York to Submitter).

7. "For Monday we are very long 3m cash here in NY and would like the setting to be set as low as possible . . . thanks" (December 14, 2006, Trader in New York to Submitter).

8. "PIs. go for 5.36 Libor again tomorrow, very long and would be hurt by a high setting . . . thanks" (May 23, 2007, Trader in New York to Submitter).[28]

In dramatic fashion, these e-mails not only show that market variables failed to set Libor rates, but also that trader positions in interest rate swap contracts controlled Libor submissions. The desire to keep profits steady was all that mattered.

Barclays' employees responsible for Libor submissions raised no problem with the rate-rigging scheme. For instance, these e-mails from Libor submitters in 2006 illustrate across-the-board cooperation in rigging rates:

- "[Senior Trader] owes me!" (February 7, 2006, Submitter's response when swaps trader called him a "superstar" for moving Barclays' US dollar LIBOR submission up a basis point more than the submitter wanted and for making a submission with the intent to get "kicked out").[29]

- "For you . . . anything. I am going to go 78 and 92.5. It is difficult to go lower than that in threes. looking at where cash is trading. In fact, if you did not want a low one I would have gone 93 at least" (March 16, 2006, Submitter's response to swaps trader's request for a high one-month and low three-month US dollar LIBOR).[30]

Apart from sheer greed, deceit motivated false Libor submissions by member banks. Lower Libor submissions meant that banks were more solvent, liquid, and safe than reality showed.

This was not just an effort directed by traders, but rather, by high-ranking management at many banks to falsely mislead the market. The idea was that misplaced trust in the market could spur increased investment in companies that were reporting materially inaccurate information regarding their fiscal health. Libor manipulation intended to dupe investors by misleading them on the perceived security of their investments.

Sadly, for Libor manipulating banks, this was not a game of monopoly. Libor rigging drastically affected people's lives, their retirement savings, credit card rates, pension plans, mortgage payments, and overall trust, faith, and confidence in the market.

Knowingly Asleep at the Wheel

Regulators were reduced to accomplices. Despite knowing Libor rigging was occurring on a wide scale, international regulators, collusively, did nothing. The "watch dogs" were not just asleep—they knew they were asleep and did not take any proactive steps to ensure their role as global market caretakers.

For example, on June 27, 2012, the UK Financial Services Authority (FSA) issued a scathing report admonishing Barclays for its knowing market manipulation. Yet, where was the FSA throughout the prosecution of the possibly decades-long fraud? The London counterpart to the US Securities and Exchange Commission (SEC) was asleep at the wheel.

Ditto for the Bank of England. In fact, Diamond has handwritten notes of conversations from high-level Bank of England personnel, such as Paul Tucker, from October 29, 2008, indicating that banking officials were concerned with Barclays reporting higher-than-average borrowing costs.[31]

Mr. Tucker stated "the level of the calls he was receiving from Whitehall were 'senior' and that while he was certain that we (Barclays) did not need advice, that it did not always need to be the case that we appeared as high as we have recently."[32]

Most troubling, the Federal Reserve Bank of New York admitted it had questions regarding the accuracy of Libor, beginning in the summer of 2007.[33] New York Fed officials met in April and May 2008 looking to address the falsehoods of Libor, however they did nothing other than talk. No action was taken to publicize the fraud and put pressure on the BBA and its members to cut out the fraud or change the way they did business.

In fact, Barclays itself acknowledged to the Fed in the spring of 2008 that it had been submitting untrue Libor rates.[34] In the aftermath of the fraud, the Fed tried to defer blame to its British counterparts, insisting it informed British regulators of the mess to no avail.

Regardless, regulators, including the New York Fed, had a responsibility "to force greater integrity and cooperation," and it had clearly reviewed the situation and had the resources to investigate, said Andrew Verstein, an associate research scholar at Yale University. "Obviously they considered this to be within their orbit."[35]

According to the calendar of then New York Fed President Timothy Geithner, the Fed even held a "Fixing LIBOR" meeting between 2:30 and 3:00 P.M. on April 28, 2008. At least eight senior Fed staffers were invited.[36]

As The New York Times reported in the summer of 2011, "Timothy F. Geithner, who served as the head of the New York Fed during the crisis years, and other regulators raised concerns about Libor. But they did not stop the problem."[37]

Darrell Duffie, a Stanford University finance professor, said that he believed regulators were "on the case reasonably quickly" after questions were raised in 2008."[38] It appears that some regulators, at least at the New York Fed, indeed knew there was a problem at that time. Duffie said, "I am surprised, however, that the various regulators in the US and UK took this long to identify and act on the misbehavior."[39]

Despite the Fed's knowledge, the FSA did not conduct any official Libor investigation until 2009.[40] This was the case even though the FSA knew in December of 2007 (from a Barclays compliance officer whistleblower) that Barclays was proactively manipulating the Libor index.[41]

According to the Barclays whistleblower, Libor was manipulated by various "problematic actions" by some banks, an illiquid market, and the fear that a stigma would attach if institutions reported their actual borrowing costs to the market.[42]

While this might have constituted white-hot evidence of the fraud, three years later, the FSA had a flaming-hot gun. In 2010, its probe revealed that a top Barclays executive, Jerry del Missier, had instructed the firm's traders to submit false Libor data.[43]

Even then, the FSA pressed no charges against del Missier, who had a sterling career and was even promoted to be Barclays chief operating officer in 2012 until the Libor house of cards came crumbling down.

Former FSA officials who spoke with *The Wall Street Journal* in the summer of 2012 say they never viewed monitoring Libor as the agency's responsibility. Worse, they indicated that until recently, the FSA didn't see Libor as posing a threat to market integrity.[44]

This belief that Libor rigging simply wasn't a big deal was echoed by the Governor of the Bank of England Mervyn Allister King in 2012 British Parliamentary testimony:

> I was very struck and surprised, when reading these three reports [from the regulatory authorities], to discover that changing LIBOR by one basis point was the kind of rigging that people were interested in. You would never have noticed that from market activity. We were worried about tens of basis points.[45]

King went on to say that Libor manipulation was not proactive fraud, but rather, a product of an illiquid market:

> I say again, if you go back to the inquiries that the regulators made, it took them three years to work out and find the evidence of wrongdoing. If it was so obvious and all in the newspapers and everyone was talking about it, one might ask why everybody did not say, "This is wrong." The reason was that it wasn't wrongdoing. It was a market that was dysfunctional and was not operating in any effective way.[46]

In response to these cavalier remarks, the House of Commons Treasury Committee indicated that they were "surprised" and "disappointed" with the tone of the governor's comments.[47]

The lack of care and concern for investors—the group international regulators are charged to protect—is worrisome to say the least. If watchdog agencies continue to abdicate from their responsibilities by blaming "dysfunctional markets" it will not solely be markets that can become dysfunctional but business and society as a whole.

The ineptitude of institutions, regulators, and third parties to raise a hand to the knowing prosecution of the fraud might be the most frightening result of the Libor scandal.

A Troubling New Normal

The Libor market manipulation is not just another financial scandal. Shoulder shrugs and complacency that this was a market-based issue ignore the epic failure of business ethics and governance on a wide scale.

Over time, the values that helped found the Libor rate—faith, accountability, and cooperation—became so substantially eroded that systemic fraud became the new normal. In a selfish game of deceit, lies, and greed, no one dared to care about the outcome for investors who rely on the Libor rate for their own economic livelihood.

The Libor crisis is hard evidence that we are approaching the end of ethics. Institutions, CEOs, CFOs, traders, and regulators saw nothing wrong with manipulating this most important rate for personal gain. Some still see nothing wrong with this market kidnapping. Transparency was rejected in favor of opaque smoke and mirrors. Keeping the Libor process secretive allowed an immense betrayal of trust to occur for years without prosecution or reprisal.

The Libor fraud was a systemic head nod that manipulation, fraud, and rigging to the detriment of someone else is acceptable behavior. We can stand by and accept this as the "new normal," as so many of us with power have done already. Or, we can fight to find a way back for the betterment and sustainability of markets and our global economy.

We hope that the reader chooses the latter and reads on.

Notes

1. See generally, Financial Services Authority, Barclays Bank PLC, Final Notice, June 27, 2012.
2. Jean Eaglesham, "Suits Mount in Rate Scandal," *The Wall Street Journal*, August 26, 2012.
3. The Corporate Responsibility Index 2009.
4. See generally, Financial Services Authority, Barclays Bank PLC, Final Notice, June 27, 2012.
5. John Carney, "Libor Rates: A Readers Guide," CNBC, July 6, 2012.
6. Ibid.
7. Ibid.
8. Ibid.
9. Landon Thomas Jr., "Trade Group For Bankers Regulates a Key Rate," *The New York Times*, July 5, 2012, www.nytimes.com/2012/07/06/business/global/the-gentlemens-club-that-sets-libor-is-called-into-question.html?pagewanted=all.
10. Pierre Brochet, "The Libor Scandal and Libor Explained," Association of Corporate Counsel, *Lexology*, August 13, 2012.
11. Kirstin Ridley and Huw Jones, "Insight: A Greek Banker, the Shah and the Birth of Libor," Reuters, August 7, 2012, www.reuters.com/article/2012/08/08/us-banking-libor-change-idUSBRE87702320120808.
12. Times Topics, "Libor (Barclays Interest Rate Manipulation Case," *The New York Times*, August 10, 2012, topics.nytimes.com/top/reference/timestopics/subjects/l/london_interbank_offered_rate_libor/index.html.
13. Ibid.
14. Sean Vanatta, "Libor Risks Emerged From Clubby London Banking Culture," *Bloomberg*, August 14, 2012, http://www.bloomberg.com/news/2012–08–14/libor-s-risks-emerged-from-clubby-london-banking-culture.html.
15. Rosa M Abrantes-Metz, Michael Kraten, Albert D. Metz, Gim S. Seow, "Libor Manipulation?" August 4, 2008 (working paper).
16. Black Rock, View Point 2012, "Libor, Where Do We Go From Here."
17. Ibid.
18. David Malpass, "The Libor Scandal's Threat to Growth," *The Wall Street Journal*, July 11, 2012, http://online.wsj.com/article/SB10001424052702303567704577516804050467544.html.
19. Abrantes-Metz, Kraten, Metz, and Seow.
20. Ibid., citing Mollkenkamp and Whitehouse, *The Wall Street Journal*, 2008.
21. Ibid.
22. Ibid., citing Gillian Tett and Michael Mackenize, *Financial Times*, 2008.
23. Gillian Tett, "Libor Affair Shows Banking's Big Conceit," *Financial Times*, June 28, 2012, www.ft.com/intl/cms/s/0/24ee82f4-c12b-11e1–8179–00144feabdc0.html#axzz25vEZjE2p.

24. Ibid.
25. "First Mover Disadvantage," *The Economist*, July 7, 2012.
26. "The Rotten Heart of Finance, A Scandal Over Key Interest Rates Is about to Go Global," *The Economist*, July 7, 2012, www.economist.com/node/21558281.
27. In the Matter of Barclays PLC, Barclays Bank PLC, and Barclays Capital Inc. CFTC Docket No. 12–25 (2012).
28. Ibid.
29. Ibid.
30. Ibid.
31. Ibid.
32. "Barclays Reveals Bank of England Libor Phone Call Details," *BBC Business*, July 3, 2012, www.bbc.co.uk/news/business-18695181.
33. Carrick Mollenkamp, "Fed Knew of Libor Issue In 2007–08 Proposed Reforms," Reuters, July 10, 2012.
34. Michael S. Derby, "Fed Aware of Libor Problems in Fall 2007," *The Wall Street Journal*, July 13, 2012, online.wsj.com/article/SB10001424052702303919504577524830226504326.html.
35. Mollenkamp.
36. Ibid.
37. Ibid.
38. Ibid.
39. Ibid.
40. Louise Armitstead, "Libor Scandal: FSA Chief Lord Turner to Face MPs over Rate Abuses," *Telegraph*, July 15, 2012.
41. David Enrich and Max Colchester, "Embattled FSA Is under Fire for Libor Policing," *The Wall Street Journal*, July 5, 2012, online.wsj.com/article/SB10001424052702303684004577508880361170286.html.
42. Ibid.
43. Ibid.
44. Ibid.
45. House of Commons, "Treasury Committee Fixing Libor, Some Preliminary Findings, Second Report of Session 2012–2013," Ordered by the House of Commons, to be printed August 9, 2012, pursuant to Standing Order No. 137.
46. Ibid.
47. Ibid.

Chapter 2

Jon Corzine's Fallen Empire of Risk: MF Global

Take calculated risks. That is quite different than being rash.

—*General George S. Patton*

2008 was the year the rules should have changed.

The fall of proud US banking institutions such as Lehman Brothers and Bear Stearns was both shocking and disturbing to those on Wall Street and Main Street. These banks survived major world events—in Lehman's case, even the Civil War. In only a matter of months, in 2008, they ceased to exist. Their names were reduced to stories of "what not to do" for hotshot traders and MBA students alike.

Yet, in March 2010, along came Jon Corzine.

The former New Jersey Senator and senior managing director of Goldman Sachs was looking for a new opportunity in the world of finance. After searching for the right position, he was approached by a dear old friend, J. C. Flowers, to lead the nearly 230-year-old brokerage firm, MF Global.

MF Global was known in international finance circles as strictly a brokerage house that placed futures contracts for its diversified client base. MF Global had no investment banking business lines and did not engage in proprietary trading. Proprietary trading is banking on the firm's own account, not a client's.

Admittedly, Corzine was drawn to MF Global by the allure of making massive profits and reliving his own self-perceived Goldman Sachs glory days.[1] To recreate his image, once Corzine gained control of MF Global, he hastily worked to create a new business plan that called for the commodities firm to aggressively transform into an investment bank in three to five years.[2] This was despite the fact that MF Global had no experience, infrastructure, or talent to make this pipe dream a reality.

The firm lacked any of the tools to operate as a successful investment bank, yet Corzine believed that through his talents, he could defy reality and rapidly transform MF Global into a brazen, risk-taking investment bank in a limited amount of time.

We all know how the story ended. Less than 18 months after Corzine assumed the CEO position of MF Global, his policies of destruction led the firm into bankruptcy. Most notably, Corzine placed dramatically risky bets with billions of dollars of firm and customer capital in European debt.

These investments largely occurred off-balance-sheet in repo-to-maturity deals, which were similar in purpose to the transactions that earlier hid the toxic assets which eviscerated Lehman Brothers and Bear Stearns.

At least Lehman and Bear had decades-old investment banking infrastructure, the best talent, layers of risk personnel, and other governance controls. MF Global had few if any of these essential tools to navigate the complex new order of investment banking, leading to the nascent bank's rapid demise.

The bankruptcy of MF Global demonstrates that three years after the onslaught of the worst financial crisis since the Great Depression, the rules of the game remain unchanged. Similar to 2008, regulators were left with egg on their faces and helplessly looking for answers.

Just as the SEC had not acted to prevent the collapse of the mortgage-backed security house of cards, the Commodities and Futures Trading Commission (CFTC) stood idly by as MF Global recklessly used customer capital as collateral to place bad bets on risky Euro zone debt. The CFTC only implemented a band-aid to the problem after the bankruptcy of MF Global, when it issued a rule prohibiting the use of customer collateral in complex derivative swap trades.

The regulatory gloves were off during Corzine's leadership, giving him the freedom to mold the bank in his image, unchecked. A disturbing incestuous relationship between the CFTC and Corzine existed that likely contributed to the "hands-off" policy to MF Global's new risk taking agenda.

The CFTC chairman at the time, Gary Gensler, like Corzine, was a former Goldman Sachs senior managing director. At Goldman, the two worked together closely.[3] Incredibly, according to Corzine, the two maintained a cozy relationship throughout 2010 and 2011, including Corzine inviting Gensler to speak at his class at Princeton, various meetings and conference calls, and wedding trips together.[4]

Because of his obvious conflict of interest, Gensler had to recuse himself from arguably the most important investigation his agency has faced.

The systemic collapse evident from the fall of MF Global is reminiscent of the troubled times of 2008. It is a major sign that little has been done to rid our financial system of pervasive economic vice.

History of MF Global

The history of MF Global traces back to the eighteenth century. James Man founded the original parent company in 1783 as a super cooperage and brokerage at 23 Harp Lane in the City of London. Through James' connections, the rise of Man was swift. In only one year, the brokerage won the exclusive contract to supply rum to the Royal Navy. The company retained this exclusive contract until 1970.[5]

In 1802, Man expanded the company's brokerage business to include sugar, coffee, cocoa, and other commodities. In eight years it moved its offices to Mincing Lane, the City of London's center of commodity trading. Throughout the nineteenth century, the brokerage house moved forward with product diversification and opened up new markets to expand its business. In 1860, the company was named E.D. & F Man after James Man's grandchildren, Edward Desborough Man and Frederick Man.

As time wore on, the company continued to expand, diversify, and become a trusted commodities trader—not just in Britain but also around the world. Today, the parent company has trading offices in the Americas, the Far East, Africa, and around the world.[6]

Beginning in the 1970s, the commodities business changed as customers looked for ways they could invest in goods and make a sizable return. The days of conservatively placing bets as insurance to insulate against future price movements was over.

In 1983, after celebrating the company's 200-year anniversary, the company announced it would enter the alternative investment industry. This segment of the business was called Man Financial. By this time, E.D. & F Man had over 650 employees around the world. E.D. & F Man not only had a diversified array of commodity deals to broker but was diversifying products offered to clients.

E.D. & F Man was still operating as a partnership until it went public on the London Stock Exchange in 1994. The company changed its full name to the Man Group in 2000. Only the company's agricultural business retained the E.D. & F Man name.

Jon Corzine's Midwestern Roots

He isn't sure where he came from, but Jon Corzine has always known where he was going.

Corzine thinks his family might be from England, France, or Italy, but he isn't sure. Ethnicity and traditions were never of personal importance to him out of the public eye.

Corzine grew up in the town of Taylorville, Illinois, close to Decatur.[7] His roots were small-town and agrarian. Corzine's father worked as a farmer and sold insurance. Corzine's mother taught first and second grade at the local middle school.[8]

His grandfather lost nearly everything he had during the Great Depression. As a result, Corzine's father was very stingy with money and careful about amassing too much credit. "My father never had a credit card, was afraid of any kind of financial risk because he saw what happened to his father," Corzine said.[9]

The family lived a few miles north of Taylorville, Illinois, in a small white house on the other side of the railroad tracks. He only lived 200 yards off the interstate highway.[10] While his roots were modest, Corzine came from a highly supportive family: "I grew up in a positive environment," Corzine said. "My father, Roy, was a grain farmer who worked long hours. My mother, Nancy, was an elementary school teacher. The Taylorville community was positive."[11]

Corzine was an engaged student and used sports as a motivation tool, particularly basketball. "Thinking about the things that shaped me, basketball encouraged kids like me to think beyond the life they were living," Corzine said to a local reporter in 1995. "I remember hearing about the Taylorville state champs (1944) when I was in fifth grade. This was something to aspire to. It was a tremendous learning experience."[12]

Corzine was immediately a hit on the basketball court and the local high school coach believed he could be a top prospect for the town's team. "I handpicked Corzine out of seventh grade. I expected him to be outstanding," Taylorville High School basketball coach, Al Sherline, said.[13]

Corzine was the prototypical high school jock. He was the basketball team captain and football quarterback. He went to college at the University of Illinois at Champaign–Urbana in 1969 and graduated Phi Beta Kappa. Unfortunately, he was drafted into the armed forces fairly soon after graduation and enlisted in the US Marines. His drill sergeant nicknamed him "the Professor."[14]

After basic training and other-full time Marine obligations, Corzine returned to Taylorville and then on to Chicago with his wife. He sent around his resume to various banks and finally got a job working in the back office of Continental Illinois National Bank and Trust in 1970.[15]

The Rise of "Fuzzy"

After spending some time at Bank One selling government bonds, Corzine was brought on at Goldman Sachs in 1975 as a trainee on the government bonds desk. Corzine had been making about $15,000 per year at Bank One. He was now making over $50,000 at Goldman, a major improvement.[16]

Looking back on the beginning of his career at Goldman, Corzine recounts that he showed up for his first day of work "in a sport coat" and that he looked "like a country hick."[17] Corzine felt somewhat out of place because of his middle-America country roots. Goldman was young Corzine's first job on Wall Street.

Initially, Corzine only answered phones and retrieved coffee for his superiors, doing little substantive work. However, he got his big break when a large group of government bond traders walked out of the firm to join E.F. Hutton.[18]

Goldman took months to hire replacements, and in that time, Corzine's ambition and moneymaking talent proved valuable to the firm's partnership. "I made more money than the desk had made in the previous couple of years," he said. "Pure luck, I'm sure but it caught people's attention."[19]

Corzine's future quickly became attached to that of firm partners Eric Schoenberg and Victor Chang, who took him under their wing.[20] Corzine worked hard and had a unique knack for making the firm money. These traits were noticed and appreciated among Goldman partners immediately.

Corzine's fortunes quickly skyrocketed. In one year he received a $150,000 bonus. In response, his father prudently said, you ought to come home.[21] Corzine did not. In 1979, he became head of the Government Bonds Desk. He was made partner the next year. At the age of 33, the Midwestern farmboy with Wall Street dreams rose from firm lackey to partner—in only four and a half years.[22]

Corzine's dramatic rise would continue. In the mid-1980s, Corzine was appointed co-head of the increasingly powerful Fixed Income Department. Through this position, he worked hand in hand with powerful Goldman partner Mark Winkleman. The measured Winkleman was viewed as a necessary counterpoint to Corzine's rising power and brashness.

For example, there was a famous incident in 1986 where Corzine flexed his muscles as a confident and equally stubborn trader. He was largely responsible for a gigantic bet in US Treasuries that exposed the partnership to the tune of $150 million. Goldman had bought Treasury securities with a coupon of 8.75 percent and shorted Treasury securities with a coupon of 9.25.[23]

Corzine had to report to the Management Committee every other day to defend his decision. Lucky for him, the market came around as he initially imagined and he made a $10 million profit. "That's the last time I was a day-to-day trader," Corzine explained.[24]

Corzine's rapid rise to power did not go unnoticed. His Midwestern charm in some circles was seen as a camouflage for his behind-the-scenes power drive. "He comes in an attractive package," one Goldman partner noted. "So although he has got a huge ego and huge ambition which far exceeds his ability in both those things—he comes across in a laid-back, low-key disarming style."[25]

His rivals and fellow Goldman partners called him "Fuzzy." Not just because of his fuzzy beard but because he wasn't respected as a thinker and communicator. "He wasn't crisp and wasn't black and white. He fuzzed things when he communicated," a former partner noted.

When longtime Goldman Sachs Chairman, Stephen Friedman, resigned in 1994, the partnership became Corzine's to lead. Because of Freidman's departure, clients and the market lost confidence in the company. Corzine was responsible for mitigating the firm's dramatic client and trading losses, which were exacerbated by Goldman's 50–1 leverage ratio, meaning that at this time roughly $100 billion of assets was supported by $2 billion in partner capital.[26] Further, partners were leading an exodus from Goldman, creating liquidity issues for the firm, which was supported by partner funds.

Corzine was faced with his first crisis. Along with his second in command Hank Paulson, Corzine brought in 58 new partners to the firm and cut costs by 25 percent to solidify and raise capital. Corzine used the promise of a lucrative, imminent public offering as a means to lure new partners to the firm and retain talent.[27]

Making matters worse, in 1994, the Corzine-led Fixed Income Department had lost tremendous amounts of capital. There was a considerable amount of backlash against him leading the firm when he was the very partner who had steered the firm towards hundreds of millions of dollars of losses. Paulson attempted to explain away Corzine's important role by emphasizing, "There had to be someone from the fixed-income side because that's where the problems were."[28]

As William D. Cohan wrote in his book *Money and Power: How Goldman Sachs Came to Rule the World*, the appointment of Corzine to chairman was awarding someone the top position in one of the most prominent banks in the country after he had just presided over a "complete meltdown" in the Fixed Income Department.[29]

Corzine welcomed the challenge despite the turbulent times and lack of faith in his leadership. He said that facing such a grave obstacle was the "art of leadership" and it was unacceptable to "sit around accepting that just because the immediate past was what it was, that's what the future was."[30]

At Goldman, as at MF Global, Corzine unfoundedly believed he was a deft risk taker who could never lose—even when the cards were stacked against him. The banker was part and parcel of the Goldman "myth." As described by Janet Tavakoli, who once worked at Goldman Sachs and is now president of Tavakoli Structured Finance, this myth holds that Goldman Sachs traders are adept risk takers astute at navigating the always-choppy market waters.[31]

The Establishment of MF Global

During the latter half of the twentieth century, E.D. & F Man decided to capitalize on the increasing demand for hedging financial instruments, a business that was enlarging dramatically since the 1970s.[32] In 1983, E.D. & F consummated a joint venture with Mint, a New Jersey–based fund management firm that helped assist clients looking not just to hedge but to speculate on the trading of the instruments.

The E.D. & F financial services arm soon became dominant within the industry. In 2000, the pure commodities group splintered off, and in 2007 the E.D. & F American brokerage arm was spun off in an initial public offering and listed as MF Global on the New York Stock Exchange.[33]

MF Global went public in June 2007 and immediately capitalized from greater public exposure. The mortgage market was tanking, yet newly minted MF Global's brokerage business was thriving because it did not partake in the investment banking business.

In its first public press release announcing quarterly results, MF Global announced GAAP net revenues of $374.4 million and net income of $72.9 million. CEO Kevin Davis explained at the time, "This was a solid quarter for MF Global driven by continued strong performance in Europe and Asia. Our unique diversification across products, markets, and clients continues to deliver consistent results."[34]

The company emphasized its ability to stay consistent despite market turbulence. "Our business is one which tends to thrive in times of market turmoil and uncertainty," Davis said. "We remain confident in our long-term financial objectives as well as the overall growth potential for MF Global."[35]

MF Global's approach was to create income through traditional commodities brokerage operations with a focus on diversification. Critically, the company was designed to remain stable even in times of market distress.

Only months after announcing its first public results, MF Global boosted the capability of its board of directors.

CEO Kevin Davis brought on board Eileen Fusco, an attorney and CPA with 25 years of financial services experience. Fucso last worked as a financial expert for the SEC and as a senior partner at Deloitte and Touche. With the recent IPO, Fusco's appointment provided an important voice on the board to ensure compliance with GAAP, GAAS, and CFA and SEC regulations.

By September 30, 2007, MF Global was thriving. It recorded net revenue of $809.9 million, up 19 percent from 2006.[36]

Rogue Trader Scandal

Although 2007 was an exciting time of rebirth for MF Global, its reputation took a major nosedive in 2008 because of a small but devastating glitch in its newly implemented internal control and risk-management structures.

Brent "Evan" Dooley joined MF Global as a commodities trader in 2006. He had previously worked at six commodities firms in a short period of time. He had left all of them on bad terms.

Dooley was a degenerate gambler. His personal balance sheet was illiquid. In September 2002, Brent Dooley filed for bankruptcy, listing $153,600 in assets and $669,816 in liabilities. He gave up his house and a leased 2003 Cadillac DTS, court records in Memphis show. His US income tax return that year reported \$87,910 in trading losses.[37] He repeatedly failed to pay required alimony and child support payments from a prior marriage. In 2006, a judge placed a lien on his car for failing to pay court-required support payments.[38]

Dooley joined MF Global's Memphis branch. However, two years later, his lust for personal gambling intruded on the workplace. He placed an unauthorized wheat futures bet while trading for his own account. His financial gamble amounted to a huge \$141 million loss for MF Global. Dooley had no apparent way to pay, so the firm was forced to make good on the contracts.[39]

As a result of the firm's bad-hiring decision, MF Global faced serious market questions regarding its liquidity. Confidence in the MF Global brand spiraled in a market race to the bottom.

Weeks after Dooley's rogue trading was disclosed to the market, on St. Patrick's Day 2007, MF Global shares decreased 65 percent because of rumors of the firm's limited liquidity. The firms stock traded at the lowest levels since the initial IPO at \$3.64.[40]

While CEO Ken Davis valiantly enacted new risk controls and oversight procedures, this was not enough. He had to find a way to fight back against viscous market rumors that MF Global lacked liquidity to support its business.

In May 2008, the firm announced a deal with former Goldman Chief, J. C. Flowers, one of Jon Corzine's closest friends. Flowers purchased a \$300 million piece of the company so it could meet its various debt obligations. As part of the deal, Flowers was given the power to appoint new directors to MF Global.

This deal with the devil enabled Flowers to exert tremendous control over the future of MF Global. The arrival of his old buddy Jon Corzine was imminent.

From Gubernatorial Disgrace to MF Global CEO

J. C. Flowers helped place Corzine in control of MF Global in late March 2010. Corzine was looking to revitalize his career and reputation. He had recently lost his New Jersey gubernatorial reelection bid to Republican upstart Chris Christie.

The latter years of Corzine governorship were mired in salacious corruption. In fact, in the heat of the race on July 31, 2009, 44 members of New Jersey's government were arrested on charges of money laundering and corruption, including three mayors, two state assemblymen, and several city councilmen.

Many of the public figures arrested and under FBI investigation were "close allies" of Corzine, according to *The New York Times*.[41]

The FBI searched the home and office of Corzine's commissioner of the Department of Community Affairs, Joseph V. Doria Jr. Another important Corzine ally, Mayor Jeremiah T. Healy of Jersey City, the state's second-largest city, was alleged to have been involved in allowing improper campaign donations with the promise of anticipated help on massive real estate projects.[42]

Whether Corzine knew about such political abuse is debatable. However, in 2009, the New Jersey populace had had enough and voted him out of office. Nonetheless, Corzine wanted to get back into finance, a profession that he perceived supported risk taking, big bets, and close relationships with the right people (like Flowers).

In his congressional testimony after the fall of MF Global, Corzine explained why MF Global's CEO position was attractive to him:

> It [MF Global] had several positive attributes such as memberships on multiple derivative exchanges around the globe, solid market shares on those exchanges, and an extensive set of client relationships. I saw the possibility of taking part in the transformation of a challenged company by restructuring existing businesses and capturing opportunities available in the post-2008 financial environment.[43]

Notably, Corzine did not mention "the ability to transform the brokerage into an investment bank in his image."

MF Global under Corzine

In late 2010, MF Global was on its heels and had posted consecutive losing years. The company's income depended on commissions earned from placing commodities futures bets for its clients, execution, and clearing services, and from interest on customer accounts.[44] With interest rates remaining at historic lows, MF Global struggled to generate enough income to remain perennially profitable.

To reverse the firm's fortunes, Corzine enacted a three- to five-year plan designed to place MF Global on the fast track to becoming a broker-dealer, and then a living, fire-breathing, risk-taking investment bank. There was a major catch. MF Global had sparse existing infrastructure to conduct traditional investment banking services such as underwriting, asset management, proprietary trading, and managing complex derivative risk.

Inclusive of the new MF Global business plan was a fateful decision, in the summer of 2010, to make a major investment in European sovereign debt. European nations issue bonds as debt securities that are actively traded in international markets. Corzine believed quick profits in these securities were possible through off-balance-sheet repo to maturity (RTM) transactions.

Similar in purpose to the nefarious Lehman REPO 105, these unique arrangements allowed MF Global to keep these investments off balance sheet because of an accounting technicality that enabled the deals to constitute "sales" rather than traditional repurchases under generally accepted accounting principles (GAAP) rules governing securities transactions.

Corzine routinely transacted with other banks, as counterparties, to "sell" millions of European sovereign bonds, knowing they would be sold back to MF Global in a fixed period of time, on the maturity date. Counterparty banks were required to sell the bonds back to MF Global along with their respective interest rates.

Corzine foresaw profits from the "spread" on the difference between the interest rate of the European bonds and MF Global's obligation to pay the interest rate of the RTM deal.

In a stable market, where prices remained static, the RTM deals could work beautifully. MF Global would receive the bonds back at the same price and, additionally, higher interest payments from its counterparty. Yet, there was a reason the interest rate of the European bonds was so high. They were intrinsically risky bets that could spiral out of control based on market confidence in the Euro zone.

For example, in a stressed European debt market, where bond prices steadily decrease, the RTM transactions created significant liquidity and capital risk. Counterparty banks could demand additional collateral from MF Global through "margin calls" that required the firm to sweeten the pot. Further, if the prices of the bonds severely decreased, MF Global would receive the assets at lower values than it sold them for. Corzine was taking a huge gamble on the European sovereign debt market, with $6.3 billion of company funds hanging in the balance.

A year after MF Global made the decision to invest in Euro zone bonds, the Financial Industry Regulatory Authority (FINRA) realized that MF Global was substantially exposed off balance sheet after conducting a routine review of MF Global's May 31, 2011, financial statement.

Accordingly, FINRA and the SEC had "detailed" discussions with MF Global in mid-June 2011, where they insisted that the firm was not allocating enough capital against the risky RTM European bond portfolio.[45] MF Global was not compelled to reserve any firm capital against its exposure to the European bonds because the RTM deals were graced with precious GAAP "sale" status.

In October of 2011, Corzine's hand folded in spectacular fashion. Once the credit rating agency, Moody's, learned of the RTM portfolio exposure, it downgraded MF Global to "junk" status on October 24, 2011. This, along with weakened market confidence in European debt, precipitated investors to sell their stock, clients to remove their money, and counterparties to demand additional collateral on the $6.3 billion RTM portfolio.[46]

Making matters much worse, the MF Global bankruptcy trustee, James Giddens, reported on February 6, 2012, that MF Global routinely used customer funds to meet margin calls or other obligations to counter parties in conducting regular business.[47] As MF Global's exposure to the European debt market intensified, Giddens explained that the company used much larger sums of customer funds to satisfy various obligations until there was no more cash to keep the firm's doors open. Corzine's MF Global was entirely bankrupt in less than two years. Immediately after the company bankruptcy, $1.2 billion in customer funds remained unaccounted for.[48]

Risk Governance Failures

In congressional testimony, former MF Global Chief Risk Officer Michael Roseman explained that Corzine, and the MF Global board of directors, had several opportunities to reduce the firm's exposure to bad Euro zone sovereign debt.[49] Nonetheless, MF Global stubbornly stayed the course even though management (i.e., Corzine) was repeatedly made aware of growing market risks.[50]

Roseman joined MF Global in August of 2008. During his employment with the firm, he provided regular reports to the board and executive officers on the firm's various market exposures. He also was charged with establishing risk thresholds for MF Global's European sovereign investments.

Immediately after Corzine's arrival in late March 2010, Roseman received direct requests from Corzine to "adjust" the European sovereign trading limits. Roseman stated in testimony to Congress that he shared "different views" with Corzine because of the "continued political and financial uncertainty in the relevant countries."[51] The two first agreed on a $1.0 billion trading limit in MF Global's European debt portfolio. This number would drastically rise in the coming months.

In mid-September 2010, Roseman expressed "increasing concerns" regarding the capital risk associated with MF Global's European positions. Rather than addressing Roseman's concerns, Corzine convinced the board to raise the European portfolio-trading limit to $2 billion.[52] Remarkably, in November 2010, the European portfolio was "adjusted" once again to $4.75 billion, despite Roseman's continued warnings of margin calls and price declines.[53]

Corzine and the board fired Roseman in January of 2011. Michael Stockman, a former Goldman Sachs mortgage trader, was hired as the next MF Global chief risk officer. According to his congressional testimony, he "believed that the risk profile associated with the company's European sovereign debt position was acceptable in light of then market conditions."[54]

Stockman stood idly by as the firm dramatically increased its risk exposure during the summer and fall of 2011. Just like his old pal Flowers had hand-picked Corzine to lead MF Global, Corzine hand-picked Stockman because of their shared Goldman ties and stubborn allegiance to risk, speculation, and doubling down on big bets.

The story of MF Global is a tragedy. Its bankruptcy demonstrates how Wall Street casino values destroyed a traditional commodities brokerage that traced its roots back nearly 230 years. Once again, industry regulators failed to prevent speculative risk taking from destroying a prestigious banking institution. As a November 2012 Congressional Report on MF Global concluded, the watchdog effort was "disorganized and haphazard."[55]

Yet, MF Global's demise was not self-inflicted. After the damaging rogue trader crisis, the firm's leadership turned to Flowers, a known Wall Street raider.

Flowers shaped the board of directors and handed control of the firm to Corzine, who changed the very cultural essence of MF Global. The firm was intended to be Corzine's shining accomplishment, after his reputation had been mired in corruption and disappointment. Instead, MF Global turned out as another blemish for the Wall Street titan.

The reshaping of MF Global as a giant exotic derivative Wall Street risk taker was no accident. Corzine willfully eroded risk, governance, and any risk management the company had left, all for the hope of fast money. He is no longer "Fuzzy," the charming Midwesterner. Corzine's addiction to Wall Street values of risk, speculation, and synthetics brought down a centuries-old firm all because his personal ethical compass determined it was acceptable. When an out-of-control CEO ego transforms and overtakes decency and prudence for unattainable short-term glory, the results can be catastrophic.

Notes

1. Corzine stated in his December 8, 2011, congressional testimony that he provided a new business plan that would "evolve" MF Global "into a broker-dealer and ultimately into an investment bank, which would provide broker, dealer, underwriting, advisory, and investment management services."
2. Ibid.
3. Review & Outlook, "The Talented Mr. Gensler," *The Wall Street Journal*, December 12, 2011, online.wsj.com/article/SB10001424052970204903804577080480063317856.html.
4. Ibid.
5. Man Group Timeline. http://www.edfmancapital.com/ed-f-man/history.
6. ED& F Website edfman.com, "about us."

7. Craig Horowitz, "The Deal He Made," *New York Magazine*, July 10, 2005, http://nymag.com/nymetro/news/politics/12194/.
8. Ibid.
9. William Cohan, *Money and Power, How Goldman Sachs Came to Rule the World* (New York: Anchor Books, 2011), p. 341.
10. Bob Fallstrom, "Former Taylorville Basketball Coach Recalls Corzine Skills," *Herald Review.com*, January 23, 2012, www.herald-review.com/news/opinion/editorial/columnists/fallstrom/fallstrom-former-taylorville-basketball-coach-recalls-corzine-s-skills/article_089bf9c4–461f-11e1-a9ee-0019bb2963f4 .html.
11. Ibid.
12. Ibid.
13. Ibid.
14. Cohan, p. 342.
15. Ibid.
16. Robert Farzad and Matthew Leising, "Corzine Lived up to Risk-Taking Reputation at Helm of MF Global," Bloomberg, November 3, 2011, www.bloomberg.com/news/2011–11–03/corzine-lived-up-to-risk-taking-reputation-at-mf-global-before-bankruptcy.html.
17. Ibid.
18. William D. Cohan, "Goldman's Alpha War," *Vanity Fair*, May 2011, www .vanityfair.com/business/features/2011/05/goldman-sachs-201105.
19. Ibid.
20. Ibid.
21. Cohan, "Money and Power," p. 344.
22. Ibid.
23. Ibid.
24. Cohan, "Money and Power," p. 345.
25. Ibid.
26. Ibid.
27. Ibid.
28. Ibid., p. 361.
29. Ibid., p. 362.
30. Ibid., p. 369.
31. Roben Farzad and Matthew Leising, "Corzine Lived Up To Risk-Taking Reputation at Helm of MF Global," Bloomberg, November 3, 2011, www .bloomberg.com/news/2011–11–03/corzine-lived-up-to-risk-taking-reputation-at-mf-global-before-bankruptcy.html.
32. "Evolution of Man From Barrel Maker to Hedge Fund," *The Telegraph*, 28, September 2011, www.telegraph.co.uk/finance/newsbysector/banksandfinance/8793938/Evolution-of-Man-from-barrel-maker-to-hedge-fund.html.
33. Ibid.

34. 2007 Second Quarter MF Global Press Release. Available at SEC Edgar website.
35. Ibid.
36. 2007 Third Quarter MF Global Press Release. Available at SEC Edgar website.
37. Elliot Blair Smith and David Scheer, "MF Global's Dooley Lost House Before Bad Bet on Wheat," Bloomberg, March 6, 2008, www.bloomberg.com/apps/news?pid=newsarchive&refer=home&sid=axeRxkfcktg4.
38. Ibid.
39. Kevin McCoy, "Bankrupt Brokerage MF Global Showed Appetite for Risk," USA Today, November 9, 2011, www.usatoday.com/money/industries/brokerage/story/2011–11–10/mf-global-warning-signs/51145024/1.
40. FTSE Global Markets, "Bernie Dan Leads MF Global's Fight Back," www.ftseglobalmarkets.com/index.php?option=com_k2&view=item&id=191:bernie-dan-leads-mf-globals-fightback-&Itemid=78.
41. David M. Halbfinger and David W. Chen, "Corruption Case a Blow to Corzine's Campaign," The New York Times, July 24, 2009, www.nytimes.com/2009/07/25/nyregion/25jersey.html.
42. Ibid.
43. Corzine congressional testimony, December 8, 2011.
44. Ibid.
45. Luparello congressional testimony, December 8, 2011.
46. Jeannette Neumann and Aaron Lucchetti, "Moody's: MF Bet Was Surprise to It," The Wall Street Journal, January 31, 2012, online.wsj.com/article/SB10001424052970203920204577193542047863420.html.
47. Nick Brown, "MF Global Shortfall Worsened as Bankruptcy Neared," Reuters, February 6, 2012, www.reuters.com/article/2012/02/06/us-mfglobal-idUSTRE8151YK20120206.
48. Ibid.
49. House Committee on Financial Services, Memorandum: "Oversight and Investigations Subcommittee Hearing on the Collapse of MF Global," March 23, 2012.
50. Ibid.
51. Statement of Michel K. Roseman, . . . Before the U.S. House of Representatives Committee on Financial Services Oversight and Investigations Subcommittee, February 2, 2012.
52. Ibid.
53. Ibid.
54. Michael Stockman congressional testimony, February 2, 2012.
55. Ben Protess and Michael J. De La Merced, "House Report Faults MF Global Regulators," The New York Times "DealBook." November 15, 2012, http://dealbook.nytimes.com/2012/11/15/house-report-details-collapse-of-mf-global/.

Chapter 3

The Continued Rating Agencies Game: Will Rating Agencies Be Reined in for the Sake of Global Market Stability?

Truth will lose its credit, if delivered by a person that has none.
—*Bishop Robert South*

I n today's markets, investor confidence, counterparty trust, and reputational risk are critical to the longevity of capitalism, sustainable investment, and the effective spread of globalization. Without investor faith in the world markets that connect us, our financial system crumbles, stock markets descend into death spirals, and banking institutions struggle for liquidity injections.

CEOs, CFOs, risk managers, and government treasury departments are charged with ensuring that their balance sheets are solvent and that investors, shareholders, and market participants can trust in their long-term legitimacy. To prevent worst-case scenarios, good governance and internal controls are essential.

Yet, in the last five years, an external force has dropped an atom bomb on the best-laid plans of boards of directors, risk managers, and sovereign governments. In the name of their own bottom line, credit rating agencies have selfishly flexed their muscle through "pay-to-play" agreements for golden AAA ratings and downgraded seemingly stable sovereign governments. Slight differences in credit rating can decrease the stock prices of private companies, erode investor confidence, and destroy institutional reputation. Because of this phenomenon, rating agencies have taken advantage by asking for lavish sums in return for a cursory review and the treasured AAA rating.

In fact, from mortgage-backed securities to the sovereign debt crisis, credit rating agencies have had a dangerously virulent effect on global markets and, in the process, have disrupted the essential flow of accurate information critical to efficient markets.

Most alarmingly, rating agencies have knowingly disregarded their original mission of providing accurate AAA ratings. This has been close to a conspiratorial effort between banks and rating agencies, solely to boost profit and raise investor capital in risky investments that are falsely deemed safe. Indeed, duping investors into believing their money is protected in worthless securities with a AAA or high rating allowed banks to peddle subprime securities during the credit crisis and unsustainably inflate the mortgage bubble.

A Duke University Kenan Institute for Business Ethics case study on rating agencies illustrates the very essence of this failure:

> With the rise of subprime mortgage securitization, conflicts of interest formed in the securitization supply chain. . . . The most significant conflicts of interest involved the way the investment banks would procure ratings on their securitizations. In essence, banks would only do business with the CRAs [credit rating agencies] that provided the favorable ratings that banks wanted to show investors. The more complex the securitization product, the more the CRA would get paid.[1]

Perhaps more than any other institutions within the financial community, rating agencies have contradicted their very mission and duties to global market investors.

For example, Standard and Poor's (S&P) proudly states on its website that its organization facilitates "better informed investment decisions with market intelligence in the form of credit ratings, indices, investment research, and risk evaluations and solutions."[2]

Yet, during the great credit crisis, Standard & Poor's, along with its two brothers in arms Fitch and Moody's, categorically misled investors by knowingly bestowing their top credit ratings to worthless subprime mortgage assets.

The root of the problem is that S&P's business model is undiversified and entirely reliant on "pay-to-play" credit rating services.

In fact, Bloomberg reported that S&P's parent, New York–based McGraw-Hill Cos., depended on credit ratings for 27 percent of its $6.19 billion of revenue in 2010—down from 33 percent of $6.77 billion in 2007, but still an extremely large percentage of its business revenue.[3]

Credit rating agencies cling to this undiversified business model because it is lucrative and legal. Moody's revenue from grading company debt and financial borrowers rose 26 percent in 2010 to $843 million from 2009, according to company filings. That compared with a 10 percent increase from giving grades to public securities.[4]

S&P doesn't provide a granular level of profit detail garnered from debt rating services. Yet, in 2010, its sales rose 10 percent to $1.7 billion and profit increased 7 percent, driven in part by record-high yield corporate bond issuance.[5]

Fitch, a unit of Paris-based Fimalac, said revenue grew 6.3 percent to 488 million euros ($678 million) in 2010 from a year earlier, without disclosing the breakdown of contributions.[6]

The collateral debt obligation (CDO) financial instrument, in particular, provided tremendous wealth during the financial crisis to agencies such as S&P through pay-to-play agreements with subprime mortgage originators. Indeed, S&P collected as much as $750,000 to grade pieces of a collateralized debt obligations before the credit market meltdown in 2008.[7]

It's "just another demonstration of the fact that ratings have historically been skewed by the parties that are compensating the raters," Byron Georgiou, a commissioner on the Financial Inquiry Commission Panel, said. "You can frequently demonstrate the accuracy of ratings by following the money."[8]

The promises of continued revenue have stymied any internal reformist effort within credit rating agencies themselves. In August 2011, S&P provided AAA grades to 59 percent of Springleaf Mortgage Loan Trust 2011–1, a set of bonds tied to $497 million lent to homeowners with below-average credit scores and almost no equity in their properties.[9]

How can subprime assets justifiably be categorized as safe assets?

Our judicial system is similarly puzzled. On May 7, 2012, the Southern District of New York refused to dismiss complaints against S&P, Fitch, and Moody's. The complaints alleged that the agencies collaborated with banks in arranging for ratings as high as AAA for assets with low quality and subprime underlying collateral.[10]

In contrast to their considerable profits from rating debt securities, rating agencies receive little to nothing in commissions from sovereigns. As a result, rating agencies are far more strict on sovereign nations because of this differing relationship.

Despite their inherent conflicts, global market participants still rely on rating agencies for future indicators of bond performance. Therefore, when a major "big three" rating agency (Moody's, S&P, Fitch) issues a negative outlook or lower credit rating on a sovereign or municipality, it can have drastic consequences for stock markets and the perceived vitality of an individual sovereign.

Rating agencies can be a critical force in ensuring that accurate information is disseminated to global investors about the vitality of global economies. Yet, in recent months, they have neglected this duty in favor of making brazen statements regarding the financial health of the most trusted economies in the world.

Rather than calming global investors during these times of market crisis, the big three credit agencies are quick to show their immense power by rapidly downgrading countries, and issuing dire warnings of apocalyptic doomsday scenarios.

Famously, in August 2011, S&P downgraded the United States from AAA to AA. In response to this bold statement of rating agency authority, savvy investor Warren Buffett (and a shareholder of Moody's) insisted that the decision could change his opinion of S&P as a fair and balanced entity.[11]

In January 2012, France lost its top rating status along with a number of other stable European counties. Only one month later, in February 2012, Moody's went farther, suggesting that the United Kingdom's AAA rating was in dangerous decay and that there was uncertainty of UK default. This rather ridiculous prognostication for one of the most stable economies in the world only promulgates fear, uncertainty, and distrust in the performance of sovereign bond notes.

Apart from the most notable downgrades, between October 2006 and April 2010 there were 71 total announcements on sovereign nation outlooks.[12] According to a recent IMF working paper, all of these announcements had serious effects on international markets, none greater in effect than the rating downgrade announcements concerning the "PIGS" countries of the rating zone (Portugal, Ireland, Greece, or Spain).[13]

Are investments in these countries really more risky than putting millions of dollars in subprime securities?

These continual downgrades of Euro zone sovereign nations have tremendously destabilized the region during a time in which investor confidence is most critical. Disgusted with the influence that the big three credit rating agencies have had in Europe, the EU has sought out other alternatives.

On February 28, 2012, only two weeks after the negative outlook on the United Kingdom was issued, a draft report from the European Parliament proposed sweeping regulatory powers that included the right to ban sovereign credit ratings if countries do not want them.[14]

"The prime aim is to restore credit rating agencies to their rightful place," Leonardo Domenici, a member of European Parliament, said in an e-mail to *The New York Times*, "This implies that their ratings should be treated as information to be taken into account, but that agencies should not themselves enjoy special status or automatically influence the activities of economic and financial operators and public institutions."[15]

On April 16, 2012, a blueprint for establishing a global nonprofit credit rating agency for sovereign debt was outlined by the Bertelsmann Foundation.[16] This effort was aimed at eviscerating the power of the big three rating agencies to affect the ebbs and flows of global markets.

"In light of these downgrades and their critical timing, the acceptance, transparency, and legitimacy of sovereign ratings have been put into question," said the foundation in a public statement.[17]

Annette Heuser, executive director at Bertelsmann and one of the authors of the proposal, said, "We believe that we have to make a decision now, either to live with the shortcomings of the sovereign-risk sector or to have an international debate about how we can improve the system."[18]

Heuser's blueprint aims to establish an international nonprofit credit rating agency, known as Incra, that would be funded by a $400 million endowment and be structured so that management and rating decisions are independent from its financiers.[19]

Even former big three executives realize that the system is fundamentally broken. Vincent Truglia, former head of the sovereign risk unit at Moody's, helped craft the Incra proposal. In formulating Incra, Truglia's stated purpose is to destroy the conflicts of interest from the rating process.

"There is widespread concern that the profit motive might contaminate the decision-making process," Truglia and his fellow authors noted, "Since Incra is not based on the classic for-profit structure for ratings, the agency is therefore not dependent on solicited sovereign ratings."[20]

Regardless of what solutions are suggested and potentially implemented, we are currently facing a pay-to-play rating agency system where a cherished AAA rating is based on the wads of cash provided to the big three rating agencies. The result is that the AAA rating means nothing. Investors can no longer rely on and trust the very entities designed to provide them with the valuable service of forward-looking market prognostications and performance.

The failure of rating agencies only further demonstrates that in the rubble of the great credit crisis, prudence, thrift, and responsibility has been sacrificed for selfish short-term profit.

History of Rating Agencies

The idea of a "rating" agency was a twentieth century creation. During the mid- to late-nineteenth century, the Industrial Revolution, and specifically, the railroad industry, required sophisticated financing. Banks like Goldman Sachs and Lehman Brothers stepped in. They issued railroad bond debt notes to investors looking to make a profit off the railroad boom. Investors actively traded these bonds, which could be worth a great deal at their maturity date.

With so many railroad bonds floating in the marketplace there grew a need for guidance on their quality. In 1860, Henry Varnum Poor published a *History of the Railroads and Canals of the United States*. This was the first attempt at generating a comprehensive account of the financial and operational strength of the railroad industry.[21]

Varnum Poor founded the company H.V. and H.W. Poor Co. with his son, Henry William Poor. In 1868, the father and son team published *The Manual of the Railroads of the United States*. This document received far more exposure than their previous manual. In only a few months, the Poors sold all 2,500 copies they produced. The foundation for the modern Standard & Poor's was laid.

A few decades later, John Moody furthered the growth of the future ratings business. Originally a Wall Street errand boy, Moody saw a need in the market for specific, accurate performance information for various institutional bonds. In 1900, he founded John Moody & Company and published the Moody's *Manual of Industrial and Miscellaneous Securities*.[22]

This manual provided information and statistics on stocks and bonds of a wide array of entities, including financial institutions, government agencies, manufacturing, mining, utilities, and food companies.[23] Remarkably, within two months the publication sold out. In only three years, Moody's circulation exploded, and the company's index of bonds became known as the definitive literature on the state of the bond market.

However, when the stock market crashed in 1907, Moody's company did not have adequate capital to survive, and he was forced to sell his manual business.[24]

In 1909, Moody returned to the financial market with a new idea: instead of simply collecting information on the property, capitalization, and management of companies, he now offered investors an analysis of security values. This time, he focused on expert valuation and analysis of bond quality. His company published a book that analyzed the railroads and their outstanding securities. It offered concise conclusions about their relative investment quality. He expressed his conclusions using letter grades adopted from the mercantile and credit rating system that had been used by the credit-reporting firms since the late 1800s.[25] This new manual soon became the industry standard for weighing investment options.

Moody was fiercely entrepreneurial. In 1913, he expanded his business to include rating industrial companies and utilities.[26] One year later, he founded Moody's Investors Services in New York City. In 1917, Moody's began rating bonds issued by the US government and other municipalities.[27] By 1924, Moody's ratings covered nearly 100 percent of the US bond market.[28]

Shortly after John Moody's rapid success in the bond rating business, John Knowles Fitch founded the Fitch Publishing Company in 1913. A former florist, Fitch saw an opportunity to become a fixture in an emerging industry. *The Fitch Stock and Bond Manual* soon became another widely distributed ratings publication. In 1924, Fitch began conducting detailed analysis of securities on a rating scale from AAA to D in a similar fashion to Moody's.[29]

Prior to the Great Depression, credit ratings served a major purpose. The SEC did not yet exist; therefore, market actors were responsible for self-regulation. Credit ratings provided the information services required for investors to make informed decisions.[30]

Like the real estate bubble, the booming years of the 1920s had its expiration date. In the aftermath, there were accusations of *banksterism* because of the massive fees collected by those who sold speculative and inherently risky securities to the public.[31] Sound familiar?

The Great Depression served as the spark that resulted in the significant market reliance we have on credit agencies today. During the 1930s, in order to attack the proliferation of speculative securities in the market and to reverse the downward spiral of the financial system, the US Office of the Comptroller of the Currency (OCC) made an emergency decision that elevated the role of rating agencies to national importance.

The OCC decided to institute formulas based on rating agency credit ratings to book the valuation of US national bank bond portfolios.[32] Moreover, in 1936, the important role of credit rating agencies was furthered when the OCC restricted the purchase by banks of securities with lower credit ratings.

Yet, the OCC failed to take into account that the rating agencies' projections were overly optimistic in the boom years of the 1920s, with upgrades greatly outnumbering downgrades.[33] The rating agencies were blissfully ignorant. A famous example involved a default by the Chicago, Rock Island & Pacific Railroad on bonds that all of the major rating agencies had given the highest possible ratings during the 1920s.[34]

If the 1920s were a decade in which rating agencies established a presence in US markets and the 1930s were a time when they were relied on to stabilize markets, the period after World War II only continued to exacerbate their decline.

According to a study of 207 corporate bond rating changes from 1950 to 1972, credit ratings were ineffective, out of date, and of little to no value for investors.[35] Changes merely reflected information already incorporated into stock market prices—and lagged that information by as much as 18 months in certain instances.[36]

As a result of the credit rating industry's inability to serve as a leading voice on market trends and stay ahead of the curve, the public argued for its regulation as early as the 1950s.[37] Rather than regulate credit rating agencies, however, the SEC continued to rely on them as a supposed reliable benchmark on the financial services industry. For instance, during the early 1970s the SEC made the decision to elevate the status of credit ratings considerably.

The agency proclaimed that the ratings of a handful of major credit rating agencies would now be necessary in order to ascertain suitable net capital requirements for broker dealers.[38] The SEC mandated that only nationally recognized statistical rating organizations (NRSROs) would be able to be used for this important purpose. The big three, Moody's, S&P, and Fitch, were grandfathered into this category.

To profit from their emergence as the critical benchmark for market participants, credit rating agencies wisely changed their economics. Around the 1980s, the big three agencies decided to charge *security issuers* for credit ratings rather than rely on fees from investors.[39]

While not immediate, this led to the boom of rating agency revenue that occurred during the 1990s. By 1997, Moody's was rating 20,000 public and private issuers in the United States and about 1,200 non-US issuers, including both sovereign states and corporations.[40]

Taking note of the boom in credit rating agencies, in 1996, journalist Tom Freidman stated on *News Hour with Jim Lehrer*, "There are two superpowers in the world today in my opinion. There's the United States and there's Moody's Bond Rating Service. The United States can destroy you by dropping bombs, and Moody's can destroy you by downgrading your bonds. And believe me, it's not clear sometimes who's more powerful."[41]

In fact, Moody's, in particular, experienced a tremendous boom in revenue, especially after going public in 2000. By 2005, Moody's market capitalization exceeded *$15 billion*, roughly equal to the international investment bank, Bear Stearns.[42] Moody's revenue as of 2005 was nearly $1.5 billion.[43]

The dramatic rise in profitability was largely due to the SEC's role as gatekeeper. Since establishing the concept of an NRSRO, the SEC approved only four additional credit rating agencies as possible NRSROs, substantially increasing the monopoly of the big three.

As Lawrence J. White at the Stern School of Business writes, "Without the NRSRO designation, any would-be bond rater would likely be ignored by most financial institutions; and, since the financial institutions would ignore the would-be bond rater so would bond issuers."[44]

Lack of competition in the market allowed the big three to flourish and increase profits exponentially as new financial instruments such as mortgage-related securities were introduced into the market. In fact, since the big three NRSROs were grandfathered in, the next officially admitted NRSRO organization was Dominion Bond Rating Services in 2003.[45] Therefore, outside of the big three, there was no other official NRSRO until 2003, allowing the SEC to act as gatekeeper to a booming rating agency monopoly.

The conflict of interest in rating a bond issuer and receiving a profit from them for that rating coupled with literally no competition in the market creates a disastrous situation where rating agencies abdicate their duties to investors.

Indeed, the record of the big three credit rating agencies was blemished long before the mortgage-backed security debacle. Most wantonly, only five days before Enron declared bankruptcy in 2001, the big three uniformly held that Enron's bonds were "investment grade."[46] The rating agencies were similarly tardy in recognizing the supremely weakened state of WorldCom during its own accounting crisis.

The SEC was required to issue a report on the credit rating industry by Sarbanes–Oxley legislation, yet its report failed to mitigate any of the troubling trends for NRSRO credit rating agencies that had plagued the "big three" companies since the 1920s.

Where were the aggressive investigations of these failed companies on behalf of investors?

Although rating agencies receive funds from bond issuers, rating agencies receive no funds from sovereigns or municipalities. Curiously, these ratings are downgraded far more ravenously.

Mortgages and the Ratings Boondoggle

The tremendous growth of securitized mortgage products in the late 1990s and 2000s was a case study of the rating agencies' conflict of interest at its worst. In fact, credit rating agencies acted as a knowing accomplice to the subprime mortgage crisis boondoggle.

The big three were critical to the development of the securitized subprime mortgage market. As Lawrence White explains, ratings had the "force of law" with respect to the SEC-regulated financial institutions' abilities and incentives through net capital incentives to invest in the bonds.[47] Higher ratings meant the securities were far more marketable in the market.

The reputation and preeminent role of credit rating agencies in the global economy encouraged the trust of market participants that their investments in mortgage-backed security assets would be safe with a AAA rating.[48]

Based on the structure of the mortgages underlying a specific security during the mortgage boom, the securitizer of the asset would make a higher profit if the relevant investment vehicle attained a higher rating on a larger percentage of the tranches of securities that were issued against those mortgages.[49]

Why? Because the higher rated tranches carried lower interest rates, resulting in an enhanced profit spread for the specific securitizer.

Accordingly, there was a coordinated effort by mortgage-securitizing banks with credit rating agencies to ensure that their assets were top-rated regardless of what the market was doing.[50]

The mortgage securitization rating process was nothing short of a giant hoax. In 2009, James Crotty wrote in the *Cambridge Journal of Economics*:

> The growth of mortgage securitization generated fee income— to banks and mortgage brokers who sold the loans, investment bankers who packaged the loans into securities, banks and specialist institutions who serviced the securities and ratings agencies who gave them their seal of approval.

Since fees do not have to be returned if the securities later suffer large losses, everyone involved had strong incentives to maximize the flow of loans through the system, whether or not they were sound. Total fees from home sales and mortgage securitization from 2003 to 2008 have been estimated at $2 trillion.[51]

This was not a scheme that was simply unnoticed during the credit crisis. In 2005, attorney David J. Reiss drafted an article, "Subprime Standardization: How Rating Agencies Allow Predatory Lending to Flourish in the Secondary Mortgage Market."[52] On the cusp of the great credit crisis, Reiss noted that credit rating agencies' "privileged regulatory status" created a lack of effective responsibility:

> They [credit rating agencies] have been granted a privileged regulatory status by the Securities and Exchange Commission and other government regulators, they have not been assigned a reciprocal responsibility to the public, as the GSEs have been. As a result of this mismatch between privilege and responsibility, those concerned with the rights of homeowners should meet the Privileged Raters' efforts to impose standardization on the mortgage market with greater skepticism.[53]

Despite Reiss's warnings of mortgage market skepticism because of credit rating agencies' lack of accountability, there was no push to investigate the true worth of ratings for mortgage-backed securities and other real estate–related products.

No investigations occurred, in large part because of the dangerous conflict of interest in how the big three rate securities. A recent study by scholars at Indiana University, American University, and Rice University examined the actual defaults of securities rated A by Moody's over a 30-year period. Sovereign bonds rated A had no defaults over a 30-year period, compared to 27.2 percent of securities backed by debt such as mortgages and loans assigned that ranking, the study of Moody's Investors Service data reported.[54]

"There's a problem here of conflicts, credibility and competence," said Phil Angelides, chairman of the Financial Crisis Inquiry Commission. "The current model is tragically broken, it needs to be abandoned," he said in an Oct. 14, 2011, interview.

Obviously, in response to the study by three major university scholars, the big three fought back. "We disagree with the study's methods and findings," said Michael Adler, a spokesman for Moody's. "It attempts to draw broad conclusions about the comparability of Moody's ratings over time by relying disproportionately on the ratings performance of US housing-related securities during the financial crisis." S&P spokesman Edward Sweeney said its criteria are "developed and applied independent of any commercial considerations."[55]

Although the rating agencies have a right to defend themselves, their actions during the credit crisis were self-serving and lacked any tangible value to investors. Most heinously, during the credit crisis, the rating agencies were intimately involved in luring investors into purchasing knowingly risky AAA-rated subprime securities.

In a Southern District of New York Court Opinion by Judge Shira Scheindlin, Scheindlin noted that the rating agencies (S&P, Fitch, and Moody's) had controlling interests in a special investment vehicle (SIV) called *Rhinebridge* that issued subprime securities to investors.[56] The Rhinebridge SIV collapsed because of the worthless nature of its debt issuances.

Scheindlin's opinion is particularly illustrative of the rating agencies' special relationship with subprime mortgage origination:

> The Rating Agencies had a significant ongoing role in the operation of Rhinebridge, which included (among other rights and responsibilities) the right to veto changes in management

and the right to review and potentially veto any changes in how Rhinebridge obtained funding, modified its operating instructions, or changed its investment guidelines. Regardless of their historical roles, the Rating Agencies did not merely provide ratings; rather, they were deeply entrenched in the creation and operation of Rhinebridge.

The Rating Agencies were compensated for their involvement with Rhinebridge, and had significant economic incentives to provide falsely high Ratings. Each of the three Rating Agencies gave the Senior Notes the "Top Ratings" without which Rhinebridge could not have existed. Yet these ratings were false or misleading, in part because all three Rating Agencies used information that was stale and inaccurate, and models that were outdated.

Moreover, the Rating Agencies knew that their ratings were false or misleading because they: (1) had access to confidential information about the assets held by Rhinebridge; (2) had knowledge unavailable to the public regarding the assumptions and methodologies used in rating the SIV; and (3) knew that, although the goal of an SIV is to acquire high-quality assets making it worthy of a "Top Rating," the Rhinebridge SIV included low-quality toxic mortgage-backed assets.

The Rhinebridge "SIV" is an example of rating agencies running dangerous amuck of their mission statements to global investors. John Moody, John Fitch and Varnum Poor established companies to assist investors in making informed investment decisions of their hard-earned cash. Today, these three companies have diverged so far from this noble original mission that they are now parties to law suits from investors alleging fraud and negligent misrepresentations.[57]

Rating agencies have the brazen audacity to conduct pay-to-play schemes with subprime originators—crafting AAA ratings for worthless securities and at the same time issuing dire warnings that some of the most successful economies in the world (France, Germany, the United Kingdom, and United States) are in dangerous decay.

While governments certainly confront difficult twenty-first-century challenges, specifically in regards to growing deficits and capital creation, rating agencies are more concerned with their own bottom line. This means that their own profit and losses and international stature often take prominence over ensuring markets are safe for investors.

In raising the importance of the big three rating agencies during the NRSRO legislation of the 1970s, the SEC allowed a cartel of rating agencies to hold public and private markets hostage for their own personal gain.

Accountability and responsibility are critical to rein these agencies back into their original and noble missions to global investors. The SEC and other international regulatory agencies need to take action to eliminate the enormous existing conflict of interest by barring agencies from receiving revenue from debt bond ratings. Revising NRSRO legislation to allow necessary competition in this market could be a start.

In these turbulent times, it is imperative that rating agencies serve the interests of investors, rather than those of special interests, predatory mortgage lenders, and a few giant investment banks.

Notes

1. Kevin Selig, *Greed, Negligence, Or System Failure? Credit Rating Agencies and the Financial Crisis* (Durham, NC: The Kenan Institute for Ethics at Duke University, no date). http://kenan.ethics.duke.edu/wp-content/uploads/2012/07/Case-Study-Greed-and-Negligence.pdf.
2. Standard & Poor's "About Us," http://www.standardandpoors.com/about-sp/main/en/us.
3. Zeke Faux and Jody Shenn, "Subprime Mortgage Bonds Get AAA Rating S&P Denied to U.S.," *Bloomberg Businessweek*, Aug. 31, 2011, http://www.bloomberg.com/news/2011-08-31/subprime-mortgage-bonds-getting-aaa-rating-s-p-denies-to-u-s-treasuries.html.
4. John Detrixhe, "Credit Rating Companies Favoring Firms Paying Most Over Nations," *Bloomberg Businessweek*, November 8, 2011, http://www.businessweek.com/news/2011-11-08/credit-rating-companies-favoring-firms-paying-most-over-nations.html.
5. Ibid.
6. Ibid.

7. Ibid.
8. Ibid.
9. Zeke Faux & Jody Shenn, "Subprime Mortgage Bonds Get AAA Rating S&P Denied to U.S., *Bloomberg Businessweek*, August 31, 2011, http://www.bloomberg.com/news/2011–08–31/subprime-mortgage-bonds-getting-aaa-rating-s-p-denies-to-u-s-treasuries.html.
10. Thomson Reuters Legal, "NY Judge Won't Dismiss Law Suits vs. Moody's, S&P," *Thomas Reuters News and Insights*, May 7, 2012, http://newsandinsight.thomsonreuters.com/Legal/News/2012/05_-_May/NY_judge_-won_t_dismiss_lawsuits_vs_Moody_s,_S_P/.
11. Becky Quick, "U.S. Rating Still AAA, No Matter What S&P Says," CNBC, *Bloomberg Businessweek*, August 8, 2011, http://www.cnbc.com/id/44056326/Buffett_US_Rating_Still_AAA_No_Matter_What_S_P_Says.
12. Rabah Arezki, Bertrand Candelon, and Amadou N.R. Sy, "Sovereign Rating News and Financial Markets Spillovers: Evidence from the European Debt Crisis," IMF Working Paper.
13. Ibid.
14. Stephen Castle, "Europe Seeks to Reduce Debt Ratings' Influence," *The New York Times*, February 28, 2012, http://www.nytimes.com/2012/02/29/business/global/european-parliament-proposes-sweeping-european-powers-over-credit-ratings.html.
15. Ibid.
16. Michael Mackenzie, "Non-Profit Credit Rating Agency Challenge," *Financial Times*, April 16, 2012, http://www.ft.com/intl/cms/s/0/302e5b38–84ab-11e1-b6f5–00144feab49a.html#axzz1vdTJhCeV.
17. Ibid.
18. Ibid.
19. Ibid.
20. Ibid.
21. "A History of Standard & Poor's," http://www.standardandpoors.com/about-sp/timeline/en/us/.
22. Moody's History, A Century of Market Leadership.
23. Ibid.
24. Ibid.
25. Ibid.
26. Mark Mobius, *Bonds: An Introduction to the Core Concepts* (Singapore: John Wiley & Sons Singapore Pte. Ltd., 2012).
27. Ibid.
28. Ibid.
29. Ibid.
30. Lawrence J. White, "The Credit Rating Agencies, How Did We Get Here? Where Should We Go?" Stern School of Business, www.ftc.gov/be/seminardocs/091112crediratingagencies.pdf.

31. Marc Flandreau, Norbert Gaillard, and Frank Packer, "Ratings Performance Regulation, and the Great Depression: Evidence From Government Securities," Conference on the Financial Crisis, May 8–9, 2009.

32. Ibid.

33. Ibid.

34. Frank Partnoy, "How and Why Credit Rating Agencies Are Not Like Other Gatekeepers," University of San Diego School of Law, Research Paper No. 07–46 May 2006.

35. Ibid.

36. Ibid.

37. Ibid.

38. Ibid.

39. Ibid.

40. Ibid.

41. Ibid.

42. Ibid.

43. Ibid.

44. White.

45. Matthew Richardson and Lawrence J. White, "The Rating Agencies: Is Regulation the Answer?" in Viral V. Acharya and Matthew Richardson, eds., *Restoring Financial Stability: How to Repair a Failed System* (Hoboken, NJ: John Wiley & Sons, 2009).

46. Ibid.

47. Ibid.

48. Ibid.

49. Ibid.

50. Ibid.

51. James Crotty, "Structural Causes of the Global Financial Crisis: A Critical Assessment of the New Financial Architecture," *Cambridge Journal of Economics*, 33 (2009): 563–580.

52. David J. Reiss, "Subprime Standardization: How Rating Agencies Allow Predatory Lending to Flourish in the Secondary Mortgage Market," The Berkeley Electronic Press, September 10, 2005, http://papers.ssrn.com/sol3/papers.cfm?abstract_id=797164 (available for download here).

53. Ibid.

54. John Detrixhe, "Credit Rating Companies Favoring Firms Paying Most Over Nations," *Bloomberg Businessweek*, November 8, 2011, http://www.businessweek.com/news/2011-11-08/credit-rating-companies-favoring-firms-paying-most-over-nations.html.

55. Ibid.

56. *King County v. IKB, Morgan Stanley, Moody's S&P & Fitch*, 09- Civ.8387 Opinion and Order, May 4, 2012.

57. Ibid.

Chapter 4

Belligerent Leadership and the Demise of Lehman Brothers

The tigers of wrath are wiser than the horses of instruction.
—William Blake

O n Wednesday, September 17, 2008, US Secretary of the Treasury Henry "Hank" Paulson had one of the most disturbing conversations he can remember.[1] It was the "gorilla" of Wall Street on the line, former Lehman Brothers CEO Richard (Dick) S. Fuld.

A day earlier, Paulson had guided the bailout of American Insurance Group (AIG). Fuld was in total disbelief. How could Paulson have informed Fuld that federal bailouts were undesirable "moral hazards" and then rescue AIG in a landmark deal the day after? In fact, Paulson had insisted to Fuld that a federal bailout of Lehman was "illegal."

Fuld desperately begged Paulson to reverse the Lehman failure. "I see you bailed out AIG," Fuld said. "Hank, what you need to do now is let the Fed come into Lehman Brothers. Have the government come in and guarantee it. Give me my company back. I can get all the people back. We will have Lehman Brothers again."[2]

In his biography, Paulson omitted to explain what he said next to Fuld, but history tells the story. Curiously, the US Treasury and Federal Reserve never rescued Lehman Brothers. One of the proudest banks in US history—a bank that had survived the Civil War, the Great Depression, and 1987's "Black Friday"—was now entirely bankrupt.

Two figures predominately ran Lehman Brothers in the 1990s and throughout the financial crisis: Dick Fuld and Joe Gregory. While in power, Fuld and Gregory displayed a business "wrath."[3] Industry analysts and former Lehman Brothers managers and employees report that the rule of Fuld and Gregory was marked by outward anger and extreme "aggression."[4] Former Lehman Vice President Larry McDonald explained, "There were mind-blowing tales of the Fuld temper, secondhand accounts of his rages, threats, and vengeance. It was like hearing the life story of some caged lion."[5] Larry McDonald recounted that Fuld believed "everyone was out to get him."[6]

Lehman Brothers' bankruptcy examiner, Anton R. Valukas, reported that Fuld and Gregory's "aggressive growth strategies" clouded the firm's risk management, accounting, and complex product valuation that might have mitigated Lehman's rapid downfall.

Valukas specifically wrote that Fuld's aggressive accumulation of long-term real estate assets, a dramatic increase in short-term liabilities, weak risk management, accounting manipulation, misleading asset valuation, and a refusal to acknowledge the illiquidity of mortgage-backed security assets such as collateralized debt obligations (CDOs) led to Lehman Brothers' bankruptcy in a manner of months—not years.[7]

In some books and articles written about the fall of Lehman, Fuld is identified as a CEO that ruled the firm like a general.[8] Although most generals conduct regular visitation with their troops, this Wall Street general apparently rarely visited managers, traders, bankers, and other staff.[9]

While many CEOs rule their companies with an iron first, Fuld's chosen leadership strategy won him few friends at Lehman, on Wall Street, and in the government community. McDonald suggests that Fuld's own rise to power was marked by deceit, manipulation, and anger.[10] In fact, Fuld's reputation in the Wall Street and government community as a belligerent, wrathful figure may have contributed to Lehman's demise.[11]

Lehman was the only top-five investment bank allowed to "fail" by the government since the Great Depression.

History of Lehman

The birthplace of Lehman Brothers was in Montgomery, Alabama. In 1844, Henry Lehman, a Jewish Immigrant, son of a Bavarian cattle dealer, immigrated to Montgomery. A year later, Lehman opened a dry goods store, H. Lehman. Three years later, Henry renamed the store H. Lehman & Bro in honor of his brother Emanuel's arrival.

Astutely, the Lehmans' start-up enterprise focused on the South's most lucrative export, cotton. Montgomery was situated on an inland waterway that flowed into the Gulf of Mexico. The Southern city was the epicenter of the cotton trade and part of the trade routes that shipped cotton to Mobile, New Orleans, and international markets.

The Lehman brothers first saw cotton as a commodity its customers could convert to cash prior to purchasing merchandise in their store. However, as the price of cotton swiftly escalated, the Lehmans began to accept cotton bales as payment, rather than cash. This resulted in profitable cotton trades for the Lehmans.

The onset of the Civil War disrupted the Lehmans' cotton trading business. Nonetheless, the crafty family was able to use the crisis to their advantage. Annual cotton yields dropped considerably in the south, from 4.5 million bales in 1861 to 300,000 in 1864.[12] As a result of lower supply, consumer demand took off, and the Lehmans decided to take advantage of higher prices. In 1862, the entrepreneurial family established a joint venture with John Wesley Durr, a cotton merchant with an excellent reputation.[13]

Durr and the Lehmans termed the business "Lehman Durr & Co." They purchased a large Alabama warehouse that could discretely store cotton. Lehman purchased cotton when prices were low, held bales until prices were higher, and then sold at very attractive prices. Using this business model during most of the Civil War, Lehman Durr & Co.

solidified itself as one of the most profitable cotton firms in the Montgomery area.

Upon the imminent defeat of the Confederate army, the Lehmans destroyed much of their cotton inventory to ensure northern forces could not secure it. Loyalty to the southern cause came from an unlikely source, German Jewish immigrants. The powerful Alabama aristocracy appreciated the Lehmans' loyalty to the southern cause. The Lehmans and Durrs became important figures in refinancing Alabama's debt during reconstruction.

Financial success, smart business, networking, and new connections allowed the Lehmans to set up a New York office. The Lehmans realized that the cotton trading market had permanently moved to the commission houses in New York City.

In conjunction with their move to New York, the Lehmans wisely diversified. They soon became traders in all sorts of commodities, including coffee, sugar, grains, and petroleum. In 1870, the Lehmans helped found the New York Cotton Exchange and were also active members of the Coffee Exchange and New York Petroleum Exchange.[14]

During the late nineteenth century, Drexel, Morgan & Co. (later known as JP Morgan) had a considerable market share in the Industrial Revolution. J. Pierpont Morgan and Anthony Drexel had strong ties to European markets and high-worth investors. The firm began underwriting new issues of stocks for wealthy investors. In fact, the company successfully issued New York Central Railroad stock for owner William Vanderbilt, in the most massive stock offering of its kind in the late nineteenth century.[15]

However, Drexel, Morgan & Co. had an unwritten business policy of not transacting with Jewish companies or investors.[16] Heavy industry segments, including railroad and steel, worked with an underwriting oligopoly of banks that did not include any Jewish clients.[17]

This provided firms like Lehman and Goldman Sachs & Co. (another predominately Jewish-run company) the opportunity to work with a client base without competition from other banks. Working very closely with the Goldmans, the Lehmans helped pioneer the use of commercial paper as a lending tool, which began to be traded in the investment bank community.[18]

Lehman continued to make smart business decisions that helped develop their burgeoning company. The company acquired a seat on the New York Stock Exchange (NYSE) in 1887. In 1899, the Lehmans assisted in the sale of the Rubber Tire Wheel Company (predecessor of Goodyear), and shares of this company were subsequently offered in a public offering. The firm then underwrote a public offering in 1899 involving the International Steam Pump Company.[19]

Next, in 1906, Lehman and Goldman partnered to take United Cigar public, and both banks were able to sell the stock at a 24 percent markup, resulting in sizable profits.[20] This success led Lehman to specialize in retail IPOs, including Sears, Roebuck & Co., F.W. Woolworth Co., R.H. Macy, Gimbel Brothers, Brown Shoe Company, and May Department Stores Company.[21]

In 1924, the first non–Lehman family member became a partner, John Hancock. Philip Lehman was running the bank at the time, and he had already made significant progress in transforming the partnership from a commodities house to an aggressive investment bank. At this time, it had become a major player in the securities underwriting business. Hancock wisely believed that control of the partnership should be in the hands of talent, not family members.

Philip officially retired in 1925. He placed control of the firm in the able hands of his son, Robert "Bobbie" Lehman. Bobbie was perhaps the most important leader in the history of Lehman, other than Dick Fuld (Fuld was influential for other reasons). Under Bobbie's leadership, the firm expanded its products to include equities, bond underwriting, investment advising, and brokerage services, survived the Great Depression, and turned Lehman into one of the most respected and powerful firms on Wall Street.[22]

During the Great Depression, Lehman concentrated on its bread and butter, investment bank underwriting services, and distanced itself from commercial banks and deposit taking activities. Retail underwriting remained a profitable enterprise for the firm despite the disintegrating economy. In the 1930s, Bobbie Lehman helped bring Dumont public, the first American television manufacturer. Bobbie followed the depression economic climate closely. He sought to exercise the appropriate amount of risk in light of the turbulent economy.[23]

Bobbie Lehman continued to prudently steer Lehman through the market turbulence of World War II. With many members of the partnership fighting overseas, Bobbie sold government bonds to keep the company's balance sheet liquid. After World War II, Lehman profited immensely. Its expertise in underwriting retail and other commercial transactions was now in high demand. By 1967, Lehman was responsible for $3.5 billion in underwriting revenues.[24] Prospering through difficult times, Lehman became one of the top underwriters in the world.

Bobbie Lehman died in 1969. The Wall Street tycoon brought Lehman from relative obscurity to one of the most respected and profitable investment banking firms in the world. However, with Bobbie gone, the firm plunged into a power struggle that nearly destroyed it entirely.

After four years of leadership turmoil, the arrival of Peter G. Peterson at Lehman Brothers was a stabilizing force that enabled Lehman to once again prosper. Peterson, the former CEO of Bell & Howell, and secretary of commerce in the Nixon administration, was brought in to rebuild the bank. Like Bobbie had done decades before, Peterson restructured Lehman's product base and restored its reputation and grandeur. Peterson was personable, thrifty, and a Wall Street outsider, having grown up in Nebraska. Lehman was his first job on Wall Street.

Immediately, Peterson was in awe of Lehman's decadence. "It [the Lehman offices] dripped with amenities like the Partners Dining Room where the partners ate at a long table covered with ornate china and silverware. A large fireplace dominated one side of the dining room, and the walls were hung with portraits of the founders."[25] In his biography, Peterson noted that when he arrived in 1973, the business community considered Lehman Wall Street's oldest and most distinguished banking partnership.[26]

Brewing Anger

In addition to Lehman's obvious extravagance, Peterson dealt with growing anger within the firm's product divisions. Since the early twentieth century, Lehman had expanded outside the family. Many of its new arrivals were elite Protestants who found a home in Lehman's investment banking division. In contrast, many of the Jewish partners worked in commercial paper and fixed income, run by Lew Glucksman. Peterson recalls:

> They [Glucksman's commercial paper division] waited resentfully, poised for their opportunity to strike . . . The traders, including Glucksman's peddlers of commercial paper, considered the investment bankers a bunch of spoiled and rather unproductive Park Avenue brats—white-shoe elites who were more show than real dough. The investment bankers thought the traders were crude and uncultured, and that they gave having money a bad name.[27]

Peterson explains that "opinions were so ingrained that . . . according to one frequently repeated story, most of the senior partners had their desks in a single room because none of them trusted the others out of their sight."[28] Incredibly, at this time, Lehman was largely divided on religion and class status and the bank suffered from a lack of trust and faith in one another.

Glucksman angrily envied Peterson and the firm's investment bankers, who wined and dined the media, showed up in the society pages, and received wide Wall Street community recognition. Glucksman and the traders believed they were the engine that ran Lehman profits through brash trading, a never-ending work effort, and supreme confidence. This lingering resentment and anger within the firm would eventually result in another power struggle in which the traders' envy and anger (including Glucksman and Fuld) finally prevailed.

Peterson tried to delicately manage both divisions and focus upon diversifying Lehman's product base significantly, as Bobbie Lehman had done years before him. A major decision was cutting expenses and reducing the number of employees from 955 to 663 to reduce overhead. Peterson's work soon became recognized. In November of 1975, Peterson appeared on the cover of *Business Week*—the story was termed "Back from the Brink Comes Lehman Bros."[29] In 1978, Peterson had led Lehman to five straight years of profits.

At the same time, trading was emerging as a highly profitable segment of Lehman's business. Lew Glucksman was the so-called trading "boss" of Lehman during the 1970s. His background was an American success story. Glucksman was born into a second-generation Hungarian Jewish family in New York City. He served as a teenage volunteer with the navy in World War II and later got an MBA from NYU. Glucksman was a feisty, belligerent man and used his personality to his advantage. In the 1970s he oversaw Dick Fuld, and he became Fuld's unofficial mentor.

In contrast to Glucksman, Peterson was a statesman. He was concerned about the dissension within Lehman and wanted to make a move to bridge the gap between the investment banking and trading sectors. In 1983, he promoted Glucksman to share the position of co-CEO. Glucksman saw this as his opportunity. He exercised power, making personnel changes and redistributing partnership interests that solely benefited Lehman's traders.

As a result of these moves, more anger, resentment, and ill will resulted between the investment banking and trading sectors. Peterson's olive branch to Glucksman entirely backfired.[30] Glucksman gave Peterson a hefty severance check and informed him that the firm was his. Peterson begrudgingly agreed, leaving Glucksman and his protégé Fuld in control of Lehman.

Uncaging the "Animal"

Dick Fuld was born in New York City to Richard Severin Fuld, Sr., and Elizabeth Schwab. The Jewish family resided in Harrison, New York, a wealthy suburb of New York City. Fuld's father was an entrepreneur and ran a company that wrote short-term loans for textile companies. Betsy Schaper, a media publicist who grew up across the street from him, remembers that young Fuld was doted on by his parents and was thought of as a local adolescent heartthrob.[31]

As a youth, Dick attended Wilbraham & Monson Academy, a boarding school in Massachusetts. Fuld did not leave a lasting impression outside the athletic fields and party scene. "If you'd asked me back then, is this a man with burning ambition? I would have said absolutely not," said a former faculty member of the school.[32]

Instead of academic fortitude, Fuld's lasting impression on his peers was his nickname "animal." Richard Carreno, a former classmate of Fuld's at Wilbraham, said Fuld received this nickname because he was an athlete, with a reputation for "aggression" and a "pumped up" personality.[33]

Unlike many of his classmates, Fuld did not attend an elite, Ivy League institution. He studied at the University of Colorado. Again, his undergraduate legacy had nothing to do with his classroom endeavors. As author Vicky Ward writes, "He stood out mostly for the reckless passion he brought to parties, and for the fierce loyalty he showed his friends and demanded in return."[34]

Apart from passion and loyalty, Fuld's gorilla-like anger began to explode as a college student. As a member of the Reserve Officer's Training Corps (ROTC), Fuld was expected to demonstrate discipline, loyalty, and honorable behavior to his superiors. Instead, he was expelled for insubordination and assaulting a commanding officer.[35]

Fuld grew upset in weekly meetings when his commanding officer repeatedly asked him to shine his shoes. The officer would step on Fuld's shoes and then send him back to his dorm to shine them again. On one such occasion, Fuld grew belligerent when an officer stepped on a fellow cadet's shoes. The exchange went as follows:

"Hey, asshole," Fuld said. "Why don't you pick on someone your own size?"

"Are you talking to me?" the officer asked, astonished at Fuld's audacity. "Yes," Fuld said.[36]

Immediately, the two men started fighting. After the incident, Fuld was kicked out of the ROTC program for insubordination.

Fuld was the grandson of a high-level Lehman client. After graduating from Colorado in 1969, the connection landed Fuld a job at Lehman.[37] "People at Lehman said Dick Fuld's grandfather was an important man," said Paul Newmark, then a senior vice president and treasurer of Lehman Commercial Paper Inc. (LCPI). "No one was going to turn down his grandson. And anyway, Dick's father had accounts at Lehman. That's how he got the interview."[38]

Culture of Anger

Fuld's mentor at Lehman was Lew Glucksman. Glucksman and Fuld had much in common. In fact, Glucksman would hurl office material across the room when he was in a bad mood, which, according to many financial historians, was quite often. Former Lehman Vice President Paul Newmark explained that he saw Glucksman rip the shirt off his back in anger and on another occasion, throw a 20-pound adding machine on the trading floor.[39]

Fuld found inspiration in a man who had a similar brash personality. As author Vicky Ward explains, "Fuld and Glucksman were in many ways alike. Both were taciturn, ruthlessly competitive men, who swore loudly, and often, in and out of the office. Both thought the most effective tool for managing a trading floor was fear."[40] In fact, Glucksman and Fuld's combined personalities resulted in unchallenged, autocratic power on the Lehman trading floor.

As the ideal complement to Glucksman, Fuld earned the new nickname "gorilla" in recognition of his loud grunting on the trading floor and obsession for intense physical workouts. With these two volatile personalities in power, no one felt that they could oppose the emerging gorilla/animal and the intimidating Glucksman. If they did, "There was hell to pay."[41]

After wrestling the CEO position from Pete Peterson, the man who in many ways had rescued Lehman from the brink of collapse, Glucksman's control resulted in the collapse of the Lehman partnership—in less than one year. Indeed, because of his belligerent and volatile leadership style, Glucksman lacked statesmanship and the ability to inspire loyalty or confidence in his employees.

After Peterson's exit, many important, high-worth Lehman investors pulled their capital from the firm. At this point, Lehman was suffering from a capital crisis. Glucksman and Fuld could have reduced risk, evaluated costs, and taken other measures to encourage market trust. Instead, they decided to sell the company.

Lehman was sold to Shearson/American Express for $360 million in 1984. The storied Lehman partnership incorporated in the antebellum south, rescued by Bobbie Lehman and Pete Peterson, existed no more.

As part of the Shearson–American Express takeover, Peter Cohen of Shearson took over the CEO position. Since this disturbed his foothold and influence on firm leadership, Fuld's internal anger brewed. To protest the merger, Fuld assembled a large group of traders and other employees loyal to him and threatened to defect to rivals Paine Webber or Dean Witter Reynolds.[42]

Unfortunately, there was little market interest in Fuld's demands. Lacking leverage, Fuld settled. He accepted a vice chairman position at Shearson-Lehman and he took a voting member position on the board.

Although he would have preferred more centralized leadership, Fuld continued to manage the fixed income department of Shearson Lehman, taking Lew Glucksman's former position. Trading continued to be profitable for the firm throughout the late 1980s, although the other sectors of Lehman products suffered greatly, especially after the events of "Black Friday."

In 1990, Shearson-Lehman reported losses of approximately $1 billion. Due to these startling losses, the firm's leadership decided it needed to make a change.

Accordingly, Cohen was forced out and was replaced by American Express CFO, Howard L. Clark. Once again, the investment bank and trading sectors of Lehman were merged as Fuld and Tom Hill (a highly respected investment banker) were elevated to positions of co-CEO. Fuld and Hill cut employees in their divisions to encourage profits. However, this strategy backfired. Employee utility was very low and capital losses kept mounting. Like the tensions during Peterson's and Glucksman's time, relationships among the investment banking and fixed income divisions were intensely fractured.[43]

Again, the fixed income group prevailed as Fuld refused to work with Hill and forced him out, consolidating his control over the firm. In 1993, American Express's CEO made this consolidation of power official. Fuld was appointed CEO of Shearson-Lehman and Chris Petit was named COO. Petit had known Fuld for years; he was also a friend and another Glucksman protégé. The hope was that they would coexist in peace.

Despite their history and friendship together, Petit soon threatened Fuld's power base and was the object of his continuing belligerence. Petit was a proactive former bond salesman. He was charismatic, beloved by his employees, and an accomplished public speaker. He was the absolute counterpoint to the introverted Fuld. Fuld demanded respect, but Petit earned it.[44]

In 1993, Lehman's retail brokerage operations were sold to Smith Barney; the rest of Shearson Lehman was spun off in an initial public offering (IPO). The new company was called Leman Brothers Holdings Inc., in honor of the company's partnership prior to the sale.

Increasing Risk and Authority

When Lehman went public, it was thrust in the public spotlight once again. It was up to Fuld to increase profits, employee morale, and raise capital. Yet, instead of diversifying Lehman's product offerings, Fuld increased risk by deciding to enter the junk bond market. As would prove fatal later in his career, Fuld's strategy was always that higher risk would lead to higher returns.

To accomplish this end, Fuld hired Tom Bernard from Kidder, Peabody & Company. Bernard's expertise was "junk bonds." Yet, Bernard was fresh out of a job because illiquid junk bond assets had just destroyed Kidder's balance sheet only months earlier, forcing Paine Weber to buy the firm.

Junk bonds are what their name indicates: "junk," noninvestment-grade assets with the possibility of booming returns in ideal market circumstances. Fuld's junk bond hire signaled that Lehman's leadership was determined to prove that speculation and high risk could work, regardless of the possible consequences.

In addition to taking on new risk, Fuld also decided to embark on major austerity initiatives. Fuld appointed a cost-cutting czar and sent an internal memo to all employees insisting that no cost was too small (including pencils and electricity). For example, Lehman's air conditioning was turned off at 7 P.M. rather than 8 P.M.[45]

Three percent of employees were let go September 8, 1994. One year later, even more employees were laid off. Free employee lunches were eliminated (which had been a prized Lehman tradition since Bobbie Lehman). As you might imagine, employee morale was considerably low.[46]

Rather than assuming personal blame, Fuld made Petit the scapegoat for the employee dissension. As the years went by, Fuld increasingly viewed Petit's strong relationships with fellow managers and employees with envy. Petit was, in many ways, the Peterson of the 1990s Lehman era. He was another statesman who spoke at major public events, and he was respected by staff and the Wall Street community.

In Fuld's eyes, Petit had to go. Petit had hired his brother-in-law to run Lehman's equities division, and Fuld believed the hire was not based on merit. Moreover, whether true or not, it was rumored that Petit was having an affair with the head of fixed-income research.[47]

In April 1996, Fuld stripped Petit of his COO title and then fired all of Petit's close friends and loyalists in the top tiers of Lehman management. Petit resigned under immense pressure six months later. To avoid any friction, Fuld handpicked Petit's replacement, Joe Gregory. Gregory was the perfect soldier, a fiercely loyal right-hand man with no CEO ambition. This hire cemented Fuld's autocratic power. Lehman was now the personification of Dick Fuld.

Walsh's Rise

During the late 1990s, a man established himself as the most brilliant real estate financer on Wall Street. His name was Mark A. Walsh. Walsh set the bar for commercial real estate deals through smart maneuvering. As *The New York Times* explained, "In the 1990s, he [Walsh] pioneered the art of lending to office building developers and then slicing up and repackaging the debt for investors. Less risky pieces went to institutional investors; the lower-rated chunks to hedge funds and others hungry for juicier returns. Lehman pocketed a fee every step of the way, and it often retained a risky piece or two to give its own earnings a kick."[48]

Walsh led Lehman's Global Real Estate Group (GREG), located in the Fixed Income Group. GREG's primary business was underwriting, origination, securitization, warehouse lending, and bridge equity.

Fuld became enamored with the waves of profits coming in from GREG. He saw commercial real estate as an important tool for Lehman's diversification. Fuld believed that rapid expansion of Lehman's commercial real estate practice and the ensuring profits could distinguish the firm on Wall Street and considerably raise Lehman's reputation and stature. In fact, in the commercial real estate sphere Lehman was competing with and sometimes winning deals over Goldman Sachs—all because of Walsh's reputation, skill, and acumen.

Yet, Fuld was never satisfied. Walsh's successes led to Fuld wanting more and more—more commercial real estate deals, more risky bridge lending, and less diligence. While other banks such as Goldman Sachs and JP Morgan required weeks of diligence before approving any commercial bridge loan, Fuld moved fast. It was this strategy of increased risk taking that allowed Lehman and Fuld to do major deals with entities like Starwood Hotels and beat rival banks, including JP Morgan and Goldman Sachs.

On Fuld's marching orders, Walsh fostered close relationships with the top real estate developers in New York. Beginning in the late 1990s, these relationships enabled Lehman to handle the largest real estate acquisitions worldwide. For example, in 1997, Lehman facilitated Tishman Speyer's purchase of the Chrysler Building. A year later, Lehman financed Steven C. Witkoff's purchase of the famous Woolworth Building and Aby Rosen and Michael Fuch's purchase of the ritzy Lever House and Seagram Building. Remarkably, Walsh closed the Lever House deal in four weeks.

With these successes in mind, Fuld's appetite for more deals and profits only grew, exponentially. In the process, Fuld decided to double-down and risk more firm capital to invest in these transactions. The only massive downside was if the bullish real estate market turned, which to Fuld was simply not an option or possibility.

By 2000, Walsh was promoted to the co-head of a new private equity group that was solely focused on earning returns on commercial real estate deals. Through this group, Lehman began to lend out its balance sheet to real estate developers for the right price. Fuld was convinced, despite the obvious risk of putting the Lehman balance sheet at stake, that investments in commercial real estate would never fail.

Early 2000 deals like the Beacon Capital Partners–John Hancock Tower deal made Fuld look like a commercial real estate financial genius. Lehman provided Beacon Capital Partners with a $200 million bridge equity line with a 6 percent commitment fee. In only a few weeks, Beacon was able to find permanent financing so the loan never had to be funded, and Lehman earned $12 million in interest.[49]

A risk, certainly, but the profits kept rolling in. Additionally, on the same deal, on Fuld's direction, the difference between the buy and finance price was securitized and sold as commercial mortgage-backed securities (CMBS).

Lehman believed it had found the formula for quick profits. Fuld assumed that real estate prices would remain high and lenders would be willing to provide financing to complete deals, and the market would thirst to have a piece of such transactions through CMBS.

From 2004 to 2006, Walsh's group increased capital market revenues by 56 percent. This rate was more than double the growth rate of asset management and investment banking combined and at one point accounted for 20 percent of Lehman's total revenues.[50]

A Gorilla Bursting the Bubble

As CEO of Wall Street's fourth largest investment bank, Fuld felt that he could not be complacent. Goldman Sachs and JP Morgan enjoyed premier status in the industry, particularly with regard to firm capital levels, reputation, and investor confidence. This was unacceptable to Fuld. He felt extreme internal pressures (from his own aggressive personality) that demanded perfection, preeminence, and absolute power for Lehman Brothers, which in many ways he saw as an extension of himself.

Author Mark T. Williams writes that Fuld and Walsh were committed to playing with "monopoly money" in the commercial real estate business and believed this was the only means to raise profits and overcome rivals.[51] For example, Walsh had full authorization to purchase two prestigious office buildings in Paris for development for $2.8 billion, because Goldman Sachs was the competitor for the property. Lehman used its own funds to purchase the real estate.

Fuld's downright aggression in the commercial real estate market continued to escalate. At the peak of the market, Lehman perhaps made one of its most dire "monopoly" transactions. In 2006, Walsh put $2 billion of Lehman's balance sheets on a SunCal Bakersfield 6,000-unit residential community development project where the Lehman commercial paper department took an exposure of $235 million. Lehman, with Fuld's eager blessing, committed 10 percent of its entire capital to the deal.

However, the deal was based on only the developer's architectural blueprint. There was no structure on the land. Lehman had placed $2 billion on empty land in Bakersfield, California.

Fuld was again overly eager. His endless ambition to chase Goldman Sachs ruled the day. In fact, "We had Goldman Sachs and other people who were clamoring to do business with us," says Louis Miller, a lawyer for SunCal. "Lehman said, 'No, we want you to be exclusive with us.'"[52]

The Bakersfield project never commenced. Lehman never experienced Fuld's massive profits, only staggering millions in losses.

In October 2007, Lehman continued to double-down on commercial real estate despite a rapidly falling market. Looking back, Lehman made its most infamous real estate investment when it decided to finance Tishman Speyer's purchase of Archstone Smith Trust, the owner of more than 360 large high-end apartment complexes. Lehman offered to commit $22.2 billion to the leveraged buy-out (LBO) of Archstone. Incredibly, the developer Tishman Speyer only agreed to invest $250 million of its own money to the deal. Again, Fuld felt pressure because Goldman Sachs was the main competitor.

Lehman found a partner in Bank of America to finance the deal, but this did not lessen the immense cost to the bank. This time Lehman exposed 20 percent of its balance sheet for Tishman's Archstone LBO. Although this was at the very top of the real estate bubble and Lehman had a $1 billion escape clause (after it had spent $22.2 billion), Lehman did not exercise it. It was now left with a massive black hole of real estate debt in a rapidly declining quicksand market. Walsh desperately sought a way out. He sold $8.9 billion of debt to Fannie and Freddie Mac and had Bank of America and Barclays buy $2.4 billion of bridge equity.

Nonetheless, Lehman had more than $5 billion in liability still sitting on its balance sheet, sending its leverage ratios to astronomical levels. Fuld's gorilla-like tactics and competitive streak that insisted on going toe to toe with Goldman Sachs (and winning) led to massive balance sheet exposure, tremendous risk, and extreme leverage ratios. Lehman was on the path to failure.

Like other big investment banks, Lehman fueled the mortgage-backed securities derivative bubble. Wall Street was generating massive amounts of profits by securitizing pools of homeowner mortgages (mortgage-backed securities) with the price of homes (the collateral) rising exponentially.

However, what separated Lehman from other banks was its reliance on the mortgage-based derivate products and its repeated refusal to recognize in-house and outside experts who cautioned management that the market was in a bubble that would burst.

In 1938, Congress amended the National Housing Act to create the Federal National Mortgage Association (Fannie Mae). The goal was to provide a government-supported enterprise (GSE) designed to assist Americans in having sufficient capital to purchase a home. Further increasing support for home ownership, in 1970, Congress created another GSE, the Federal Home Loan Corporation (Freddie Mac). Both of these companies were devoted to providing mortgage capital to Americans in need of help.

Over time, Lehman product innovators and others in the investment banking and financial community saw the GSE as an ideal backstop. They believed mortgage portfolio derivatives had little risk of default because of the federal guarantee protections of Fannie Mae and Freddie Mac.

In fact, Lehman and other banks were so convinced of the invincibility of these products that they began selling CDOs that were synthetic and not backed by physical assets. Because of the GSE model, Lehman believed the real estate market was immune to failure. Accordingly, the firm crafted synthetic real estate derivatives securities in assembly line–like fashion, betting its house of cards on plastic assets that did not hold tangible value.

Extreme Leverage

Lehman was one of the first Wall Street banks to sell mortgage-related derivatives. In 1997, Fuld bought an interest in Aurora Loan Services, a Colorado-based mortgage lender that issued Alt-A loans. The term "Alt-A" indicates that the loans were not quite dangerously subprime but originated from buyers whose credit was not of the highest degree. Lehman also decided to take a small ownership stake in BNC Mortgage LLC, a West Coast subprime mortgage lender. These moves were all part of Fuld's strategy: increased risk, increased returns.

Fuld continued to intensify Lehman's exposure to the subprime and Alt-A market. As of 2003, Lehman owned 9 percent of the market, with $18.2 billion in loans to subprime borrowers. Ameriquest and New Century were the only two companies more exposed than Lehman, and both were mortgage lenders.

Despite its existing exposure, from 2002 to 2003, Fuld decided to increase its lending in the subprime market by 71 percent. In 2004, Lehman purchased BNC outright, and at the end of 2004, Lehman owned $40 billion in subprime and Alt-A mortgages. At the end of 2006, Lehman was lending $4 billion a month in subprime and Alt-A mortgages.

Many subprime and Alt-A loans offered by Aurora, a Lehman subsidiary, required no credit checks and documentation—essentially a never-ending credit line with a massive interest rate. Aurora personnel were rapidly entering mortgage deals with uneducated subprime buyers without any oversight or governance by Lehman.

Billions upon billions of Lehman's Alt-A and subprime loans from questionable homebuyers were securitized into CDOs and hedged against with seemingly safe credit default swaps (CDS). Because CDOs were debt securities, Lehman's leverage ratios began to skyrocket. In a falling market, if the CDO assets could not be moved, Lehman was bound for a liquidity and capital crisis.

Fuld was taking on $4 billion in debt every month. Combined with the commercial real estate losses, this was an exceptional amount of debt on Lehman's 2006 books.

While the Fixed Income Group's traders made dependable money for Lehman from 2004 to 2007 through smart short and long positions, Fuld marginalized their opinions and place within the firm. Rather than worry about long-term sustainability, Fuld was transfixed with the rapid profits he saw coming in from his massively leveraged positions in the mortgage market.

Top talent at the firm, such as Director of Fixed Income, Mike Gelband, cautioned Fuld as early in 2005 that the market was at its peak and would soon burst. Gelband insisted that Lehman diversify and place less importance on the mortgage market. Despite the strong warnings of his own top personnel, Fuld resisted. Gelband eventually left Lehman, as did star trader Larry McCarthy.[53]

In the back of Fuld's mind he knew that investor confidence was critical to Lehman's success and day-to-day operations. Fuld had been through the LTCM crisis of the late 1990s when a confidence failure in the markets nearly doomed Lehman Brothers' very existence. Nonetheless, Fuld turned a blind eye to the known lessons of the past and financed Lehman through the short-term repurchase agreements (repos) where confidence in Lehman was absolutely critical to the bank's everyday survival.

Indeed, to open its doors daily, Lehman routinely transferred assets to another party as collateral for a short-term borrowing of cash, while agreeing to repay the cash and take back the collateral at a specific point in time. The other party would receive the cash back plus interest. This understanding between the two parties is called a repo. Every day Lehman conducted repos to finance its entire bankwide operations.

Unfortunately, the *black swan scenario*, that Lehman's essential repo partners would turn their backs on the firm, was never considered.

The Deception of Repo 105

As Lehman's leverage ratios grew increasingly higher and its assets more illiquid, Fuld became extremely concerned. Fuld did not want the market to lose confidence in his bank. In times of trouble, Fuld often saw himself at "war" with the financial services industry and markets in general.[54] Indeed, this was his strategy during the 1998 LTCM crisis, where he drove an investor relations onslaught to encourage market confidence in Lehman.

This time, Fuld's "war" on the precipice of the mortgage crisis consisted of downright deception. Lehman employed off-balance-sheet devices, known within the bank as "Repo 105" transactions, to temporarily remove illiquid securities from its balance sheets prior to a quarterly report, materially misleading investors in the process.

As Lehman's bankruptcy examiner explains, "Repo 105 transactions were nearly identical to standard repurchase and resale transactions . . . with a critical difference . . . by characterizing the transaction as a 'sale,' removing the inventory from its balance sheet."[55]

For numerous required quarterly reports from 2007 to 2008, Lehman conducted Repo 105 transactions to reduce its reported leverage and balance sheet. The public, investors, and the market were entirely unaware of these transactions that in effect borrowed tens of billions of dollars. A few days after the new quarter began, Lehman would borrow the necessary funds to repay the deceptive cash borrowing plus interest, repurchase the securities, and restore the illiquid assets to its balance sheet.

Fuld failed to disclose the Repo 105 practice. Incredibly, Martin Kelly, Lehman's former global financial controller, explained that a careful review of Lehman's annual Forms 10k and quarterly 10-Q would not reveal Lehman's use of Repo 105 transactions.[56] Kelly repeatedly contested the validity of Repo 105 transactions to two Lehman CFOs, Erin Callan and Ian Lowitt, the management. He felt there was no substance to the Repo 105 deals and advised Callan and Lowitt that the transactions could substantially damage Lehman's reputational risk.[57]

Lowitt and Callan were both getting orders from Fuld. Beginning in late 2006, Fuld was extremely concerned with market perception issues. He believed that raising equity had negative consequences for Lehman's capital reputation. Accordingly, he tried to sell inventory to raise capital. However, Lehman's inventory through Walsh's commercial real estate and CDO exposure was fundamentally illiquid. Because of these factors, Fuld relied on the Repo 105 deception to keep investors happy and stock prices at comfortable levels.

Notably, during Lehman's 2008 earnings calls, the firm's management touted its leverage reductions. Analysts repeatedly asked through what mechanism the firm was deleveraging. CFO Erin Callan told analysts Lehman's goal was to increase balance sheet transparency and that the firm had sold a considerable amount of less liquid assets.

Lehman deceptively reduced its net balance sheet at quarter-end through its Repo 105 practice by approximately $38.6 billion in fourth quarter 2007, $49.1 billion in first quarter 2008, and $50.38 billion in second quarter 2008. These amounts illustrate the rapid accumulation of toxic assets and leveraging at the firm from 2007 to 2008.[58]

Because Lehman characterized Repo 105 deals as sales rather than financial transactions, management's position was that accounting and legal rules did not require the firm to list the billions of dollars as liabilities. However, this was simply a technicality, as the substance of

Repo 105 deals was financial transactions, not sales. The Lehman bankruptcy examiner concluded that colorable legal claims of breach of fiduciary duty existed against Fuld, Lehman's CFOs, and Ernst & Young (Lehman's accountant) for nefariously hiding illiquid assets off-balance through Repo 105.[59]

Fuld's Marginalization of Risk Management

In the late 1990s Lehman began to use quantitative market risk measurements for the firm's risk management, primarily value at risk (VaR). VaR is a statistically based tool that estimates how much a trading book or entire portfolio could lose over a given time frame and is communicated in terms of dollars of potential loss. The metric uses computer algorithms to measure potential market risk.

When accurate, the VaR model provides insights into what to expect in the future. If risk appears to be growing, its purpose would be to encourage risk-reduction strategies. VaR is designed to measure worst-case scenarios on a daily basis so firm risk personnel can then prudently adjust their balance sheet positions.

Yet, VaR formulas come with one glaring shortcoming. The quantitative risk measurement does not accurately capture risk in turbulent markets. Rather than seeing volatility as an uncertain variable, VaR's algorithms see volatility as a constant. VaR makes determinations with a 95 percent confidence interval, not accounting for the 5 percent possibility of worst-case financial disaster events. Accordingly, in order to successfully employ VaR as a risk manager, it must be used with other important tools such as stress tests, maximum risk appetite ceilings, and regular audits.[60]

After the 1998 LTCM crisis, the metric's reliance in the industry should have been devalued. In August 1998, VaR represented that LTCM had $45 million of daily VaR—meaning that the fund could lose/gain $45 million on a single day of trading. However, on that same day, the LTCM fund lost an astounding $550 million. Famous hedge fund manager David Einhorn has stated, "VaR is like an airbag that works all the time, except when you have a car accident."[61]

Despite VaR's shortcomings in turbulent markets, Fuld viewed the risk metric with full confidence. Like LTCM failure's to understand the risks associated with the Russian debt crisis, Fuld failed to comprehend the potential volatility in the commercial and residential real estate market.

Fuld pushed Lehman ahead with aggressive new commercial and residential real estate initiatives that risked exceedingly more of Lehman's balance sheet. The firm was overleveraged and ambivalent to the onset of the subprime mortgage crisis in late 2006. Lehman had drastically changed its product base to focus upon mortgage-derived products. The firm was now focused primarily on the securitization and origination of risky assets that were distributed to counterparties. Nonetheless, Lehman's risk management willfully did not keep up with the risky changes in business strategy and the massive increases in leverage, debt, and illiquidity.

Again, Fuld's judgment was clouded by his intense ambition to overcome his perceived rivals. Not only was he at war with the markets, but also, he felt continually at war with his competitors. Fuld believed that while other banks were mitigating leverage and risk in response to the financial crisis, he had a golden opportunity to pick up ground on competitors like Goldman Sachs, JP Morgan, and Merrill Lynch. Fuld termed this aggressive plan as *countercyclical growth strategy*.

Moreover, because of Fuld's ravenous appetite for such growth, senior risk managers within the firm were marginalized and entirely disregarded. Any opposition to Fuld's increasingly risk-centric policies was a death sentence to relevancy at the firm.

For example, press reports prior to Lehman's bankruptcy stated that in 2007 Lehman had removed Madelyn Antoncic, Lehman's chief risk officer, and Michael Gelband, head of fixed income, because of their opposition to management's accumulation of risky and illiquid investments.[62]

In order to meet Fuld's plan of countercyclical growth, Lehman exceeded its own risk appetite limits, did not include illiquid assets in stress tests, and modified traditional firm risk policy to suit Fuld's whimsical needs. Fuld actively took the following actions to avoid risk managers from averting his aggressive business strategies:

- Lehman's management decided to exceed risk limits with respect to Lehman's principal investments, namely, the "concentration limits" on Lehman's leveraged loan and commercial real estate businesses.

- These limits were designed to ensure that Lehman's investments were properly limited and diversified by business line and counterparty. Lehman management excluded risky and highly leveraged instruments from its stress tests.
- Lehman did not strictly apply its balance sheet limits, which were designed to contain the overall risk of the firm and maintain the firm's leverage ratio within the range required by credit rating agencies, but instead decided to exceed those limits and use Repo 105 to camouflage illiquidity.[63]
- Lehman's management willfully decided to enlarge the firm's risk appetite and treat limits as "soft" guidelines, despite the fact that Lehman represented to the SEC that the firm's risk appetite limit was a meaningful constraint on the firm's leverage ratios and risk taking.

The shift in Lehman's risk profile became strikingly apparent. Between December 2006 and 2007, Lehman raised its firmwide risk limit three times from $2.3 billion to $4.0 billion.[64] Between May and August 2007, Lehman omitted some of its largest risks from its risk usage calculation—most notably, the Archstone transaction, in which 20 percent of their balance sheet was offered. When Lehman finally included Archstone in its risk usage calculation, it raised its risk appetite limits once again to make the transaction permissible.

Clearly, Fuld and Lehman's senior managers decided to place a higher priority on countercyclical business growth than taking any action to mitigate the firm's illiquid positions, excessive leverage, and expanding balance sheet. Fuld was supremely confident in himself and marginalized risk metrics, quantitative formulas, and his top risk management personnel.

Fuld's Last Chance to Save Lehman

On May 2, 2007, Roger Nagioff succeeded Mike Gelband as head of Fixed Income.[65] By August 2007, Lehman's leveraged loan exposure had grown to $35.8 billion.[66] Nagioff became alarmed once he learned about the size of Lehman's leveraged loan exposures from Alex Kirk, head of Global Credit Products. Nagioff thought that the possibility of a sudden market downturn was high and Lehman was not diversified enough to withstand its extraordinary leverage and illiquidity.

Nagioff arranged for a meeting with Fuld to discuss his concerns on May 31, 2007. Nagioff told Fuld that Lehman was overleveraged and could lose a massive amount of capital in a potential market downturn. Nagioff recommended that Lehman reduce its forward commitments from $36 billion to $20 billion, impose rules on the amount of leverage in the deals, and develop a framework for real estate risk management.[67]

At this time, with the walls of his empire falling around him, Fuld was responsive. He said he would plan a meeting with Nagioff and the Lehman executive committee. Yet, such an urgent meeting did not take place until several weeks later. Nagioff was authorized to conduct a cross-firm initiative to reduce commitments to $20 billion by the end of 2007.

Fuld and the executive committee listened to Nagioff with deaf ears. There was no action to deleverage Lehman; instead, the firm continued to double-down. Incredibly, after speaking with Fuld on May 31, the firm entered $25.4 billion in new leveraged loan commitments over the next two months.[68] Nagioff's Fixed Income department ended the quarter roughly $2 billion over its net balance sheet limit. Disgusted, Nagioff retired only months later.

After Nagioff's departure, head of Equities, Bart McDade, tried to save Lehman Brothers in the third quarter of 2008. Two days after the second quarter earnings were announced, McDade walked straight into Fuld's sprawling private office and bravely explained to Fuld:

"This firm has to make a change. The division heads are unhappy with the leadership . . . and the investment community has lost a degree of confidence in our stock."

Fuld was furious. "What the hell is all this about?" he yelled. "This was all done behind my back!"[69]

Fuld could not believe one of his lieutenants was challenging his right to power. In the first ultimatum Fuld had heard in 30 years, McDade explained that either Fuld or his right hand man, Joe Gregory, had to go. Gregory's head was first on the chopping block, but Fuld's time would come soon enough.

With McDade in control, Mike Gelband and Alex Kirk were rehired to try and salvage the firm from upcoming default. However,

Fuld's damage was too far gone. After merger deals with Bank of America, Barclays, Warren Buffett, and the Korean Development Bank fell through (all for different reasons), Lehman Brothers filed for bankruptcy September 15, 2008.[70]

Subsequent to the bankruptcy, Dick Fuld and other senior managers have been defendants in a number of civil lawsuits and bankruptcy matters that are ongoing. Fuld has not been accused of criminal conduct. Other than serving as a party to lawsuits, testifying to Congress, and the sporadic news interview, Fuld has been largely out of the public eye.

Notes

1. Henry M. Paulson, Jr. "On the Brink," *Business Plus*, New York, 2010, p. 243.
2. Ibid.
3. Mark T. Williams, *Uncontrolled Risk* (New York: McGraw Hill, 2010), pp. 84, 85, 86.
4. Lawrence G. McDonald, *A Colossal Failure of Common Sense* (New York: Crown Business, 2009), pp. 89, 90, 91.
5. Ibid., p. 91.
6. Ibid., p. 90.
7. In "Re Lehman Brothers Holdings Inc., Report of Anton R. Valukas," *Examiner*, Introduction, Executive Summary & Procedural Background US Bankruptcy Court, S.D.N.Y. March 11, 2010, pp. 2–15.
8. See generally, McDonald; see also Vicky Ward, *The Devil's Casino: Friendship, Betrayal, and The High Stakes Games Played Inside Lehman Brothers* (Hoboken, NJ: John Wiley & Sons, 2011).
9. McDonald, pp. 89, 90, 91.
10. Ibid.
11. Ibid.
12. Williams, p. 14.
13. Ibid.
14. Ibid.
15. Ibid., p. 15.
16. Ibid., p. 16.
17. Ibid.
18. Ibid., p. 17.
19. Ibid.
20. Ibid.
21. Ibid., p. 17.

22. Ibid., pp. 18–19.
23. Ibid., p. 20.
24. Ibid.
25. Peter G. Peterson, *The Education of an American Dreamer* (New York: Twelve, 2009).
26. Ibid.
27. Ibid.
28. Ibid.
29. Williams, p. 24.
30. Ibid., p. 28.
31. Ward.
32. Ibid.
33. Richard Carreno, "Dick Fuld: Wall Street's Camel Trader," *Salon*, October 7, 2008, open.salon.com/blog/richard_carreowriters_clearinghouse/2008/10/07/dick_fuld_wall_streets_camel_trader.
34. Ward, p. 19.
35. Ibid.
36. Ibid.
37. Ibid.
38. Ibid.
39. Ibid.
40. Ibid, p. 20.
41. Ibid.
42. Williams, p. 60.
43. Ibid., p. 68.
44. Williams, p. 75.
45. Ibid., p. 72.
46. Ibid.
47. Ibid., pp. 75–76.
48. Devin Leonard, "How Lehman Got Its Real Estate Fix," *The New York Times*, May 2, 2009, www.nytimes.com/2009/05/03/business/03real.html.
49. Ibid., p. 132.
50. Williams, p. 132.
51. Ibid., p. 133.
52. Leonard.
53. McDonald, p. 246.
54. McDonald, pp. 89, 90, 91; see also Williams,
55. In "Re Lehman Brothers Holdings Inc., Report of Anton R. Valukas," p. 732.
56. Ibid.
57. Ibid., p. 735.
58. Ibid., p. 739.

59. "Examiner's Findings Of Claims Against Lehman Officers," Reuters, March 11, 2010, www.reuters.com/article/2010/03/12/us-lehman-examiner-factbox-idUSTRE62A5NU20100312.
60. Williams, p. 114.
61. Ibid.
62. McDonald, pp. 268–269.
63. In "Re Lehman Brothers Holdings Inc., Report of Anton R. Valukas," p. 50.
64. Ibid., p. 51.
65. Ibid., p. 119.
66. Ibid., p. 122.
67. Ibid., p. 120.
68. Ibid., p. 122.
69. McDonald, p. 293.
70. See generally, Paulson.

Chapter 5

How Out-of-Control Pride Brought Down Bear Stearns

It was pride that changed angels into devils; it is humility that makes men as angels.

—*Saint Augustine*

On July 17, 2007, Bear Stearns was in crisis. CEO Jimmy Cayne announced the firm was forced to close two of its most profitable hedge funds: the High-Grade Structured Credit Strategies Enhanced Leverage Fund (the Enhanced Fund) and the High-Grade Structured Credit Fund (the High Grade Fund). The two funds were awash with toxic mortgage-backed securities, including substantial amounts of subprime loans. The fund's liquidity could not shoulder massive amount of institutional investor redemptions and margin calls. The SEC and Justice Department disclosed that they were investigating the fall of the funds, specifically the actions of two Bear fund managers, Ralph Cioffi and Matthew Tanin.

Industry analysts responded with dire outlooks. Brad Hintz, research analyst at Sanford Bernstein, wrote that the mortgage-backed security issue was "more than a Bear Stearns issue . . . it is an industry issue. How many other hedge funds are holding similar, illiquid, esoteric securities?"[1] Bill Gross, CEO of PIMCO, predicted defaults on sub-prime loans would "grow and grow like a weed in your backyard tomato patch."[2] Due to the events, Bear Stearns stock was down 18 percent from its all-time high only five months earlier.

The investment bank was in need of tough, decisive action to reverse Bear's stock plunge, encourage investor confidence, and mitigate the company's growing reputational risk.

Instead, on July 18, 2007, one day after announcing the dismantling of the two hedge funds, CEO Jimmy Cayne and Bear President Warren Spector traveled to compete in the ten-day Spingold Knockout bridge tournament in Nashville, Tennessee. Cayne, Spector, and Bear's management team knew that the bank's two most powerful men would be out of contact because cell phones and Blackberry devices were not permitted at the competition.[3]

At arguably the most important juncture in the history of Bear Stearns, its leaders were playing a bridge tournament. This failure of corporate governance was self-created. For decades, Bear was steeped with immense pride among its top management, with an admitted focus on hiring personnel who were selfish, ambitious, and greedy. Bear believed it could prosper with a brash, swashbuckling, fraternity-house mentality.

Since 1970, Bear Stearns had discouraged looking for MBA-level talent. Instead, hiring personnel sought people with "poor, smart and a deep desire to become rich" (PSD) degrees.[4] Long-time Bear Stearns CEO Alan "Ace" Greenberg said of the firm's expansion of entry-level talent from 1973 to 1981, "Our first desire is to promote from within. If somebody with an MBA degree applies for a job, we will certainly not hold it against them, but we are really looking for people with PSD degrees."[5] Many of these "greedy poor persons" would be in senior positions during the financial crisis.

In reflection, Greenberg tried to reconcile this statement (and his legacy) by stating that he actually meant "smart, aggressive persons" and that he conducted his own "self-policing initiatives." Greenberg explained, "If the guy at the next desk was spending every week end in Atlantic City, that had a bearing upon his behavior and performance the other five days of the week—and by extension had a potential effect upon our bottom line."[6] However, if Bear's official policy was to hire poor persons with a deep desire to become rich, it is unfathomable for Greenberg to expect personnel to exercise thrift and caution or care in the volatile capital markets.

The events surrounding Greenberg's hiring of Cayne illustrates the toxic corporate culture of pride at Bear Stearns. In 1969, Harold C. Mayer, one of the founders of Bear, called Greenberg and indicated that he wanted Cayne to become a retail broker. Cayne reached Mayer's desk through a bridge connection. Cayne was a former taxi driver and scrap metal salesman with no college degree and no experience in finance. He was a "bridge bum," a perpetual gambler, who risked everything for the rush of winning a hand of cards. He needed a job at Bear to pay his bills and avoid inevitable personal bankruptcy.

In 1969, Cayne told Greenberg that he was a competitive bridge player. Greenberg, also an avid gambler, asked Cayne, "How good are you?"

"I'll put it this way," Cayne said, "If you play for the rest of your life, if you really work at it and play with great partners, you'll never be as good as I am now." This statement, demonstrating Cayne's extraordinary arrogance, remarkably won him the job.

"That, in my estimation, was a good sign," Greenberg recounts in his autobiography. "We were looking for PSDs—even though I hadn't yet coined that phrase—and Jimmy's brash confidence suggested that he was a live one."[7]

Hiring persons based on brawn, supposed invincibility, gambling prowess, and greed turned out to be an unsustainable model of corporate culture at Bear Stearns. A blindly prideful firm run by traders, salesman, and management who were motivated by "PSD" degrees and arrogance was bound to eventually fail.

History of Bear

Robert B. Stearns, Harold C. Mayer, and Joseph Ainslie Bear established the partnership of Bear Stearns in 1923. The company was founded with

$500,000 in capital. The partners formed the investment bank partnership largely in response to the booming years of the 1920s, where there was a surge of capital in markets and a high demand for investments.

Bear was 45, the oldest partner. He had been educated in France, Germany, and Switzerland, and before founding the firm was a partner at J.J. Danzig, a small bond trading firm. Stearns graduated from Yale University and joined Danzig as a statistician. Mayer was the most precocious of the original Bear partners. He owned his own import-export business in his early twenties and had a seat on the New York Stock Exchange prior to joining the Bear partnership.

With the initial investment of these three partners, Bear was able to generate enough profits during the six years before the Great Depression to remain in business. In fact, smart, thrifty policies enabled Bear to grow to 75 employees by 1933. In only ten years, the partnership increased its capital levels by 60 percent.

In the midst of the turbulent times of the Great Depression, Bear partner Theodore Low pushed for the firm to open a corporate bond department. Corporate bonds are long debt instruments issued to raise capital. They are subsequently traded in the marketplace based on investor confidence in the bond repayment plus interest.

At this time, it could be said that the first PSD was brought into Bear Stearns to run the firm's new corporate bond department, Salim "Cy" Lewis. Lewis was born in Brookline, Massachusetts, to a family of Orthodox Jews. His childhood was marked by health and economic struggles. Lewis had debilitating asthma, and sometimes, as a child, "He got it so bad he used to have to crawl up the stairs to get into his house."[8]

Lewis was bright, but was only able to attend Boston University for three semesters because his parents did not have enough funds to pay his tuition.[9] To earn some extra money at this time, Lewis played professional football. However, football during the 1920s did not provide much career stability. Lewis's only choice was to follow a girlfriend to Philadelphia and became a shoe salesman.[10]

Through this job, Lewis became enamored with the process of selling and pitching products. He believed Wall Street was the ideal destination for him. Like other PSDs in the future, Lewis got to Wall Street through exposure to rich executives.

For example, although Lewis did not know how to drive a car, his son, Sandy Lewis, explains that he got a brief job as a North Shore Country Club valet in the hopes of driving Herbert Salomon's car for him.[11]

"Cy Lewis stuck to Herbert Salomon because he was hoping to get himself a job at Salomon Brothers," Sandy said, "He ended up getting Herbert Salomon's car for him in the parking lot of the country club, which is pretty remarkable because he didn't know how to drive. That didn't bother him any. He got the car over to him. Salomon said to my father, "Come in on Monday morning, son. We'll have a talk."[12]

Before Bear, Lewis's Wall Street career was marked by a series of failures and firings. Lewis was let go from Salomon Brothers soon after working in its sales and trading department. He then worked for Barr, Cohen & Co. and was fired in three short years. He was brought on at two smaller investment banks and was fired abruptly from both.[13]

When Lewis got to Bear Stearns, he was a seasoned Wall Street salesman. His capital contribution to the firm was $20,000.[14] Lewis was convinced that enhanced risk would mean more profits for the partnership.

Lewis sold the Bear partners on the business opportunities of risk arbitrage.[15] Risk arbitrage is trading in companies that have the same business line at their highest level of stock price difference. Risk arbitrage involves shorting the stock of the highly priced company and longing the stock of the undervalued company.

Through smart trading, Lewis was able to build Bear's risk arbitrage business when other banks were frightened away by the practice's inherent risks. It was in this manner and shrewd trading that Lewis built the foundation for Bear's tremendous success in the latter half of the twentieth century.

During the Great Depression, Bear Stearns survived, but barely. Stock market trading was at highly diminished levels and most of Bear's clients were Park Avenue German Jewish widows.[16]

During World War II, Lewis made the investment decision that made his career. Applying his theories of risk arbitrage, Lewis saw railroad bond trading levels as low as 5 cents on the dollar. These bonds were being paid without interest because the government had seized American railroads to transport essential goods for the war effort. Lewis believed that if he bought the bonds at such a low rate and the United States won the war, the bonds would bounce back at much higher prices plus interest.

When Lewis secured a loan to Bear Stearns in order to purchase massive amounts of railroad bonds, he was taking a giant risk.[17] Lewis and Bear had to continue to pay interest on the loans to buy the war bonds. Additionally, Lewis could not move the bonds because they were without interest and, accordingly, not attractive to investors.

However, Lewis's plan worked to perfection. By February 1946, railroad bonds were selling at record high prices with a yield only slightly higher than dependable US Treasury bonds.[18] Cy's son, Sandy Lewis, explained, "Things got awful good awful fast. All of a sudden, these bonds rose to par. And you got par plus accrued interest back when . . . things got different. We got better cars . . . golf cars. The apartment was well furnished. All kinds of things started happening. We had parties. There were six servants. There was a chauffeur."[19]

Cy Lewis made the firm and himself a massive amount of money through his World War II railroad bets. As in most investment banks, accumulating this kind of money led to increases in personal power within the firm. Lewis was Bear's new all-star trader. He centralized power by marginalizing rival partner Teddy Low's conservative thinking. Low did not want to risk any firm capital in taking investment risks. Lewis then focused the firm's proprietary trading efforts on merger arbitrage (e.g., betting a firm would merge or not merge).

Lewis was the quintessential PSD. He would define the kind of person Bear would look to hire until the firm's disintegration in 2008. Fired from countless previous positions, down on his luck, Lewis had a deep desire to be rich and powerful. Through one risky railroad bet, he was able to do this, change his fortune, and cement his legacy at Bear and on Wall Street for generations.

As Ace Greenberg explains, "It was Cy who had made Bear Stearns a force to be reckoned with. Previously, it [Bear Stearns] had been a small-commission firm whose survival strategy was predicated upon a very low tolerance for risk. All of that changed, however, because Cy had the vision and nerve to go into risk arbitrage."[20]

A Different PSD

The man who would lead Bear Stearns to Wall Street preeminence had largely humble roots. Alan "Ace" Greenberg grew up in Oklahoma to first-generation Jewish immigrants. His father owned a women's clothing store that had more than 11 separate locations. While Greenberg's family was not rich by New York standards, he was relatively wealthy for Oklahoma City.

As a Jew and one of the few affluent families in the neighborhood, Greenberg learned to be humble, unassuming, and quietly confident. He was very careful to blend in as well as he could. In fact, in his biography he explained that the only time he "freaked out" was when his mother ordered him to wear "knickers" to his poverty-stricken grade school—not when Bear's stock plunged in a matter of weeks.[21]

Greenberg attended the University of Oklahoma and the University of Missouri. At both of these Midwestern institutions he was an outcast. No one else shared his last name. For a short period of time, Greenberg took the advice from a friend and changed his name to "Ace Gainsboro" with hopes of enhancing his social life. The nickname "Ace" stuck; the last name, Gainsboro, was short lived.

Nevertheless, because he was an albatross for much of his youth, as a Jew in the 1940s American Midwest, Greenberg developed unassuming humility that would distinguish him on Wall Street for years to come. When Greenberg arrived at Bear Stearns on March 8, 1949, he had a deep desire to be successful and was extremely ambitious. Yet, at the same time, he had a deep sense of prudence and lacked the usual Wall Street hubris.

After World War II, Bear Stearns more or less became Cy Lewis's firm. His successful risk arbitrage in railroad bonds resulted in major profit increases for the company. With this rise in profits came greater autocratic power vested in him. Cy was soon a partner at Bear and a major voice in leading the company's fortunes.

In 1953, Greenberg made his first major move in assuming control over the risk arbitrage desk. As Ace explains, the timing was highly fortuitous. From 1953 to 1961, there was an immense bull market because companies became more aggressive in facilitating mergers and buy-outs.[22] This made the risk arbitrage policies that Bear Stearns had pioneered even that much more profitable.

Greenberg and Lewis's personalities inevitably clashed. Greenberg was an unassuming, jovial, and extroverted personality. Lewis was starkly different in nature. He was a burly, abrasive, and introverted man who regularly chastised staff in calculated attempts at intimidation. Most employees were genuinely afraid of Lewis's growing wrath. Everyone except Ace Greenberg, that is.

In 1956, Lewis's trading assistant, Davey Finkle, retired. While Greenberg did not want to be considered for the role, Bear's John Slade told Greenberg, "Only you can take that seat, because it will hold Cy's successor."[23]

The problem with Greenberg working under Cy as his potential successor was that the two couldn't be any different. Their personalities largely correlated with their trading philosophies, thereby creating an environment for signature disagreements. While Greenberg believed that market research and trends should guide Bear's securities holdings, Lewis stubbornly refused to sell any securities he purchased.[24] As Greenberg explained, "In Cy's mind, it seemed, if he bought a stock it could do no wrong. [If it headed south, it became irrelevant, ignored, forgotten—yet remained on the books.] This certitude struck me as perverse and arrogant."[25]

Seeing an opportunity to fundamentally change Bear culture and its holdings, Greenberg gradually challenged Lewis's positions. Ace was made partner in 1958. He owned only 3 percent of the firm's equity in 1960. However, despite his relatively small stature in the firm compared with Cy, in the spring of 1962, Greenberg made his stand that would definitively change the trajectory of Bear Stearns and his own path to the Bear Stearns boardroom.

Bear was having difficulty navigating the waters of a choppy stock market in the spring of 1962. In addition to the company's balance sheet woes, what made Greenberg "physically ill" was seeing Lewis' long positions in security holdings that were not performing—and had not been performing in years. Greenberg was so disgusted with Lewis's hubris and his irrational trading strategy that he announced he was going to quit.[26]

Lewis ordered Greenberg to report to his apartment later that night and explain to him the reasons he wanted to leave Bear Stearns.

Greenberg's conversation was straight to the point, and demonstrated Lewis's tremendous aversion to diligence, thrift, and market research.

"Have you ever heard of Rudd–Melikian?" Greenberg asked Lewis.

"No, what the hell is that?"

"It's a stock. You bought it. We own ten thousand shares of it. It's gone from 20 to 5. We have at least 20 positions like that. I can't stand it another day."[27]

Remarkably, Lewis relented. "Okay Alan, I'll make you a deal. From now on, you're free to sell anything you want that has a loss in it. You hear me? . . . And I also promise that I'll do my best to live with it."[28]

On the very next day, Greenberg sold Rudd–Melikian and all of Cy's other losing positions. Soon after, Greenberg created a risk committee that would evaluate the potential downside of acquiring or maintaining large holdings in specific stocks and would track how the firm's capital was invested.[29]

In a few days, Greenberg had broken Lewis's stranglehold over Bear Stearns and drastically improved both the company's governance and risk management structures.

Greenberg's Vision of Corporate Thrift at Bear Stearns

As Greenberg's power within the firm grew in the latter half of the twentieth century, he gained greater control over the firm's operations and culture. He continued the pattern of lowering costs, increasing governance, and decreasing the extravagance of Bear under Cy Lewis.

Like Lewis, Greenberg molded the company in his self-assured, practical Midwestern image. "My strategic thinking boiled down to a conviction that whatever boosted morale and camaraderie (among staff) should also help boost profits. Common sense, self-assurance and controlling costs, would guide us through up markets, down markets, auspicious circumstances and the opposite."[30]

In the early 1970s, Greenberg also pushed for a policy that required Bear Stearns partners to donate at least 4 percent of their gross income to charity. If the firm did exceptionally well in a year, Greenberg would donate more. Other big Wall Street firms called Greenberg about the policy and how they did it, but at the time, no other investment bank enacted such philanthropic efforts.[31]

In 1973, Bear moved to 55 Wall Street, burdening the firm with greater costs. Rather than cutting employees, Greenberg diversified the firm by entering the clearing business. The business didn't become profitable immediately, but by 1988, the firm was processing 10 percent of all trades on the New York Stock Exchange.[32]

In 1978, Cy Lewis officially retired from the firm. He passed away soon after—in fact, at his official Bear Stearns retirement party. Only months after Lewis's passing, another major partner at Bear Stearns also died, Ted Low. These two deaths left Greenberg squarely in charge of Bear Stearns publicly and within the power structures of the firm. Greenberg admittedly felt a considerable amount of pressure to keep Bear Stearns clients appeased, maintain revenue levels, and keep employee utility high with Lewis and Low now both gone.

In order to raise morale, Greenberg invoked a fictional business philosopher, Haimchinkel Malintz Anaynikal.[33] Greenberg used this pseudo figure to promote thrift, diligence, detail, extroversion, and hard work within Bear Stearns in hundreds of official memorandums to all Bear Stearns staff. In each memo, Greenberg warned of the dangers of complacency, cockiness, sloppiness, and carelessness. Famously, Greenberg sent out a memorandum explaining that Haimchinkel prophesized, "Thou will do well in commerce as long as thou does not believe thine own odor is perfume."[34]

Greenberg was mocked for these memorandums by future CEO and Bear Stearns power broker Jimmy Cayne and author William D. Cohan in his book, *House of Cards: A Tale of Hubris and Wretched Excess on Wall Street*. Cohan argues that many of these memos were intended to "belittle" his partners and were a sign of Greenberg's "ruthlessness."[35]

Regardless of Mr. Cohan's beliefs, these memos were in many ways instrumental in inspiring staff, encouraging firm loyalty, spurring employee production, fostering counterparty trust, and boosting market confidence in Bear Stearns. Within seven years of Cy's death, Greenberg had grown firm capital to $350 million and grown the firm to 5,000 employees.[36]

Bridge Bum Turned Bear Salesman and CEO

In 1993, Bear Stearns' company biography devoted 10 lines to James ("Jimmy") E. Cayne's achievements at the company and 13 lines to his achievements at the bridge table.[37]

In many ways, this defined Cayne's tenure at Bear Stearns. He was first hired not because of his financial acumen or talents as a salesman, but because of his bravado on the bridge table.[38] It was a lucky turn of events for Cayne. In 2005, this former self-professed "bridge bum," was named the 384th richest American in *Forbes* magazine with a net worth of $900 million.[39]

When Greenberg hired Cayne in 1969, he was 35 years old and had never sold a security in his life.[40] For all of Greenberg's bluster about risk management and Haimchinkel Malintz Anaynikal, he took a major chance on Cayne because of his passion for bridge and belief in the success of the PSD employee model.[41] "You could see the electric light bulb," Cayne recalled in informing Greenberg he played bridge. On the spot, Greenberg guaranteed Cayne $70,000 a year if he joined Bear Stearns.[42]

As an adult, Cayne wanted to be a betting bookie but chose against it because he thought it might bring shame on his family.[43] Cayne's family was professional and wealthy. His father was a patent attorney and his mother was a housewife who devoted family money to Jewish causes.[44] Cayne enrolled in the Purdue University mechanical engineering program in 1950 with pressure from his father to follow the family business of patent law. However, Cayne did not take his academic pursuits very seriously. He spent most of his studying time at fraternity bridge tables.[45]

Cayne eventually left Purdue one semester shy of his diploma. He had lost all interest in school, admits he was "massively irresponsible," shot pool, played poker, and "chased women." Cayne proudly recounts that he was "like Action Jackson."[46] He volunteered for the army draft to respectfully remove him from his academic obligations. His parents, in turn, kicked him out of the house.[47]

After serving for a short period of time as an army court reporter in Japan, Cayne became a Chicago cab driver and lived with a fraternity brother. He then lived with the sister of a family friend because she was attractive and rich.[48] At this time, Cayne was nothing more than a professional bridge player. His net worth was near zero, and by his own accounts he was living like a "vegetable."[49]

Cayne spent time at this family's scrap iron business and then joined the municipal bond brokerage, Lebenthal & Co. At Lebenthal, he spent three hours at work and the rest of the day playing bridge.[50] After five years working at Lebenthal, his new rich, attractive girlfriend, Patricia Denner, gave him an ultimatum: Find a real job, or else find a new girlfriend.[51] Finally, at the age of 35, Cayne tapped into his bridge network to interview at Bear Stearns. The year was 1969. He would not leave the company until 2008.

In the mid-1980s, business at Bear Stearns was booming. Total revenues had increased to $1.8 billion in the fiscal year ending April 1985.[52] Only four years earlier, Bear had made $393 million. Within four years, under Greenberg's thrift and quirky philosophy, the firm made over a billion dollars.

Cayne at this time was driving Greenberg to work every day. This was a calculated move by Cayne to endear himself to Greenberg. Cayne was already a firm partner by the 1980s, but he wanted more than just an equity stake in Bear's rising fortunes—fortunes that soon included going public through an initial public offering (IPO).

Cayne's opportunistic persona saw an IPO as his leverage into gaining increased power within the firm. In his depiction of events to author William D. Cohan in House of Cards, Cayne explains that the executive committee voted on going public without Greenberg. On the day after, Cayne blindsided Greenberg by explaining that the committee voted to go public. "You'll be the chairman. Johnny Rosenwald will be the vice chairman. I'll be the president." Greenberg apparently sat in silence.[53] Greenberg accuses Cayne in his memoir of blatantly lying to Cohan regarding the events leading to Bear's IPO.

Greenberg states, "This fabrication is ludicrous in every particular, starting with the fact that three of my best friends . . . sat on the executive committee."[54] Instead, Greenberg says, "What did occur is that a few months before the IPO, I returned from a vacation and was handed a memo that referred to certain details about our offering prospectus."[55] The memo listed Jimmy as the sole president of Bear Stearns and Johnny Rosenwald (Greenberg's friend) as vice. Although Cayne explained that Rosenwald agreed to it, Rosenwald told Greenberg that it had never been discussed.[56]

This exchange exemplifies the way Cayne operated. Whether either account is true, both demonstrate his opportunism, manipulation, and deep desire to move up within the Bear Stearns power hierarchy. Despite Greenberg calling Cayne "fanciful" and "unapologetically crude and bullying," Cayne's tactics worked to raise his stature at Bear during the 1980s.[57] Greenberg did not give into Cayne in 1985, but Cayne, the epitome of the ambitious Bear Stearns PSD model, became sole president of Bear Stearns in 1988.

In 1993, Cayne made an almost identical power grab with Greenberg when he decided to travel to China to cultivate business. In order to do so, Cayne reasoned he needed a greater title (i.e., chief executive officer). Like he did with the president power grab move, he did it indirectly—arguing that the title was second fiddle to the purpose of the trip. This time, Greenberg gave in to Cayne. He believed he could still be in charge of Bear Stearns in the chairman position. Cayne had once more chipped away at Greenberg's iron grip on power.

Looking back on Cayne's rise after hiring him in 1968, Greenberg recounts:

> At first Jimmy's avidity struck me as a mixed blessing, according to the PSD principle, I wanted our people to be hungry—but over time it increasingly seemed like an unfortunate character trait. As head of private client services, he pushed the retail reps out of competitive instinct and a clear awareness that their success and the consequent rewards would encourage a personal loyalty to him and enhance his stature . . . Jimmy was constantly caucusing and forming alliances. I didn't like it and I told him so, but I don't think he could help himself.[58]

Cayne was the greatest PSD success story Bear Stearns would ever know.

A Casino Culture

Mortgage-backed securities were the chosen product of the Bear Stearns PSD gamblers. The firm enjoyed peddling products and revenue opportunities that other Wall Street firms dismissed.[59] Bear cared little for appearances and what other institutions, traders, or bankers thought of them.[60] In many ways, especially beginning in the 1980s and 1990s, Bear Stearns basked in a fraternity-like atmosphere where bond traders, according to *The Wall Street Journal* and now CNBC's Kate Kelly, "were brusque, arrogant, and uninterested in anyone who disagreed with their positions."[61]

While other banks have been called quasi-casinos, Bear Stearns had a living and breathing gambling addiction, complete with model attendants and "geisha girls."[62] There were few women in the top power circles of Bear Stearns, except scantily clad models who escorted visitors to meetings.[63] In essence, it is not surprising that Bear was one of the few early firms that pioneered the art of the mortgage-backed security during the 1980s. The securitization of such loans represented the ultimate boom and bust prospect for any Wall Street trader moonlighting as a bridge or poker whiz.

In the 1980s, Bear decided that one of the ways it could fuel growth was with new fixed-income products called mortgage-backed securities. Mortgage-backed securities are a portfolio of consumer mortgages, securitized, sold, and traded by financial firms.

In 1981, Bear Stearns founded the mortgage department as a division of its fixed income group. Thrift organizations that were struggling to keep illiquid mortgages on their books were looking for a way to make profit and keep afloat in a time of high interest rates, encouraging defaults. On a smaller scale than in the twenty-first century, some banks willing to take the risks of trading and selling packaged illiquid assets founded mortgage departments to meet this demand. Bear Stearns was one of these firms. It was at the front of the line.

Tommy Marano, a Bear executive who worked in the mortgage division beginning in 1983, explained, "What you were trying to do was get the assets off the thrifts balance sheets to basically get them some liquidity to keep operating."[64]

Bear Stearns revolutionized the market by working with Fannie Mae and Freddie Mac, two government-sponsored entities, which insured mortgages, to issue real estate mortgage investment contracts (REMICS).[65] These products holding distressed mortgages were seen as nearly risk free because of Fannie and Freddie's status as GSEs.

Marano recounts, "I actually priced and traded the very first REMIC Fannie Maes 87–1 for $500 million. It was a new market, it was a growing market . . . We did deals for all the failed thrifts, among them American Savings and Loan and California Federal . . . It became kind of a real race between us, Salomon Brothers, Merrill, First Boston, Lehman Brothers, and DLJ."[66]

In response to the October 1987 stock market crash, one of the greatest one-day drops in stock market history, Ace Greenberg stated at a business conference, "Stocks fluctuate; next question."[67]

This summarized Bear's attitude and conception on Wall Street during the 1990s as well. Senior management and staff felt invincible to all volatility and crisis. Greenberg, admittedly, was confident in his own ability to navigate risk, bad deals, and market volatility. Discussing the 1987 crash, junk bonds, and leveraged buyout trends, and the opening of Russia, Greenberg claims that he knew at the time that bridge loans, junk bond financing, and Russian investments would lead to disaster.[68]

However, both Greenberg and Cayne kept wanting more. In fact, Greenberg writes that he only put up with Jimmy's hubris because "a war between us would have done the firm no good, and the fact was that on the whole Bear Stearns had been performing very well . . . In 1993, despite our decision to cut our profit share by 15 percent we still took home almost $16 million."[69] Bear revenues and Greenberg's salary overshadowed what he says was "Jimmy's need for power and the swaggering bluster that went with it."[70]

During the mid-1990s, Bear surged forward with continued expansion, new PSD hires, new real estate ventures, and historic company revenues. Cayne began negotiations in 1997 for Bear Stearns move to 383 Madison Avenue in New York City. The real estate project was massive and would include perks such as a private gym, restaurant, and, most importantly, a building that would only house Bear Stearns personnel.

Bear now had 8,300 employees, up 32 percent from June 1993.[71] The 47-story building cost Bear $700 million, but would house the largest installation of electronic and digital cable in North America.[72] Author William D. Cohan writes that in many ways, the building was Cayne's "playground" and a "monument to himself."[73]

Greenberg commented in his biography that, at the time, his firm was in "rock solid" condition and that the building project demonstrated where "Bear was headed as a major financial institution." Yet, only a few months after Bear Stearns broke ground on its sprawling new financial palace, Bear's booming balance sheet became threatened by the LTCM crisis.

Most problematic was that Bear handled LTCM's clearing business and settlement of dealings in bonds and derivatives at the time when the massive hedge fund was going bottom up. In less than four months, LTCM had lost $4.6 billion because of its exposure to the Russian financial crisis.

Despite the amount of LTCM losses, Bear's clearing exposure, and the potential market reaction of a swift LTCM liquidation, Bear Stearns flexed its muscles. Under the direction of Cayne, Bear was the only major Wall Street firm not to assist in the Federal Reserve Bank's organized private bailout of LTCM.

Federal Reserve officials were incredulous and instructed Bear they would no longer have access to LTCM's clearing business.[74] Cayne's response demonstrated Bear's growing pride and perceived invincibility: "We're not clearing anymore . . . I agree. We're not. By the way, if you want to hire us back, it's triple the rate."[75]

In the end, Bear was suffocated by its stubborn insistence that mortgage-backed securities were invincible products. Minutes from a Bear Stearns board meeting on January 10, 2007, reported that Cayne (then the firm executive) indicated that the real estate "business continued to be buoyant."[76] On March 29, 2007, Bear Stearns proclaimed on its annual investor day report that "credit products continue to produce record revenues."[77] These comments came during a time in which it was becoming patently obvious to most all Wall Street analysts that the mortgage-backed security investment vehicle was doomed for failure.

BSAM: Bear Stearns' Kryptonite

Bear Stearns continued to be immensely profitable at the turn of the twenty-first century. The firm's real estate products continued to have a great deal to do with record-breaking profits at the bank. For example, as early as April 2002, Bear Stearns announced quarterly profits of $181 million.[78] Cayne emphasized in Bear's official SEC filing that this number was due in large part to its fixed income business, "with a particularly strong performance from our industry leading mortgage-backed securities department."[79]

Low-interest rates, coupled with boilerplate mortgages, relaxation of credit standards for homebuyers, and predatory subprime lending, fueled a massive real estate boom. Banks securitized mortgages, other fixed income, and credit products into CDOs, a new financial product peddled by banks, sold and traded in the thousands. Most banks were unaware of their risks and complexity. They held a revolving door of CDOs that remained on their balance sheets, increasing Bear's debt and the firm's leverage ratios.

Bear saw a major opportunity in trading real estate–engineered products similar to Lehman Brothers and other large investment banks. Feelings of invincibility and immense pride continued to fuel the firm's decision making. From 2001 to 2003, the bank received substantial positive press regarding its glistening new building, record-breaking revenues, and seemingly "can't miss," shrewd management.[80]

Bear categorically believed it could do nothing wrong. As Bear's Warren Spector told Richard A. Marin in convincing Marin to run Bear Stearns Asset Management (BSAM), "Bear Stearns succeeds at anything it puts its mind to. And since we haven't really succeeded at asset management, we haven't put our mind to it. We want to put our mind to it now."[81]

Ralph Cioffi was selected to lead BSAM's new real estate hedge fund, termed the "Bear Stearns High Grade Structured Credit Strategies Master Fund" (High Grade Fund). The fund's premise was to invest and trade in CDO products.

Cioffi grew up in South Burlington, Vermont. He was an excellent student athlete in high school and played running back, fullback, and offensive guard for his Catholic high school team. He then attended St. Michael's College, a small Vermont liberal arts Catholic college.[82] Cioffi arrived at Bear Stearns in 1985 to work as a fixed income bond salesman.[83]

Prior to his stint with BSAM, Cioffi's only managerial level experience at Bear Stearns was the position of institutional sales manager. Perhaps not surprisingly, then, Bear Stearns Senior Managing Director Paul Friedman recounts that Cioffi's managerial position was not a success. "He was a disaster, Friedman said, "He had adult ADD. Ralph didn't do well with that stuff . . . He was just not a really good manager."[84]

However, Cioffi was very well liked at Bear Stearns. While his performance as a manager received poor reviews within the firm, the company's leadership wanted to find a well-paid, prominent position for him. The growing real estate asset management group seemed like a position that would be immune to failure for Cioffi. Yet, many within Bear questioned Cioffi's credentials for the job.

"There were a fair number of skeptics internally who couldn't figure out how this guy—who was bright but had never managed money— was now going to be running money. He knew nothing about risk management, had never written a ticket in his life that wasn't someone else's money. But we did it. I sure as hell wouldn't have given him my money."[85]

In 2003, the High Grade Fund opened for business. Matthew Tanin was brought on board to help Cioffi manage the fund's portfolio investments and trades. Tanin was somewhat more experienced in CDO and real estate derivative products. Tannin had helped structure Bear's CDO products since 1994. However, like Cioffi, he had no fund manager experience.[86]

"Never a Losing Month"

The High Grade Fund's eventual lethal fund portfolio consisted of leveraged CDO instruments.[87] These AA or AAA credit rated CDOs were insured and hedged by CDS positions that acted as insurance contracts against the risk that a bond or other security defaulted or experienced a credit rating downgrade.[88]

Cioffi and Tanin marketed these risky, credit investments as "safe" investment portfolios and an excellent tool for investors desiring capital preservation.[89] BSAM asserted that the High Grade Fund operated "like a bank" in the process, continuing to build trust and confidence with markets and investors.[90]

With the Bear Stearns brand name, attractive marketing strategies, and immediate positive returns, the High Grade Fund was soon managing more than $1.5 billion in investor capital.[91] Investors consisted of relatively high-net-worth individuals, some of whom had invested through closely held corporations, trusts, and IRAs, as well as institutional investors, corporations, and employee benefit plans.[92]

After opening in October 2003, the High Grade Fund had positive returns for 40 straight months.[93] It earned a 50 percent cumulative return. The High Grade Fund alone accounted for 75 percent of BSAM's total revenues from 2004 to 2005.[94]

For his success, Cioffi earned eight-figure compensation. He was the proud new owner of vacation homes, suburban real estate, and two new Ferraris.[95] In 2006, Cioffi was one of the highest paid individuals in all of Bear Stearns.[96] The High Grade Fund became so popular that potential investors had to beg friends at Bear Stearns to invest their capital.[97] In fact, in August 2006, BSAM established a second fund, The High Grade Credit Strategies Enhanced Leverage Fund, to meet the wild demand from investors who could not get into the first fund.[98]

In 2005, Bear Stearns fixed-income product income declined 12 percent. However, the firm's profits on the whole couldn't be higher.[99] The firm posted a record profit in 2005 of $1.5 billion, up 9 percent from the year prior.[100]

Nevertheless, by 2006, signs of the mortgage bubble became apparent. Housing prices were dropping; securitized predatory loans were being distributed in the thousands—packaged, and then traded as CDOs and CDOs squared (CDOs backed by other CDOs) in funds like Cioffi's High Grade. The High Grade Fund had little diversification and consisted almost entirely of real estate CDO products.

Cioffi was learning risk management, compliance, and SEC disclosures on the fly. For example, in the Fund's Private Placement Memoranda (PPM) (essentially, the contract signed with investors regarding managerial duties and liabilities), BSAM assured its clients that the "Fund's operating procedure required disclosure, consent, and approval before the deal could be settled."[101] The deals were trades that the High Grade Fund consummated. In 2006 alone, 79 percent of Cioffi's trades did not receive proper appropriate approval from Bear Stearns affiliates.[102]

While some might believe this is a technicality, if there is no record or approval of a trade, it is not legally valid. If a trade is not legally valid, it cannot be traced, never really occurred, and cannot be properly disclosed to the fund's investors. In fact, Cioffi believed compliance and disclosure was "a low-priority task for junior assistants at the fund."[103]

Joan Marie Pusateri, who had been at Bear since 1986, was responsible for BSAM administration and trade approvals. She claimed that neither Cioffi nor Tanin informed her of legal responsibilities under the Investment Advisers Act of 1940 nor did she know that obtaining approvals from the fund's independent directors was essential for trades between Bear Stearns and its affiliates.[104] Once Pusateri became aware of these responsibilities, she put an assistant, Jessica Borenkind, a sales assistant, in charge of obtaining approvals.

However, Borenkind was equally apathetic to ensuring that required approvals were received. Once a month, BSAM compliance sent Pusateri's team a spreadsheet showing where she had failed to get approvals for trades that had already cleared and been settled.[105] As a result, Cioffi was making hundreds of trades a month that were illegal under the Investment Advisers Act of 1940.

Since many of the High Grade Fund's trades were with Bear Stearns' own affiliates, the firm decided to place a permanent moratorium on Cioffi's trades with Bear Stearns and its subsidiaries because of repeated failures to properly disclose and approve the Fund's related company dealings.[106] For Bear senior management, this was the first sign that something was amiss at BSAM and that Cioffi needed further monitoring.

According to the Justice Department's indictment of Cioffi and Tanin, the High Grade Fund was marketed as only "slightly riskier than a money market fund" and the High Grade Fund was not designed to "hit home runs."[107] In early 2006, High Grade performance began to decline; yet, rather than changing the Fund's strategy, Cioffi and Tanin decided to open a fund that employed extreme leverage.[108]

Thus, in August 2006, Cioffi created the Enhanced Fund, which was the epitome of the Fund's swashbuckling, risk/reward investment strategy. This new fund had the flexibility to boost leverage, beyond the maximum 10 times amount of leverage used by the High Grade Fund to 27.5 times of total investor capital.[109] This dramatic increase in leverage came at a time when the real estate bubble was on the precipice of popping.

To encourage new investment in the Enhanced Fund, Cioffi and Tanin explained they were moving their own personal capital into the leveraged pool of investments.[110] By early 2007, investors in the High Grade Fund had made net contributions of $1.08 billion, while those in the Leverage Fund invested a total of $775 million.[111]

At the end of July 2006, Cioffi reported to the High Grade Fund investors that "despite the significant downturn in the housing market and deterioration in subprime credit fundamentals, overall structured credit spreads remained tight and the credit performance of the Fund assets remains strong."[112] On repeated conference calls with both Fund investors beginning in January 2007, Cioffi tried to camouflage the amount of subprime loans in the funds by insisting "we're not believers in the world-is-coming-to-an-end housing bubble scenario" in regards to the perceived subprime loan crisis.[113]

Nonetheless, despite Cioffi's assurances to Fund investors, his world and the world of his investors were all rapidly coming to an end. Cioffi's lack of experience continued to haunt him. For example, Cioffi made a critical misstep in trying to rid both funds of $720 million in illiquid CDO securities by spinning off the illiquid assets into a separate off-balance-sheet entity termed "Everquest Financial."

Cioffi idea was that Everquest would act as a financial services company that would buy illiquid CDO securities in the BSAM hedge funds.[114] For some reason, Cioffi believed Everquest would be best served by going public and there would be public demand for illiquid, predatory, subprime loans.[115] Cioffi disclosed to the SEC in Everquest's offering documents that a "substantial majority" of the CDOs are backed by subprime mortgages to homebuyers with questionable credit.[116]

Cioffi pridefully believed he could market illiquid, predatory loans to public investors during the onslaught of the financial crisis. In evaluating Everquest's IPO potential, Cioffi believed the entity would somehow bring "increased liquidity to our hedge funds" and "mark to market gain."[117] Eventually, Cioffi thought better of it and called off the Everquest IPO, but the special-purpose company was still purchasing massive amounts of BSAM's illiquid CDO and CDO squared assets.

In February 2007, the High Grade Fund reported a gross return of 1.5 percent, but the Enhanced Leverage Fund lost 0.08 percent—the first time either fund had lost money since 2003.[118] Remarkably, despite this loss, Tanin sent an e-mail to Barclays Bank, a debt investor in the fund, misrepresenting the fund's performance. "You will be happy to know that we are having our best month ever," Tanin said, "Our hedges are working beautifully."[119] In reliance upon these statements, Barclays increased its total commitment in the fund to $400 million by March 2007.[120]

The misrepresentations continued. The two inexperienced managers were walking on thin ice in a falling "bear market" that was only become increasingly volatile. In fact, Cioffi was sending monthly statements to investors that the funds were only 6 percent exposed to subprime CDOs when, in fact, the number was closer to 60 percent.[121]

Cioffi desperately tried to masquerade the Enhanced Fund's performance by misrepresenting the returns of the Funds to investors. However, by June 2007, the Enhanced Fund was down 20 percent on the year.[122] Even though he knew the contrary was true, on April 25, 2007, Cioffi assured investors that the Enhanced Fund had "significant amounts of liquidity."[123]

On July 17, 2007, Cioffi and Tanin conceded defeat. After much posturing, investor misrepresentations, and balance sheet masquerading, BSAM finally reported that its two funds were "worthless."[124] By August 1, BSAM began the process of winding down the funds and filing for bankruptcy. Only two months earlier, Bear Stearns had invested another $25 million in the funds to help ward off investor redemption requests.

Although Bear had only invested $45 million in the funds, what was most damaging to the firm was its market reputation and investor confidence in the firm. Bear had insisted for months (through BSAM) that both funds were liquid and not subject to any dramatic downturn or potential market disruption. The opposite proved to be true.

At the time, industry analysts couldn't believe Bear invested more money in the fund only months before the funds failed: "For them to put up so much capital, just for reputational risk, wouldn't make sense unless they believe they won't lose money on it," said Erin Archer, an analyst at Minneapolis-based Thrivent Financial for Lutherans, which in the summer of 2007 owned about 200,000 Bear Stearns shares.[125]

Bear's PSD culture, defiance, and pride resulted in investments that turned markets against them. The events of the summer of 2007 created a larger reputational risk and market confidence crisis. The US Justice Department indicted Cioffi and Tanin on charges of securities fraud for their numerous misrepresentations of fund performance. In November 2009, a jury acquitted Cioffi and Tanin of all criminal charges, and the pair settled with the SEC for a total of $1.05 million in June of 2012.

The End of Bear Stearns: The Importance of Golf and Bridge during a Liquidity Crisis

In September 2007, Alan "Ace" Greenberg turned 80 years old. Greenberg stated in his memoir that it was difficult for him to conduct any sort of celebration. Warren Spector, the de facto new leader at the firm, was butting heads with Cayne, and Bear's usually strong fixed income department was reeling from market confidence issues and fractures in Bear's reputational risk on Wall Street. Nevertheless, Greenberg recounted, Cayne was largely complacent, believing he could run Bear Stearns at home, playing bridge in his pajamas.[126]

In mid-January 2007, Cayne's Bear shares were worth a whopping $1.2 billion.[127] According to Greenberg, Cayne's pride and hubris had a "maddening" correlation to the price of Bear stock.[128] For example, during the summer of 2007, while Bear Stearns was suffering from the Cioffi hedge fund crisis, Cayne and his good friend, CFO Sam Molinaro, pushed through a massive investor stock buyback at a cost of $1.5 billion.[129] Despite Greenberg's protests that the buyback would seriously affect the firm's liquidity, Molinaro stated that there would be no problem because Bear was "swimming in money."[130]

Cayne grew even more reclusive towards the end of 2007 as Bear became even more immersed in the financial crisis. Important golf tee-times and bridge tournaments conflicted with Bear Stearns business.[131]

If he was playing golf or bridge, Cayne was unreachable. As noted at the beginning of the chapter, Cayne was entirely unreachable during a weeklong Nashville bridge tournament that was held the week prior to BSAM's hedge fund liquidations.[132] Even when Cayne returned, he neglected an important industry analyst call concerning the firm's fiscal health after the hedge fund crisis.[133] Perhaps because of Cayne's absence, immediately after the call, Bear's stock dipped by 8 points.[134]

Cayne believed a capital infusion from China's CITIC Group could help boost Bear's capital and liquidity that was suffering from the fund crises and the stock buybacks. The plan was a dead-end idea, but it consumed months and investments of thousands of important man hours, in addition to hundreds of thousands of dollars.[135] Greenberg recounted that this was another decision that was dictated by Cayne's pride to do a "big deal" where he could take "sole credit."[136]

On November 1, 2007, a widely read *Wall Street Journal* article by author Kate Kelly depicted Cayne as selfish, out of touch, and more concerned with his golf game than the future of Bear Stearns."[137] With negative press, lack of market confidence, and Bear's illiquid fixed income products, the firm suffered its first quarterly loss since it went public in 1985 in the fourth quarter of 2007.

JP Morgan and the Takeover of Bear

By January 2008, according to Greenberg, no one could have reversed Bear Stearns' fate.[138] The firm was losing capital, its hedging strategies were not working efficiently, and product inventory was becoming even more illiquid. Cayne was finally out as CEO but there was little that new CEO Alan Schwartz, an investment banking whiz, could do to reverse the Bear Stearns demise.

A few days after Schwartz took over, he looked over the balance sheets Cayne had largely ignored and exclaimed to Cayne, "You have no idea how bad this is. We're long all this crap."[139] On March 10, 2008, Bear stock dropped 10 percent. On March 15, 2008, the stock was trading at $30 a share and was down a staggering 47 percent for the day. The defiant firm was in dire shape and in need of a merger or tremendous capital infusion to keep it in business for the next month.

With strong lobbying and negotiations between the Federal Reserve and Department of Treasury, Bear Stearns leadership, and JP Morgan, over a period of seven days, JP Morgan emerged as the "white knight" to save Bear Stearns from inevitable bankruptcy. On March 17, 2008, it was announced that JP Morgan would be buying Bear Stearns for $2 a share, amazingly valuing the company at only $236 million.

The fall of Bear Stearns was inevitable for a number of reasons. The company is a prime example of a grave failure of corporate culture. Throughout its history, Bear stressed PSD qualities that encouraged pride, selfish ambition, and greed among its entire staff, and lauded them it its leadership ranks. To be successful, firms require collaborators, risk management, ethics, diligence, and meticulous attention to detail. Bear overlooked many of these qualities, especially with the ambivalent Cayne in power.[140]

Bear was most successful during Greenberg's time as CEO, when thrift was stressed through cutting overhead and costs and morale was boosted through numerous memos from the CEO, even though they came from his strange alter ego.

Nevertheless, Greenberg, by his own admission, bought into the PSD culture. He proudly hired personnel that cared less about the firm and more about their own personal ambition and wealth. These persons, hired in the mid-1980s, were the leaders that Bear Stearns needed to guide them through the unprecedented financial crisis. Moreover, Greenberg made the dubious decision of hiring a young, brash "bridge bum" named Jimmy Cayne, who had no financial or banking experience.

Cayne's hiring alone demonstrates that the firm was long on bravado and short on rational pragmatism. This pragmatism is something Bear Stearns could have used during the liquidity crisis at BSAM. The PSD epidemic extended from Cy Lewis to Jimmy Cayne to Ralph Cioffi. At the highest levels of management, pride, repeated failures in governance, business ethics, and risk management doomed the fate of the firm that thought it was immune from failure.

Notes

1. William D. Cohan, *House of Cards: A Tale of Hubris and Wretched Excess on Wall Street* (New York: Random House, 2009), p. 439.
2. Ibid.
3. Ibid., p. 440.
4. Alan C. Greenberg with Mark Singer, *The Rise and Fall of Bear Stearns* (New York: Simon & Schuster, 2010), p. 69.
5. Ibid.
6. Ibid., p. 70.
7. Ibid., p. 71.
8. Cohan, p. 182.

9. Ibid.
10. Ibid., p. 183.
11. Ibid.
12. Ibid.
13. Ibid., p. 184.
14. Ibid., p. 185.
15. Greenberg, p. 69.
16. Cohan, p. 185.
17. Ibid., p. 187.
18. Ibid., p. 188.
19. Ibid.
20. Greenberg, p. 19.
21. Ibid., p. 11.
22. Ibid., p. 29.
23. Ibid., p. 35.
24. Ibid., p. 36.
25. Ibid.
26. Ibid.
27. Ibid., p. 37.
28. Ibid.
29. Ibid., p. 39.
30. Ibid., p. 45.
31. Ibid., p. 53.
32. Ibid., p. 57.
33. Ibid., p. 67.
34. Ibid., p. 68.
35. Cohan, pp. 229–236.
36. Greenberg, p. 80.
37. Allen R. Myerson, "Careful Player Moves Closer to the Top at Bear Stearns," *The New York Times*, July 14, 1993.
38. Greenberg, p. 80.
39. The Forbes 400, *Forbes*, www.forbes.com/lists/2005/54/UBGJ.html.
40. Cohan, p. 198.
41. Greenberg, p. 80.
42. Cohan, p. 199.
43. Ibid.
44. Ibid.
45. Ibid., p. 200.
46. Ibid., p. 201.
47. Ibid.
48. Ibid.
49. Ibid.

50. Ibid., p. 205.
51. Ibid., p. 206.
52. Cohan, p. 239.
53. Ibid., p. 240.
54. Greenberg, p. 103.
55. Ibid.
56. Ibid., p. 104.
57. Ibid., p. 105.
58. Greenberg, p. 102.
59. Kate Kelly, *Street Fighters: The Last 72 Hours of Bear Stearns, The Toughest Firm on Wall Street* (New York: The Penguin Group, 2010), p. 25.
60. Ibid.
61. Ibid.
62. Ibid., p. 26.
63. Ibid.
64. Cohan, p. 248.
65. Ibid.
66. Ibid.
67. Will Roberts, "It'll Be Fine, The Ten Worst Financial Predictions," *Investment Week*, July 8, 2011, www.investmentweek.co.uk/investment-week/feature/2086831/-itll-fine-worst-financial-predictions.
68. Greenberg, p. 103.
69. Ibid.
70. Ibid.
71. Cohan, p. 285.
72. Greenberg, p. 115.
73. Cohan, p. 289.
74. Ibid., p. 297.
75. Ibid.
76. Andrew Ross Sorkin, ed., "DealBook," *The New York Times*, May 5, 2010, dealbook.nytimes.com/2010/05/05/a-look-at-bear-stearns-before-its-downfall/?ref=bearstearnscompanies.
77. Ibid.
78. Cohan, p. 325.
79. Ibid.
80. Ibid., p. 326.
81. Ibid., p. 330.
82. Yalman Onaran and Jody Shenn, "Cioffi's Hero-to-Villain Hedge Funds Masked Bear Peril in CDOs," *Bloomberg*, July 3, 2007, http://www.bloomberg.com/apps/news?pid=newsarchive&refer=us&sid=azWrpTVCph08.
83. *SEC v. Ralph Cioffi and Matthrew M. Tannin, Complaint*, E.D.N.Y. June 19, 2008, p. 8.
84. Cohan, p. 333.

85. Ibid.
86. Ibid.
87. Ibid., p. 9.
88. Ibid.
89. Ibid.
90. Ibid.
91. Ibid.
92. Ibid., p. 11.
93. Cohan, p. 335.
94. Ibid.
95. Ibid.
96. Onaran and Shenn.
97. Ibid.
98. Ibid.
99. Cohan, p. 357.
100. Ibid.
101. Cohan, p. 358.
102. Ibid.
103. Ibid.
104. Ibid.
105. *SEC v. Ralph Cioffi and Matthew M. Tannin, Complaint*, p. 10.
106. Ibid.
107. *United States v. Ralph Cioffi and Matthew Tannin*, 18 U.S.C. 371, 2008, p. 6.
108. Ibid.
109. *SEC v. Ralph Cioffi and Matthew M. Tannin, Complaint*, p. 10.
110. *United States v. Ralph Cioffi and Matthew Tannin*, 18 U.S.C. 371, 2008, p. 6.
111. *SEC v. Ralph Cioffi and Matthew M. Tannin, Complaint*, p. 10.
112. Cohan, p. 362.
113. Ibid., p. 363.
114. Matthew Goldstein, "Bear Stearns' Subprime IPO," *Bloomberg Businessweek*, May 11, 2007.
115. Ibid.
116. Ibid.
117. Cohan, p. 365.
118. Ibid.
119. Ibid., p. 381.
120. Ibid., p. 382.
121. Ibid., p. 383.
122. Onaran and Shenn.
123. Cohan, p. 390.
124. Reuters, "Bear Stearns Tells Investors Funds Worthless," *Reuters*, July 17, 2007.

125. Yalman Onaran, "Bear Stearns Tells Fund Investors No Value Left," *Bloomberg*, July 18, 2007, www.bloomberg.com/apps/news?pid=news archive&sid=aQKWd1Xc2Vt4.
126. Greenberg, p. 144.
127. Ibid.
128. Ibid.
129. Ibid.
130. Ibid.
131. Ibid., p. 153.
132. Ibid.
133. Ibid., p. 154
134. Ibid., p. 155
135. Ibid., p. 161.
136. Ibid.
137. Kate Kelly, "Bear CEO's Handling of Crisis Raises Issues, *The Wall Street Journal*, November 1, 2007, online.wsj.com/article/SB1193873694740 78336.html?mod=home_whats_news_us.
138. Greenberg, p. 169.
139. Ibid., p. 170.
140. Kelly, *Street Fighters*, p. 222.

Chapter 6

Tyco: Exceptional Greed and the Destruction of a Billion-Dollar Company

The Master said, "The gentleman understands what is right, whereas the petty man understands profit."

Confucius (Analects 4.16)

In one of the most famous film monologues of the modern era, fictional corporate raider Gordon Gekko pronounced, "Greed, for a lack of a better word, is good."

The Gekko character was in fact a heinous villain, a person living in unbridled excess, lacking any respect for human dignity, the merits of hard work, or the livelihood of others. Scoffing at such an imaginary man would be a natural reaction; however, undoubtedly, some of the young professionals walking out of movie theaters shaking their heads in 1987 are now left with the remnants of their own Gekko-like demise, complete with orange jumpsuits and silver handcuffs.

Although popular culture is aware of its deadly consequences, greed remains everywhere and the vice is still hopelessly embedded as a bed rock in our global society.

In fact, Kevin Rudd, prime minister of Australia, in reaction to the spiraling events of the most recent worldwide recession, stated, "Beneath the financial jargon and dramatic stock market events, the sub-prime crisis has also reflected a fundamental failure of values. We've seen the triumph of greed over integrity; the triumph of speculation over value creation; the triumph of the short-term over long-term, sustainable growth."[1] Notably, Rudd called his speech "The Children of Gordon Gekko."

In the last ten years, there have been numerous instances where greed has usurped personal integrity, accountability, and governance at the highest levels of corporate management. Executives have mis-appropriated billions of dollars owed to investors, employees, and the public all for their own lavish, unjust enrichment and selfish pursuit of extravagance.

Under American state and federal law, the corporate management of a company is required to meet duties of care and loyalty to share-holders, the owners of the corporation. Executives must carry out their powers and responsibilities in the best interest of the shareholders who have voted them to power.

The executive is a steward of the shareholder's property, which is the corporation itself. To perfect corporate harmony, the relationship between shareholder and management must rest comfortably on trust. Trust that management has accepted its fiduciary responsibilities to shareholders and will not fail to meet its many legal responsibilities.

This relationship absolutely precludes any pursuit of personal "possessions" and material goods that are not in the corporation's line of business or related to the executives' fiduciary obligations. Personal greed among corporate management is not only a deadly vice, but it is patently offensive to the very essence of the American corporate modality and to the law.

Nonetheless, since the inception of American corporate institutions, executives have on occasion fallen prey to illicit temptations of greed— none greater than misappropriating millions of corporate funds for personal gain.

When such fraud occurs, executives, managers, and other persons involved in the purchasing and selling of securities can be held liable. Section 10(b) of the 1934 Exchange Act governs such claims.

In the most general of terms, courts require the following elements to prevail on a claim of securities fraud:

A misrepresentation or omission of
A material fact;
Reliance upon that fact;
Causation between the misrepresentation, reliance and the damages claimed;
Knowledge of the misrepresentation, otherwise known as scienter; and
in connection with the sale or purchase of a security.

Executives, managers, and others may be charged criminally in addition to civil charges brought by the Securities and Exchange Commission (SEC) or disaffected shareholders. White-collar crimes are nearly uniformly prosecuted at the state level and governed by the individual state's penal code.

Tyco History

Tyco International Ltd. is a large, diversified, global company. The company provides security products and services, fire protection, detection products, and services and valves and controls to an international consumer base in all 50 American states and more than 60 countries. In 2010, Tyco had revenue of more than $17 billion and has more than 100,000 employees worldwide.

Arthur J. Rosenburg founded Tyco in 1960. Rosenburg sought to open a research laboratory to conduct experimental projects for the US government. The business was incorporated as Tyco Laboratories in 1962, and its focus was in high-tech materials, science, and energy conversion products for the commercial sector. In 1964, the company went public.

Today, Tyco's self-stated mission focuses on corporate governance, customer satisfaction, growth, employee "teamwork," operational excellence, and flexibility. The company strives to promote governance and best-in-class operating practices that foster "integrity, compliance, and accountability," while meeting investor goals relating to consistent revenue, earnings per share, cash, and invested capital objectives.

There are corporate case studies in excess and greed among the highest levels of corporate management—and then there is the disturbing tale of former Tyco CEO, Dennis Kozlowski.

On January 14, 2002, *BusinessWeek* magazine listed Kozlowski as one of the top 25 corporate managers of 2001. Five months later, Kozlowski resigned unexpectedly, amid allegations of corporate tax evasion, securities fraud, and egregious fiduciary malfeasance. Kozlowski is now prisoner #05A4820 at a New York Mid-State Correctional Facility.

What caused such a swift fall from grace? Repeated ethical, accounting, and corporate governance abuses allowed Kozlowski unfettered access to at least $600 million of the Tyco piggybank and shareholder investments.

568 South 10th Street and 605 South 19th Street, Newark, New Jersey: these are the humble addresses Kozlowski called home growing up. His father, a second-generation Polish-American, Leo Kozlowski, started out as a reporter for the Associated Press under the name "Kid Kelly."[2]

However, at the time Dennis was born, Leo took a position as an investigator with the New Jersey Public Service Transport, a predecessor to the New Jersey Transit Authority.[3] Retired lawyer and close friend of Leo's, Peter C. Pietrucha, explained that Dennis's father did not disclose the nature of his position so he could preemptively inform his employer of false accident claims.[4] Leo effectively used such false misrepresentations to raise his own stature within the New Jersey Public Service Transport Company and to increase his income.

While using deceit to leverage his position at work, Leo had an additional second career as a Newark Polish political organizer.[5] Leo worked with politicians to help deliver the Polish and Catholic vote for local Republican candidates. "I remember him as a hard man, not a nice friendly person you could talk to," says the Reverend Bogumil Chrusciel, the pastor at Newark's St. Stanislaus, a congregation in Leo's old neighborhood.[6]

Dennis had a different view on his father's career. In an interview in 2001, Dennis mischaracterized his father as a "police officer" who "worked his whole life until he retired at 65."[7] In fact, in a series of interviews during the 1990s and early twenty-first century, Kozlowski explained that his father was a Newark city police officer turned detective who home-schooled him with a rigid ethical and moral code.[8]

The Makings of a "Bad" CEO

In an article in the MIT Sloan Management Review titled "When Bad People Rise to the Top," two chief characteristics of "bad" CEOs are identified. The first "bad" CEO quality is placing his economic and psychological needs ahead of his professional obligations (greed). The second is extreme self-centeredness, which dilutes the effectiveness of interpersonal relations with his fellow board members, management, and shareholders.[9]

Dennis Kozlowski fits this mold. He believed in the principles of hard work and ambition. Yet, he also became personally obsessed with extravagance, wealth, and power. Kozlowski's ambition centered on self-centered goals, abusing the American corporate relationship in the process, and at the expense of Tyco shareholders.

Personal failures in business ethics, morality, and governance were surprisingly a product of Catholic education institutions. Kozlowski attended Seton Hall University, the oldest Roman Catholic diocesan Catholic school in the United States, from 1964 to 1968. Kozlowski graduated with a bachelor of science in finance and accounting.

Kozlowski took a position as an auditor with SCM Corp in 1970. Subsequently, he soon assumed the position of director of audit and analysis for Nashua Corp, a New Hampshire photocopier and imaging manufacturer.

Kozlowski was a proud Seton Hall graduate. He donated $3 million to the institution between August 1997 and August 2000. Seton Hall University was equally proud of him. Until 2005, a business and education building was named "Kozlowski Hall." A rotunda of the university's library also formerly bore the Kozlowski name. It should also be noted that in 1977, Kozlowski took night classes toward an advanced business degree at River College, a Catholic college in Nashua, New

Hampshire. Kozlowski completed only three classes at the college, yet he claimed to have earned an MBA from the educational institution in a questionnaire submitted for the 1988 to 1989 edition of *Who's Who in America.*

Seeds of Greed

After Tyco went public in 1964, it quickly began to acquire 16 companies from 1964 to 1968. In the 1970s, Tyco grew steadily and established a national corporate identity. In 1974, the company's stock was listed on the New York Stock Exchange. Tyco continued an aggressive acquisition strategy that focused on acquiring new companies such as Simplex Technology in 1974, Grinnel Fire Protection Systems in 1976, Armin Plastics, and the Ludlow Corporation.

Because of such a rapid acquisition period, Tyco centralized control over its new acquisitions and their subsidiaries. It divided the company into three business segments: fire protection, electronics, and packaging.

Beginning in 1986, Tyco once again began a relatively aggressive period of acquisitions. Tyco acquired the full capacities of the Grinnel Corporation in 1986, steel pipe manufacturer Allied Tube and Conduit in 1988, and Mueller Company, a manufacturer of water and gas flow control products, in 1989.

Acquisitions were the means to build a company for Tyco. The firm did not seriously try to ensure that there was enough infrastructure in place to control all of the newly acquired subsidiaries.

In 1975, Kozlowski was introduced to Joseph Gaziano. In many ways, Gaziano, the chairman and CEO of Tyco Laboratories at the time, was the spark that ignited Kozlowski's greed gene. Gaziano spoke at length to young Dennis about the benefits of executive excess and selfishness. Because of his CEO position with Tyco, Gaziano was the proud owner of a private jet, helicopter, and three luxury apartments. Dennis Kozlowski was easily hooked. "He [Gaziano] was very engaging," Kozlowski indicated in a 2001 interview. "So I signed up for what I thought would be a year or two."[10]

A year or two became a career. Kozlowski was determined to live the extravagant life Gaziano flashed before him—a life that, for Gaziano, was fueled by a period of haphazard, aggressive acquisitions that rapidly enlarged Tyco's size without regard for long-term implications of efficiency or decentralization. Kozlowski learned a great deal from Gaziano's management style. Indeed, he mimicked Gaziano's strategies to the extreme by completing over 700 acquisitions as Tyco CEO, in order to rapidly increase Tyco stock price and boost his own personal image.

From 1975, as an assistant Tyco controller until incarceration as the company's CEO, Kozlowski did not leave the Tyco workplace.

Kozlowski's Culture of Fear at Grinnel

John Fort III took over for Gaziano as Tyco CEO in 1982. In many ways, Fort was the anti-Gaziano. He was intensely analytical, thrifty, and meticulous. Fort sought to centralize the company for stable long-term growth after Gaziano's aggressive acquisition strategy. Despite his inherent conflicts with Fort's leadership style, Kozlowski's Tyco stock rose immensely during the 1980s.

Fort put Kozlowski in charge of the Grinnel Fire Protection division. In managing Grinnel, Kozlowski engineered a series of strategic decisions designed to improve his own personal stature at the expense of due diligence, governance, and corporate accountability.

Kozlowski dramatically cut overhead expenses, eliminated 98 percent of previously required written reports on company operations, executed numerous waves of layoffs, and dramatically reduced Grinnel employee compensation. Kozlowski transformed Grinnel's corporate culture. Rather than praise employees for a job well done, Kozlowski founded a new annual award ceremony for the "Worst Grinnel Warehouse Manager." Employees and managers labored in constant fear and trepidation that they would receive this title and, in turn, be next on the Grinnel chopping block.

In Kozlowski's dog-eat-dog world, low operating costs allowed him to focus on buying out Grinnel's competitors. Kozlowski sold these deals to Tyco management as essential to the overall value of the company. Kozlowski believed that focusing on the bottom line would sell itself—no matter what he did to effectuate such results. Indeed, in 1987, Fort rewarded Kozlowski with a place on the Tyco board. He was promoted to president and chief operating officer just two years later.

Kozlowski became affectionately known as "Deal-A-Day" Dennis. Throughout the 1990s as Tyco CEO, he orchestrated deal after deal, all in the hopes of rapidly expanding the company's assets and his own personal image and stock position. In fact, Kozlowski raised Tyco assets from $40 million in 1992 to $40 billion. Kozlowski instituted a "pay for performance" system at the company that allowed him to make nearly $170 million a year.

Part of his income qualified for a "top hat" deferred compensation plan only for Tyco's most senior of executives. Throughout his tenure at Tyco, Kozlowski was adept at manipulating the Tyco compensation committee to ensure that "top hat" plans primarily benefited him and his friends on the board. The new Tyco compensation system allowed Kozlowski to pursue his passions: extravagance, excess, and unbridled greed.

Looting the Company

A new performance-based compensation system was just the beginning of the changes made at Tyco.

In 1995, Kozlowski created a relocation program that permitted him and senior executives to use such funds for real estate speculation and personal expenses. The relocation plan was meant to fund the company's headquarters move from New Hampshire to New York City. Such loans were also interest free. In his investigation of Kozlowski, prominent Attorney David Boies uncovered the many criminal breaches of Kozlowski's fiduciary duty to Tyco investors:

1. $7,011,669 in interest-free loans charged by Kozlowski for New York relocations that did not qualify under the Tyco New York relocation program.
2. $29,756,110 in interest-free loans charged by Mr. Kozlowski for the acquisition of properties that were not authorized under the Tyco Florida relocation program.
3. $24,922,849 in interest-free loans borrowed by Kozlowski for the acquisitions of other properties that were not authorized by ANY relocation program.

Only $21,697,303 was ever paid back.[11]

Prior to the enactment of the Tyco relocation plan, Kozlowski received a legal opinion directing him that individually tailoring the relocation to personal executive interests was a form of unjust enrichment and a breach of Kozlowski's fiduciary duties owed to the corporation.

The Tyco board, in reaction, approved a more modest plan that focused on ensuring relocation loans that would benefit Tyco shareholders. Unconscionably, Kozlowski willfully disregarded this development, and pushed forward his original plan, which provided generous loans personally tailored to his fellow conspirators.

Through his personally tailored relocation plan, Kozlowski was able to execute the following transactions. These transactions would have been prohibited under the board-approved plan:

1. Rent a lavish Fifth Avenue apartment (817 Fifth Avenue, New York City), with annual rental of $264,000, paid for by the company, from 1997 to 2001.
2. Purchase with interest-free loans in 2000—at depreciated book value and without appraisals—a company-owned $7 million Park Avenue apartment previously acquired by the company at his behest.
3. Sell his New Hampshire home to the company without appraisals for an amount significantly in excess of its market value in 2000. Less than 24 months later, the company wrote down the corporate asset by approximately $3 million.
4. Purchase a second, more extravagant apartment on Fifth Avenue in 2001 for $16.8 million and expend $3 million in improvements and $11 million in furnishings—all without disclosing to the board or its compensation or audit committee that the apartment was paid for and carried by the company as a corporate asset.
5. Gross-up benefits that insulated Kozlowski from all state income tax liability that he incurred after relocating to New York.[12]

Kozlowski repeatedly received unauthorized bonuses from the company's assets. While the Board had to authorize any bonuses to the CEO of Tyco or any other company, Kozlowski issued himself over $100 million in bonuses (usually after the completion of mergers) without any such Tyco Board approval. These unauthorized bonuses were diverted to his own personal funds and to those of his fellow conspirators.

Unauthorized Tyco bonus:

$32,644,338, Kozlowski's own bonus

$79,177,081, awarded to Kozlowski's fellow conspirators on Tyco board

Unauthorized "ADT automotive bonus" (including loan forgiveness, cash bonus, and restricted shares)

$17,188,034 and 148,000 shares (Kozlowski's own unauthorized bonus)

$34,822,412 and 259,500 shares (bonuses given to fellow conspirators)

Unauthorized "Flag Telecom bonus"

$8,219,650 (Kozlowski's own unauthorized amount)

$15,378,700 (funds given to fellow conspirators)

Unauthorized bonus to Director Frank Walsh

$20,000,000 (unauthorized "finder's fee" in CIT Group, Inc. deal)

The following transactions demonstrate Kozlowski's misappropriation of Tyco property and assets for his own personal use:

Personal use of the following Tyco real estate:

Runnymede, North Hampton, New Hampshire (after July 6, 2000)

471 East Alexander Palm Rd, Boca Raton, Florida (1997–2001)

817 Fifth Avenue, New York, New York (1996–2001)

950 Fifth Avenue, New York, New York (2001–2002)

167 Little Harbor Rd, New Castle, New Hampshire (1995–2002)

Misappropriation of Tyco Funds for Personal Goods:

$20,000,000, purchase of artwork, antiques, furnishings

$700,000, movie rights

$2,100,000, Sardinia birthday party for Kozlowski's wife

$110,000, use of huge *Endeavour* sailboat

$1,144,000, jewelry, clothing, florist, club memberships, wines

$150,000, personal expenses at 59 Harbor Road, Rye, New York[13]

In 1983, under the control of Fort, Tyco adopted the Key Employee Loan Program (KELP), intended to foster employee ownership of Tyco's common stock. The program was meant as an incentive for employees to put forth their best efforts for the betterment of the company.

Kozlowski decided to egregiously breach the Tyco KELP agreement with Tyco employees. By the end of 2002, he had already diverted $274,205,452 of KELP funds disguised as personal, interest-free loans to him. Kozlowski used the KELP as his own revolving credit line to the absolute extreme. Funds in the KELP were used for lavish personal art purchases, real estate costs, home goods, purchasing a yacht, investment, and paying for domestics, antiques, and lavish furniture.

Moreover, Kozlowski, along with co-conspirator CFO Mark Swartz, devised a plan to credit Kozlowski's and Swartz's accounts for $25 million and $12.5 million, respectively. Although such credits are a material change in executive compensation that should have been disclosed to the compensation committee, neither Kozlowsi nor Swartz disclosed such information to the committee. When Kozlowski resigned from Tyco, he owed the $43,840,461 to the Tyco KELP program.

Kozlowski spent millions of dollars on an extensive art collection for his $18 million Manhattan duplex apartment. He had all art invoices paid for by the company and invoiced them at a New Hampshire address to avoid paying taxes.

Kozlowski used famous art consultant Christine Berry to amass an art collection with no budget restrictions and full of well-known, famous artists, costing Tyco nearly six figures on every purchase. Berry counseled Kozlowski on expenditures of over $13 million of paintings by such greats as Claude Monet, Pierre-Auguste Renoir, and Sir Alfred Munnings.

Kozlowski's greed for expensive art actually resulted in his eventual downfall. Manhattan Attorney General Robert Morgenthau first indicted Kozlowski on tax evasion of over $1 million in New York State and local sales tax on his massive art collection. While the paintings were for Kozlowski's Fifth Avenue apartment in Manhattan, he shipped the art (or sometimes empty boxes) to Tyco's New Hampshire headquarters to avoid the heavy New York sales tax on the expensive art.

Kozlowski settled sales tax evasion charges related to his purchase of artwork for $21.2 million.

Kozlowski's Accomplices

To facilitate rampant corporate looting, a CEO needs accomplices. Here were Kozlowski's.

Mark Swartz

Mark Swartz began as an assistant controller with Tyco. He made $45,000 a year. After a few years of fostering a close relationship with Kozlowski, Swartz was named CFO of Tyco in 1995. Swartz was Kozlowski's most trusted and loyal adviser. He was the dependable company lieutenant who carried out Kozlowski's fraud to the very detail. At the pinnacle of the Tyco fraud, Mark Swartz was worth roughly $150 million.

From 1997 to 2002, an SEC investigation concluded that Swartz looted approximately $85 million from the Tyco KELP program. Only $13 million of these funds was actually for company purposes, while $72 million was used for Swartz's personal investments, business ventures, real estate holdings, and trusts. Moreover, as CFO, Swartz fraudulently credited Kozlowski's KELP account balance $25 million and his own KELP balance $12.5 million. He hid such action from the Tyco compensation committee and board.

Swartz was actively involved in the fraud relating to the shadow Tyco relocation plan. He falsified business records and hid the improper funneling of funds from the compensation committee. He willfully perpetrated this fraud on the Tyco Corporation with full knowledge of the consequences of doing so.

Swartz received lucrative unauthorized bonuses from the biggest deals of the Kozlowski Tyco era:

TyCom deal: Swartz knowingly received a $16 million unauthorized bonus.

ADT deal: Swartz knowingly received an $8 million unauthorized bonus

Flag Telecom deal: Swartz knowingly received a $7 million unauthorized bonus.

CIT Group deal: Swartz transferred a $20 million bonus to outside director Frank Walsh without authorization.[14]

Swartz personally engaged in real estate transactions involving the Trump Tower property in New York City. The building address is iconic: One Central Park West.

Swartz improperly had Tyco wire him $1.2 million to cover losses relating to Swartz's real estate dealings with Trump Tower. Swartz was convicted in court proceedings of 22 felony counts with Kozlowski. He is currently serving time in a New York state penitentiary.

Frank E. Walsh

In late 2000, Frank E. Walsh, a director of Tyco since 1992, recommended the acquisition of the CIT Group, Inc. (CIT). He held the prominent position of chairman of the company's compensation committee. He also was a member of the board's corporate governance committee.

Prior to the official Tyco board vote on the CIT deal, Walsh and Kozlowski agreed that Walsh would receive a lucrative finder's fee upon consummating the transaction. However, neither Walsh nor Kozlowski disclosed the gross "finder's fee" to the Tyco board when they voted to approve the transaction. Walsh obviously voted in favor of the transaction.

When a director is personally interested in a company merger or acquisition, the law requires disclosure of such interests prior to an official vote on the matter. This is a fundamental responsibility and an element of the director's solemn duty of loyalty to the corporation. When a director fails to disclose such interests, it is a breach of his legal duty.

Making matters worse, Walsh and Kozlowski hid from the SEC, its shareholders, and the public the existence of the finder's fee agreement. The terms and conditions of the Tyco/CIT merger ("Agreement and Plan of Merger") included a provision that, other than Tyco's investment bankers involved in the merger, no other finder's fees were included in connection with the transaction.

The Agreement and Plan of Merger was incorporated by reference into the official Registration Statement filed by Tyco with the SEC for public disclosure purposes. Unconscionably, Walsh signed the registration statement knowing there was a material misrepresentation in the document. Kozlowski and Walsh agreed after the submission of the Registration Statement that Walsh's finder's fee was to be $20 million.

Walsh pleaded guilty to criminal felony fraud as well as civil securities fraud. He settled with the New York District Attorney and SEC for $22.5 million in 2002. He settled with the State of New Jersey in 2009 for $5.6 million for knowingly misleading pension fund investors in the CIT Registration Statement and insider trading abuses.

Mark Belnick

For most of Mark Belnick's career, he was a partner at the prestigious New York law firm Paul, Weiss, Rifkind, Wharton and Garrison. In fact, Belnick's legal high point was assisting in the US Senate investigation of the Iran-Contra affair. Belnick soon grew restless of his big law lifestyle. He was making $900,000 a year but still felt he was undercompensated. Along came Dennis Kozlowski.

Belnick received a large offer from Kozlowski, a three-year contract for $5.9 million in cash and bonuses with the promise of much more in stock and options. To further entice Belnick to move, Kozlowski used a $4 million relocation loan from the company (without interest) to facilitate Belnick's purchase of an expansive apartment on Manhattan's Central Park West. Belnick was already living in the Manhattan suburb of Harrison, New York, only 25 miles from Tyco's Manhattan office.

Belnick was a prominent Jewish leader in the Harrison community. He helped lead the conservative Jewish Community Center there, serving as the congregation's president for four years in the late 1980s. The American Jewish Community bestowed a human relations award on him in 1988 in recognition of his philanthropy to Jewish causes. However, Father John McCloskey III later converted him to Opus Dei Catholicism. Interestingly enough, Belnick's conversion to Catholicism coincided with his acceptance of the lucrative Tyco position.

At one point, Belnick lived a new life of extravagance as Tyco's general counsel. During one year, his annual salary approached $19 million. While most would consider $900,000 enough to make a comfortable living, Belnick's new position afforded him decadent luxuries that he self-admittedly believed he deserved. In fact, in a successful defense in New York Supreme Court, Belnick explained, "It didn't occur to me to say to the chairman of the board—my boss—'You've just awarded me a bonus. Prove it [the justification of the bonus]'."[15] The bonus at issue was $17 million.

Prosecutors argued that the Tyco board did not approve the $17 million. It was believed that the amount was used as "hush money" to buy Belnick's silence regarding the company fraud. However, Belnick explained that Kozlowski had informed him that he would get a bonus of $5 million in stock and an additional $12 million in cash and stock if the government closed an investigation into Tyco's accounting without taking action against the company.

Belnick relied on Kozlowski's assurances as CEO of Tyco that the bonus was proper. He also relied on Swartz's representations that the bonus did not have to be disclosed to SEC regulators. He did not read the minutes of the board of directors to ensure that the huge bonus was authorized.

Belnick was determined to beat charges of several felony counts, including grand larceny and falsifying business records. John Moscow, perhaps one of the most feared and respected prosecutors in the country, offered Belnick deal after deal to settle the charges, for a guilty plea. The plea would have resulted in millions of dollars in fines and the removal of his legal license, but most likely no jail time.

Belnick steadfastly refused any such admittance of guilt. Moscow's deal was still on the table hours before the jury's verdict was read. Belnick was convinced of his innocence. Despite accepting a $17 million bonus without much diligence, he argued that his moral compass was still strong. Belnick's very code of ethics and character was at issue. In order to convict, the jury needed to believe evidence that Belnick knew the bonus was unauthorized and fraudulent.

Belnick's confidence in escaping jail time proved to be accurate. In the end, the jury did not believe there was enough evidence. Belnick is today a free man and remains a practicing attorney to this date.

A Convicted "Piggy"

Kozlowski was convicted of 22 counts of criminal grand larceny, conspiracy, securities fraud, and 8 of 9 counts of falsifying business records. He was sentenced to from 8 years and 4 months to 25 years. Kozlowski is first eligible for parole in 2013. He was ordered to pay $167 million in restitution and fines.

In jailhouse interviews, Kozlowski has been unrepentant. He believes that his supposed crimes pale in comparison to the failures of the recent financial crisis.

"Why am I sitting here?" Kozlowski said in a 2008 interview with the Fox Business Network. "Tyco is still a viable company, still alive and kicking. Bear Sterns is under, Lehman Brothers is under. Merrill Lynch had to be acquired. There are all kinds of banks going under right now."[16]

Kozlowski spends his days in much the same fashion. He teaches math to fellow inmates, completes laundry services, awaits mail call, watches Yankee games (he is a minority owner), and enjoys a private supply of fresh fruit.

"I would think that the financial world would say, 'Please bring back the $6,000 shower curtain'," Kozlowski said. "You know, that seems like nothing in the middle of everything that's going on right now. Murderers that I've met, rapists, there are certainly people that have far less of a sentence than I have."[17]

Kozlowski admits he suffered from a lack of judgment. He breached his fiduciary duty of care and loyalty as CEO, put his thirst for greed before his responsibilities to Tyco shareholders, secretly looted the company of millions of dollars, and used Tyco shareholder funds as a revolving credit line.

"I was piggy," Kozlowski said. "I had bad judgment. But I don't deserve to be here."[18]

Notes

1. Kevin Rudd, "The Children of Gordon Gekko," *The Australian*, October 6, 2008, www.theaustralian.com.au/news/the-children-of-gordon-gekko/story-e6frg7b6–1111117670209.

2. Anthony Bianco, William Symonds, and Nanette Byrnes, with David Polek, "The Rise and Fall of Dennis Kozlowski, *Bloomberg Businessweek*, December 22, 2002, www.businessweek.com/magazine/content/02_51/b3813001.htm.
3. Ibid.
4. Ibid.
5. Ibid.
6. Ibid.
7. Ibid.
8. Ibid.
9. Terry Leap, "When Bad People Rise to the Top," *MIT Sloan Management Review*, 29 (2) (Winter 2008).
10. Bianco, Symonds, Byrnes and Polek.
11. *Tyco International LTD. v. L. Dennis Kozlowski*, S.D.N.Y. Complaint, September 12, 2002.
12. Ibid.
13. Ibid.
14. *Tyco International, LTD. v. Mark H. Swartz*, 03 Civ. 2247 (S.D.N.Y 2011).
15. Jayne O'Donnell, "Ex Tyco Counsel Returns to Law After Acquittal," *USA Today*, August 8, 2005, www.usatoday.com/money/2005–08–08-tyco-counsel-usat_x.htm.
16. Dan Slater, "Kozlowski: Hard to Reconcile AIG Bailout with $6,000 Shower Curtain," *The Wall Street Journal*, November 13, 2008, blogs.wsj.com/law/2008/11/13/kozlowski-hard-to-reconcile-aig-bailout-with-6000-shower-curtain/.
17. Ibid.
18. David A. Kaplan, "Why Kozlowski Should Get Clemency," *CNN Money*, November 23, 2009, money.cnn.com/2009/11/20/news/companies/tyco_kozlowski.fortune/.

Chapter 7

Insatiable Lust and Two of the Most Destructive Ponzi Schemes in American History

Temptation is the pull of man's own evil thoughts and wishes.

James 1:13–14

No one asked questions.

That is, until FBI Agent Theodore Cacioppi arrived at the opulent penthouse at 133 E. 64th Street on the morning of December 11, 2008.

"We're here to find out if there's an innocent explanation." Cacioppi said.

Cacioppi was struggling to understand how such a prominent, respected New York socialite could conceive of such a deviant Ponzi scheme.

"There is no innocent explanation," Bernie Madoff replied, admitting in one statement that the last 20 years of his life had been a gigantic securities fraud.

In the ensuing weeks and months, Madoff's face was tattooed all over CNN, CNBC, and the other major cable TV news networks. The man who had committed the most massive Ponzi scheme in world history was sentenced to 150 years in prison. Bernie Madoff was reduced to utter shame.

Peppered with insults from former angry investors, Madoff walked out of the New York Courthouse onto 500 Pearl Street, Kevlar bulletproof vest tightly secured to his chest, as he inhaled his last breaths of free air.

It wasn't supposed to end like this. Bernie Madoff had spent a lifetime building his legitimate broker-dealer business and swindling investors on the side. In New York high-society circles, Bernie Madoff, wife Ruth, and his close family were charitable, well liked, and respected.

Madoff was a Wall Street pillar. His broker-dealer business had been running since the early 1960s. The enterprise had an excellent reputation on the street. While some industry analysts and even Wall Street investors believed something might be up, no one spoke up for nearly a generation.

In retrospect, even Madoff himself displaces the blame, "Look," he recently said to *New York* magazine, "These banks and these funds had to know there were problems. I wouldn't give them any facts, like how much volume I was doing. I was not willing to have them come up and do the diligence that they wanted. I absolutely refused to do it." He said, "You don't like it, take your money out, which of course they never did."[1]

In formulating an answer to why Bernie Madoff "did it," most authors blame unbridled greed.[2] Many institutional and high-net-worth investors that lost a substantial amount of savings, income, and other capital are still seething from Madoff's securities fraud. The media, Washington, and society have captured this anger on the whole.

Contrary to public perception, however, the facts surrounding Bernie Madoff's Ponzi scheme show the man was not motivated by greed. Rather, Madoff and his many prominent investors fell prey to the temptation of lust.

For Madoff, lust was the thrill of knowing he was doing something intrinsically evil and not getting caught. For his investors, lust took the form of a chronic addiction to consistent returns, despite knowing that it was fundamentally impossible to never have a bad month in spite of market downturn, boom, bust, or crash. Despite the impossibility of Madoff's returns, no one said anything.

Unfortunately, neither Madoff nor Petters experienced an intervention or the proverbial "rehab" experience.

Seemingly legitimate businessmen falling prey to illicit temptations is not a new phenomenon. While Madoff was stealing money from his "investors," Minnesota businessman Tom Petters was offering his own investment opportunities that definitively had no substance to them.

Through the conduit of a supposed electronics giant, Petters Company, Inc., Tom Petters and his co-conspirators defrauded victims of billions. Petters claimed for years that he was using investors' money to purchase bargain electronic equipment to be sold to big-chain electronic vendors.

Petters had been conducting this scheme since he was a boy. An entrepreneurial business hustler, Petters dropped out of high school to sell overstocked electronic equipment to college students at the age of 16. But the middle-aged Petters could have learned a great deal from his former self. As time wore on, supposed electronic transactions had absolutely no substance.

As the years wore on, Petters became intoxicated with the revenue stream of his criminality. He enjoyed a hedonistic lifestyle, replete with multiple houses and lavish personal goods. This was too much to lose. Confessing to the FBI was not an option, nor was making the business legitimate ever again.

The Ponzi Scheme and Society

The Ponzi scheme concept is systemic to our culture and the human condition. Charles Dickens was the first major author to popularize the concept in the mid-1800s within his collection of stories featured in the book *Little Dorritt*.

The Ponzi pyramid scheme itself was named after Charles Ponzi, a financial swindler in the 1920s. Ponzi deceived thousands of New England investors into sending him money as part of a postage-stamp speculation scheme. Ponzi promised investors a 50 percent return in just 90 days. While Ponzi initially purchased international mail coupons to support his scheme, he soon resorted to using new investor funds to pay off older investors.

Since then, various Ponzi schemes have infiltrated Wall Street and Main Street alike. Victims include public and private institutions including universities, non-profits, retirement funds, sports teams and communities. SEC designations of qualified institutional buyers and sophisticated and accredited investors have not mattered.

In any Ponzi scheme, perpetrators need an ongoing flow of money to survive. The trust of old investors must be maintained and polished over time. A revolving door of new investors is essential, or the Ponzi scheme conspiracy unravels and becomes bankrupt.

Ponzi schemes work for generations because investors allow them to. There is an absence of due diligence, investigation, or any other normal investment research. No one says anything as long as they continue to haul in consistent profits and returns. Capital markets suffer ups and downs. Ponzi schemes are consistent regardless of market chaos. Investors always make money.

Shouldn't some of the blame be placed on the investors themselves?

Regardless of investor background, qualifications, or sophistications, Ponzi schemes work because on a systemic level, investors do not report them. Rarely, if ever, has a Ponzi scheme been brought down because a curious investor questioned why there was never a negative return on his investment.

Ponzi schemes disturb the critical confidence that investors have in private capital markets. They pose a serious threat to the reputational risk and the very legitimacy of our very capitalist institutions. Nonetheless, until money managers and investors alike face the temptations of pyramid scheme revenue streams with stern rejection, they have the potential to poison international societies for generations.

Bernie Madoff and the Seeds of Lustful Temptations

Bernie Madoff's upbringing was largely uneventful. He grew up in the sleepy post–World War II New York town of Laurelton, Queens. His parents, Ralph and Sylvia, were Austrian and Romanian Jews who had lived in the Lower East Side of Manhattan. In the early 1940s, the Madoff's moved from their cramped apartment to Laurelton.

Madoff's father, Ralph, was not easy to please.[3] Joe Kavanau, childhood friend of Bernie Madoff, recounts, "Ralph was a tough-looking guy. It was like this guy isn't going to take any shit from anyone. Back then if you had to describe the quintessential Jewish tough guy, it would be Ralph Madoff. You got the impression you didn't want to screw with him. He wasn't somebody one would go out of their way to cross."[4] According to Kavanau, Bernie was the polar opposite of his father.[5] He was smooth and looking to please, especially his rough and tumble father.

Another childhood friend of Madoff's, Jay Portnoy, explained that the elder Madoff was a "rather aggressive, intense individual who put a premium on winning."[6]

Ralph brought the mentality to win at all costs into his own personal affairs and those of his wife. Ralph and Sylvia enjoyed living beyond their means. During a nine-year period, they had a $13,245.28 tax lien (worth over $100,000 today, taking inflation into account), which was continually unpaid and ignored on the family's balance sheets.[7]

Sylvia was not immune from the Madoff cycle of deceit, temptation, and an intense drive to beat the system. With Ralph's approval, she set up the broker-dealer firm Gibraltar Securities. Gibraltar bought and sold securities for Sylvia's family and friends. Like her son, it is uncertain whether Sylvia even placed trades for her clients. In August 1963, the SEC announced it was "instituting proceedings . . . to determine whether Gibraltar Securities had "failed to file reports of their financial condition . . . and if so, whether their registration should be revoked."[8]

For young Bernie Madoff, the traditional route of working hard, going to college, and crafting a professional niche was not an option. Bernie wanted to be very successful but was drawn to the temptation of shortcuts in order to achieve his preferred outcomes.

Madoff was a lackadaisical, average student. Yet, when it came to making quick money, Bernie became an expert. He lusted after any opportunity to make a fast buck.

At 15 years old he saw his friends, Eddie Heiberger and Sheldon "Shelley" Fogel, making very good money installing sprinkler systems in local Long Island neighborhoods under the company name "Shedwin."[9] With his father's eager approval, Bernie dove right in. Fogel said:

> It was the beginning of tract homes in Nassau County, on Long Island and people were putting a lot of money into landscaping and we were able to convince them not to water their lawns by hand with a hose. I'd see a guy watering his lawn and I'd stop by and start smacking my arms and smacking my legs like mosquitoes were biting me and I'd show them their shoes were getting all muddy. We'd get them that way.[10]

Fogel recounts that he and Madoff went into "black neighbor-hoods" to procure cheap labor. "They would think we were cops when we walked in," he said. "We used to pay $1.50 an hour when we needed guys."[11]

Rather than giving away his money to partners, Madoff wanted to branch out to retain maximum profits. While in high school and college at Hofstra University, he started his own sprinkler company—a company he would continue even for a few semesters during his short tenure at law school, using even more creative marketing strategies.[12]

For example, Madoff decided to hire attractive young men because he knew his company clientele largely included suburban housewives.[13] Mike Ondis, a recruit of Madoff's to work in his sprinkler business, explains:

> Bernie was the salesman. Mike and I did the labor. Bernie would take us around when he priced jobs. He'd knock on the door and he'd have Mike and me walk around the property talking loud enough for the homeowner to hear about where the sprinkler heads were needed. Typically, the homeowner would come out and invariably he would be with his young wife . . . [14]

Armed with this can't-lose marketing ploy, Madoff was pocketing nearly $2,000 a week, a sizable sum for the mid-1960s.[15] Money was going into Bernie's pocket with little labor, hard work, or diligence. Madoff knew this was the life he wanted. He soon dropped out of Brooklyn Law School. The temptation of fast money without investing time and effort into a bona fide enterprise was too great.

In the 1960s, Bernie Madoff was a no-name broker, but he propelled himself to prominence through smart networking and capitalizing on industry changes. Madoff's small firm, Bernard L. Madoff Investment Securities (BLMIS), got its start by matching buyers of inexpensive "penny stocks" with sellers in the growing over-the-counter (OTC) market.[16]

However, soon BLMIS would adapt to revolutionary technological changes in the securities market. Spending money on new trading technology differentiated Madoff and made him attractive in the emerging broker-dealer market. "He was a man with a good idea who was also a terrific salesman," said Charles V. Doherty, former president of the Midwest Stock Exchange. "He was ahead of everyone."[17]

Madoff sought to grow his small trading business and knew that in order to do so, and compete with the titans on Wall Street, he had to have a technological edge. Madoff became one of the first to see that technology could match buyers and sellers more efficiently than pink slips and yelling and screaming across a trading floor.[18]

In 1970, Madoff hired his brother, Peter, solely to designate new trading technology to make Madoff's broker-dealer operations automated.[19] New technology allured clients that had previously dealt with the traditional power players on Wall Street.

As word spread of Madoff's technologic advancements, he soon became intimately involved in the formation of NASDAQ and the Intermarket Trading System (ITS). Madoff tied his reputation and business to the formation of NASDAQ. He was one of the first five broker-dealers to join the organization.[20]

One of the original NASDAQ directors, Peter DaPuzzo, said, "Just creating a real-time market on computer screens for over the counter stocks was a very big deal [at the time]."[21]

Armed with state-of-the-art technology, a silver tongue, and important connections, by the late 1980s Madoff was making over $100 million a year in his legitimate broker-dealer enterprise. He was attracting deals from the street's most prestigious firms, including Goldman Sachs, Merrill Lynch, Morgan Stanley, and Smith Barney.[22]

The late 1980s were the peak of Bernie's success as a legitimate businessman. Nonetheless, it wasn't enough. Madoff lusted after the illicit temptations of his Ponzi scheme.

Madoff's Culture of Sexual, Criminal, and Moral Deviance

For Bernie Madoff, uncontrollable lust was not limited to the thrill of getting away with unconscionable securities fraud. His addictions included drugs, sex, and other illicit criminal activities.

A 2009 New York Supreme Court class action complaint against Madoff stressed there was a major dark side to the Madoff enterprise.[23] According to the complaint, starting in 1975, Madoff began to send messengers to obtain drugs for himself and other employees at BLMIS. The complaint describes Madoff's messengers as "street-tough men from Harlem who were not to be messed with."[24]

Based on interviews with Madoff and other employees at BLMIS, drug use in Madoff's office was "rampant." Certain floors of the office were compared to the "North Pole," in reference to the high amount of cocaine use.[25] When other employees discovered drugs at the desk of Madoff's in-house courier, Madoff was forced to fire the employee to avoid a potential criminal investigation of the firm that could uncover the Ponzi scheme.[26]

In addition to widespread drug use, Madoff encouraged a culture of sexual deviance. Office parties would include topless entertainers wearing only G-string underwear, serving as waitresses.[27] Interviews with former employees suggest that BLMIS employees were encouraged to have interoffice affairs with married men and women in "exciting places."[28]

Madoff himself had a fetish for prostitutes. He had a personal telephone book full of sexual masseuses and escorts.[29] In fact, he allegedly used Ponzi scheme income to pay for extremely expensive hookers and brothels.[30]

In a 2009 interview with *Vanity Fair*, Madoff's longtime secretary Eleanor Squillari verified Madoff's taste for sexual deviance. Squillari recounts that Madoff had a "roving eye" and said she once caught him browsing sexual escort advertisements.[31]

While Madoff enjoyed paying for high-priced sexual companionship, he also particularly enjoyed coming on to the attractive Squillari on a daily basis (although he was married). Squillari explained, "Sometimes when he came out of his bathroom, which was diagonal to my desk, he would still be zipping up his pants. If he saw me shaking my head disapprovingly, he would say, 'Oh you know it excites you!' "

Squillari went on to say, "If a pretty young woman came in, he'd say, 'Do you remember when you used to look like that?' I'd tell him, 'Knock it off, Bernie,' and he'd go, 'Ah, you still look good.' Then he'd try to pat me on the ass."[32]

Tom Petters, the High School Dropout

Tom Petters grew up far away from Rockaway Queens, in St. Cloud Minnesota. But he, too, became quite familiar with the temptations of easy money, hustling, and rejecting the traditional model of hard work, education, and book smarts.

Unlike Madoff, Petters' family had been prominent in the Minnesota business culture for generations. His great-grandfather was a tailor whose descendants sold furs and fabrics out of the Petters building in downtown St. Cloud.[33]

The Petters family is still "very well respected for their integrity," said Michael D. Doyle. "They are considerate, modest and gracious and very much involved in the issues of the community."[34]

In high school, like Madoff, Petters was not renowned for his academic excellence. One high school friend recounts that Petters was not a "particularly good student," loved to play "practical jokes," and was the kind of kid who would offer to pay for your cup of coffee or lunch, then go to the cashier and pay for only his own, leaving friends to feel foolish when they got up to leave."[35]

Two anonymous schoolmates of Petters reported to the *Minnesota Star-Tribune* that Petters was involved in a counterfeit money scheme as early as ninth grade.[36] He told the two classmates that if they gave him $20 bills he would bring them back $400 in fake bills.[37] The classmates never saw their promised $400 profit.[38] They hounded Petters for weeks until he finally, reluctantly, returned the $20 to his friends.

When a new shopping mall nearby significantly diminished the family business, Petters had other ideas. He dropped out of high school as a junior and started hustling cheap stereo equipment to students at local colleges.[39] Essentially, young Petters would buy overstocked electronic goods at low prices and then sell them at much higher ones to local unsuspecting students. Soon, he had made thousands in profits, recruited a sales force, and rented an office.[40]

Disgusted that Petters dropped out of school to start such a business, his parents ordered him back to high school. However, traditional schooling did not last long for Petters. The temptation of easy money was too great. He dropped out of St. Cloud State College after only one semester.[41]

In the early 1980s, Petters moved to Colorado, where he had an opportunity to buy a small chain of consumer electronics stores.[42] Even at this time, Petters was conducting a criminal enterprise. The business failed, and Petters was arrested on charges of fraud, forgery, and larceny connected to the business operation.[43]

The charges were eventually dropped, however, and Petters continued to start new electronics-related businesses that were all accused of fraudulence. After the failure of his Colorado electronics business, Petters started the Amicus Trade Group, a company that operated as a "liquidator" and made money by buying overstocked, damaged, or unsold goods and reselling such items to the public.[44]

Even Amicus Trade Group was subject to allegations of fraud. In 1991, Hagen and Bargain Bin, a discount electronics supplier, claimed that Amicus failed to deliver correct orders and brought suit against Petters.[45] Petters paid damages, but was never imprisoned for the fraud.

Court documents show that Petters sent phony air-bills to Hagen and the court ordered Petters to pay Hagen thousands to compensate for goods that were never delivered.[46]

Birth of the Ponzi Scheme, Petters Company Inc.

Around 1993, Petters took his various fraudulent enterprises to the next inevitable step, and to a far grander level. Petters decided to create various special-purpose entities, including Petters Company, Inc. (PCI), Petters Group Worldwide, LLC (PGW), and PAC Funding LLC in order to carry out a massive fraudulent investment scheme.[47]

PGW and PAC Funding provided billions of dollars to fund PCI and its supposed overstocked electronics distribution. Capital was raised by leading investor-lenders to believe that their loans were being used to purchase electronics and other goods from wholesalers to be resold to "big-box" retailers.[48] In actuality, the merchandise and inventory supposedly being bought with the investors' funds was nonexistent.[49] The purchase orders and related documents intended to secure the loan documents were fabricated.[50]

As in the prototypical Ponzi scheme, investors were not repaid with earnings from their investments but, instead, with funds Petters obtained from other investors. The Ponzi scheme brought in so much capital from investors that Petters was able to purchase Polaroid camera in 2005 for $426 million. Petters had succeeded in swindling investors, enabling him to take over a giant company. This was the pinnacle of Petters' criminality.

Succumbing to Uncontrollable Lust

Petters' success was not everlasting. On October 2, 2008, FBI agents executed search warrants at various Petters company locations. Petters was arrested the day after. He was charged with and found guilty of numerous counts of securities fraud. The United States District Court for the District of Minnesota sentenced Tom Petters to 50 years in prison on April 8, 2010. His attorney's plea for a lenient sentencing delivered to the court was particularly revealing.

Paul C. Engh, attorney for Petters, stated:

> Petters is imperfect, yes, but not evil. His run at life was rooted in the sale, the moment, the transaction, the unbending faith that tomorrow all will be well. It is the belief system of many a politician who refuses to see defeat and is unbowed by the endless scrutiny, the raising of funds for the next race because life is a race. It is the gestalt of the athlete who should have left the court but who still wants the last shot . . . It is the mantra of American success to start with nothing, get up every day, work hard, and you'll get somewhere, but only if you keep going.[51]

In this short passage, Engh did an excellent job of sizing up Petters' approach to life and business: do anything to meet an insatiable demand for "success." Petters would do anything for a quick buck. Whether that meant breaking the law, taking immoral short cuts, or breaking legal fiduciary duties, Petters did not care.

Like Madoff, Petters was tragically doomed. He was a product of his own unattainable aspirations. As Engh's sentencing memorandum illustrates, Petters may not have been intrinsically evil, but he believed he was made evil by a society that provided a premium on short cuts to succeed, a society that pressures its citizens to do whatever is necessary to reach goals and satisfy out-of-control ambitions.

Life became a "race" to Petters and Madoff. However, in this race there was no finish line. Both Petters and Madoff had a tremendous desire to be successful without patience, virtue, and temperance. The only option was an endless, lifelong sprint that satisfied their lust and temptations. The result of their deadly vices were two gigantic Ponzi schemes that defrauded widespread segments of society and caused immense loss, pain, and financial ruin.

Madoff's Cast of Characters

Even the most heinous financial swindler the world has ever known needed assistance in pulling off sham transactions that lasted over a 40-year period. What follows is an overview of Madoff's most critical co-conspirators and how they helped Madoff perpetrate the largest Ponzi scheme in history.

The Alperns

As of December 19, 2008, Madoff had stolen upwards of $600 million from Jewish charitable nonprofits.[52] This was not a coincidence. From the very beginning, Madoff targeted the Jewish community and his many connections within it, in order to find clients to fuel his criminal ambition.

Bernie Madoff was building his two lifelong businesses: his legitimate broker-dealer enterprise and his secret hedge fund and eventual Ponzi scheme as early as 1960.[53] Originally, Madoff enrolled at the University of Alabama, but abruptly left after one year.

He then enrolled at Hofstra University to continue his sprinkler business and to remain close to his high school crush, Ruth Alpern. Alpern was not only Bernie's girlfriend and eventual wife, she was the conduit that enabled Bernie to cajole high-net-worth investors to give him money.

The Alperns were established Jewish professionals. Ruth's father, Sol Alpern, was a respected accountant and did business under the partnership Alpern & Heller.[54] In 1959, Bernie and Ruth were married in a traditional Jewish ceremony. This new and permanent relationship with the Alperns enabled Madoff to take advantage of financial resources that went above and beyond his sprinkler business connections.

At this time, the Catskill Mountains were a favorite destination for New York Jewish families. The tranquil setting created a sense of physical refuge but was also a place where first- and second-generation Jewish immigrants could make friends, socialize, and "live the American dream."[55] There were more than 500 retreats populated by Jewish families, including children's camps, hotels, and other summer vacation venues.[56]

The Alperns picked "Sunny Oaks Hotel" in Woodbridge, New York, as their own retreat.[57] At this Catskills retreat, guests became extremely close and developed familial relations.[58]

The hotel was owned by the Arenson family, which soon became very close with the Alperns. Cynthia Arenson, who was Bernie's age at this time, explains that the hotel was "fertile ground" for Madoff's elaborate marketing schemes.[59] In fact, Cynthia invested with Bernie, as did her parents.

With such connections in mind, Arenson recounts that Sol told "anyone who would listen" that his son-in-law worked at a firm on Wall Street and that "he was doing very well."[60] David Arenson, Cynthia's son, illustrates that Sol's depiction of Bernie's business was that of a "can't lose bank."[61]

Soon, much of Sunny Oaks decided to invest with Madoff, allowing Madoff to build the connections and network that would allow his Ponzi scheme to continue for most of his adult life.

Meeting Carl Shapiro

Despite Sol Alpern's efforts on his son-in law's behalf, Madoff was still an unknown commodity 100 miles south of the Catskills. Madoff had to make a name for himself on Wall Street. Then as well as now, on the Street everyone who matters has a reputation. In the early 1960s, Madoff had none. He was in dire need of a reference that would allow him to attract institutional investors and preeminent high-net-worth investors for his legitimate broker-dealer operation and then for his private equity hedge fund.

Jewish businessman Carl Shapiro became this important reference. Shapiro had already made a fortune in the garment industry as the founder of Kay Windsor, a women's dress design and manufacturing company.[62] With his money intact, Shapiro sought to leverage some of his fortune through risk arbitrage strategies. Shapiro wanted to rapidly move in and out of investment positions clearly to take advantage of market changes. Madoff became his man.[63]

Like the astute move he had made in the sprinkler business, Madoff thought he could close wealthy clients like Carl Shapiro by giving them the ability to make trades at speeds far more rapid than his competition. To achieve this end, Madoff invested in new electronic technology from his brother, Peter, that allowed him to trade securities and clear deals in three days.[64]

For years, archaic pink sheets and trade messengers defined Wall Street brokerage houses. Deals took weeks, sometimes even months, to be consummated. Madoff's promise of rapid transactional speed in the 1960s was enough to draw Shapiro.

As author Erin Arvedlund writes, "Once Shapiro became a client of Madoff's, word of the hustling young broker's quick turnaround time spread. Others in Shapiro's social circle began lining up to trade with Madoff, and new clients begat new clients."[65]

In 1961, Shapiro gave Madoff $100 million to start an account.[66] Over 50 years, Madoff made Shapiro a billionaire. Carl Shapiro settled with Irving Piccard, the Madoff bankruptcy trustee, for $625 million in December 2010. This astronomical amount was in consideration of the funds Shapiro transferred to Madoff for his own account and to boost Madoff's own phantom hedge fund.

When Shapiro sold his Kay Windsor Inc. dress business in 1971 for $21 million, most of this money was used to fuel Madoff's Ponzi scheme.[67]

With the promise of consistent, reliable profits, Shapiro and Madoff entered into a reciprocal relationship where Shapiro funded Madoff's enterprise and helped network for new clients, while Madoff would give Shapiro priority in receiving "returns."

Shapiro's network would prove instrumental in Madoff's perpetration of securities fraud. For example, Shapiro introduced Madoff to Robert M. Jaffe, who was married to Shapiro's daughter, Ellen.[68] Jaffe, a Wall Street broker at Cohmad Securities Corporation (Cohmad), invested millions with Madoff through the firm. Cohmad would prove to be a critical part of Madoff's Ponzi scheme. Jaffe and the firm marketed and brokered Madoff's deals through deceptive marketing, resulting in over 800 Cohmad client accounts invested in Madoff's hedge fund by 2008.[69]

Cohmad's Marketing Camouflage

Prior to dealing with feeder fund Fairfield Sentry later in his "career," Madoff worked with another feeder fund for marketing and expansion purposes. Jaffe was the ideal connection. He was the son-in-law of Madoff friend, investor, and billionaire Carl Shapiro, and a well-connected Wall Street broker. Cohmad and Jaffe helped effectively conceal massive securities fraud.

Madoff operated as his own legitimate broker-dealer, BLMIS separate from his Ponzi scheme and a member of NASDAQ.

As author Erin Arvedlund explains, "For many years, Madoff's successful broker-dealer business offered the perfect cover for his phony hedge fund. To observers in the various markets where he operated, the flow of trades from Madoff's legitimate activities was indistinguishable from those that came—or didn't come—from the investment side."[70]

However, by 1985, Madoff was using another broker-dealer to "make trades" for his private hedge fund. Madoff and his good friend Maurice "Sonny" Cohn started the firm Cohmad. Cohmad essentially served as a marketing arm and personal revolving credit line for Jaffe, Cohn, and the Madoffs. The Cohns and Jaffe received over $100 million in management fees from Madoff for recruiting new victims to his fund's accounts.[71]

According to the SEC complaint against Cohmad, Jaffe and other Cohmad personnel (namely Sonny Cohn and his daughter Marcia) deceptively marketed Madoff securities to high-worth, but unsophisticated investors with full knowledge of Madoff's fraud.[72]

Madoff used a veil of secrecy to his advantage among very wealthy persons, especially in the Jewish community. With Cohmad's assistance, he "cultivated an aura of success and secrecy surrounding BMIS, projecting to a social network of wealthy friends and investors that he was highly successful and did not need a market to solicit to obtain investments."[73] Madoff played a game of "hard to get" with investors, making it seem as if he was so profitable and liquid that he did not need any further investors.[74]

The Cohmad team preyed on areas where predominately wealthy Jewish families congregated. A prime location was the Palm Beach Country Club, a popular, prominent, largely Jewish social club in Palm Beach for members who could not get into the Everglades or the Bath and Tennis Club because of their religion.[75]

Investors would hear about Madoff from their social network, and Cohmad would promise to put in a "good word." Cohmad could not assure investors that they had the necessary status and capital to put their money in with Madoff.

From 1996 through 2008, payments by BMIS to Cohmad totaled $98,448,678.84.[76] For each year from 2000 to 2008 Cohmad's yearly revenue from Madoff ranged from $3 million to $10 million.[77]

These amounts do not even include the astronomical fees paid individually to Sonny Cohn and Jaffe. The SEC reported that Cohn received more than $14 million from Madoff during the period 2001 to 2008.[78] In November 2010, the SEC settled charges of fraud against Cohmad, Cohn, and Jaffe for an undisclosed amount. On March 30, 2011, the Financial Industry Regulatory Authority (FINRA) settled charges against Jaffe for $1.1 million.[79]

Stanley Chais

Through Madoff's emerging Jewish circles, he met the well-known California money manager, Stanley Chais, in the early 1970s. Chais ran a number of funds that simply fed massive amounts of investor capital into Madoff's hedge fund. In fact, the SEC alleged in its complaint against Chais that his funds were solely created to invest money with Madoff, essentially empty shells.[80]

Chais's investors included close friends and relatives and their own networks.[81] The number of investors eventually expanded to nearly 500 in 2008. Like Cohmad, many of these persons were unsophisticated mom-and-pop investors with high net worth or other entities who simply did not ask questions regarding the consistency of their returns. According to the account statements Madoff provided Chais and the statements Chais provided the funds, the funds yielded 20 to 25 percent in Madoff's hedge fund and did not have any returns less than 10 percent since 1995.[82]

Like Cohmad, Jaffe, and Cohn, Chais enticed investors to devote capital to Madoff through a veil of secrecy. According to the SEC complaint against Chais, if an investor asked for further information regarding specifics of the fund's positions, he would say they were confidential and if the investor wanted more information he did not have to invest in the fund at all.[83]

This strategy effectively duped hundreds of investors that their capital was well protected and safeguarded by appropriate hedges, positions, and trades—despite the fact that no actual trades were ever made. While Chais gave nearly all of his investor funds to Madoff, not a single one of them knew of the man, received a prospectus, or ever had a viable choice on whether to invest with him.[84] Despite his failure to neither make any investment management decision on behalf of his funds nor inform investors where their money was going, Chais charged the funds over $269,600,000 in fees from 1995 to 2008.[85]

Chais did not live long enough to survive the outcome of litigation against him. He died at the age of 84 in September 2010 from a rare blood disease.

Avelino and Bienes

Part of the benefit of marrying Ruth Alpern was that Madoff's new father in law, Sol Alpern, was not just an excellent networker but was a partner in the accounting firm Alpern & Heller.

The accounting firm essentially became another marketing arm for Madoff's broker dealer and private equity firm. As new clients came in, Alpern immediately referred them to Madoff, telling them what a wonderful investment manager he was.[86] Beginning in 1962, Alpern's partner Frank Avelino started fundraising for Madoff. In 1968, another partner Michael Bienes started fund-raising for Madoff, and he continued to do so over a 30-year period.[87]

In 1977, Avelino and Bienes started an accounting firm, aptly named "Avelino and Bienes," that functioned primarily to "audit" Madoff and do marketing and networking for Bernie's Ponzi scheme.[88] The SEC was tipped to Avelino and Bienes in 1992 because of the firm's marketing materials for Madoff investments promising 20 percent returns or better.[89]

At that time, Avelino was auditing 3,200 investor accounts worth $441 million.[90] In order to avert a criminal Ponzi scheme investigation, Avelino represented to the SEC that they were simply auditing Madoff's valid stock exchange trades and "would make up any money" that did not meet the 20 percent return levels.[91] "There is nothing to indicate fraud," Martin Kuperberg, an SEC Commission official, told *The Wall Street Journal* in November 1992.[92]

Nonetheless, behind the scenes, the SEC asked Pricewaterhouse-Coopers (PwC), a "big four" accounting firm, to audit Avelino and Bienes. PwC found only essential tax records on the Avelino books, and no records reflecting Madoff trades.[93] Still, the SEC did nothing. By the end of January 1993, both the SEC securities investigation and the PwC were entirely aborted.

The accounting fraud and kickbacks between Madoff, Avelino, and Bienes occurred right up to the conviction of Madoff in 2009. Avelino's profits from the Madoff scheme enabled him to own multiple homes in Nantucket, Massachusetts, Palm Beach, Florida, and New York.[94] Avelino hid his Madoff money in a shell foundation called the Kenn Jordan Foundation.[95] The foundation had $6 million in assets, much of which was invested in Madoff's private equity firm.[96]

Avelino named the foundation after his good friend Kenn Jordan, who lived in a very small Ft. Lauderdale apartment during the 1990s.[97] Even after Mr. Jordan's death in 1999, Avelino continued to use the foundation as a shell to raise money to invest in Madoff.[98]

Nonetheless, as time went on, Avelino began to doubt the sustainability of the Madoff scheme. In fact, Avelino allegedly warned his housekeeper ten days before Madoff turned himself in that her investment was not "safe."[99] Currently, Picard is pursuing a lawsuit against Avelino and Bienes for a total of $900 million.

Fairfield Greenwich

Long-lasting Ponzi schemes need strong feeder fund relationships that fuel the fraudulent operation with sustainable capital. In Madoff's case, the hedge fund Fairfield Greenwich Group (FGG) was the feeder fund that enabled his private equity "fund" to successfully prosper for decades.

Irving Picard accused 19 people and 25 affiliates of FGG of actively conspiring with Madoff's Ponzi scheme.[100] Moreover, Picard has pursued countless *claw-back lawsuits* against hedge funds that directly and indirectly invested in FGG and, accordingly, benefited from Madoff's Ponzi scheme. A claw-back suit is an action intended to recover money derived from fraud on behalf of victimized investors.

Walter Noel was the head of FGG. He grew up in Tennessee. He went to Harvard and Harvard Law School and received a master's in economics and a juris doctorate. He was a veteran of the banking business and spent decades in investment banking at large firms, perhaps most notably Chemical Bank, where he headed the firm's international banking practice.[101]

Noel met Madoff as early as the 1980s and immediately the two were taken with each other and sought ways to do business together. He effectively took Madoff's scheme international, catapulting the Madoff fraud from the Jewish country clubs of Palm Beach and Catskill retreats to major international finance hubs.

"It's fair to say that Fairfield, more than anyone else, took Madoff global," said attorney Stuart Singer of the prominent litigation firm

Boies, Schiller, & Flexner, now representing former FGG investors in a class-action suit.[102]

At the time of Madoff's arrest, FGG managed $14.1 billion and employed over 140 people.[103] Out of the $14.1 billion of assets under management, FGG had $7.5 billion of investor money placed into Madoff's funds, most notably through the Fairfield Sentry hedge fund.

FGG was loyal to Madoff's scheme until the bitter end. On December 11, 2008 (the day Madoff turned himself in), FGG salesman Andrew Douglass was on the phone with a potential investor pitching a new fund termed Emerald that would invest solely with Madoff.[104] Douglass told the investor that FGG, through Emerald, had already raised over $50 million to put in Madoff's hands.[105] Internal documents show that FGG took in more than $500 million in management fees since 2003 from the Madoff Ponzi scheme.[106]

Through Madoff, the Noel family became the toast of the affluent Greenwich, Connecticut, community. In fact, in 2002, *Vanity Fair* published an article solely about the Noels and their manifestation of the prototypical Greenwich lifestyle.[107] Through gigantic management fees associated with Madoff, the Noels lived a glamorous life, splitting time between homes in Greenwich, the Caribbean, and Florida.[108] Noel involved his entire family and relatives in managing FGG and its various funds. For example, Noel's son-in-law, Andres Piedrahita, was a key figure for FGG. He had been married to Noel's daughter, Corina, since 1989. He was one of four of the five Noel sons-in-law to work in the family business, but Piedrahita was the most critical. His "outstanding" public relations skills set him apart from others at the firm, especially in expanding FGG and Madoff's reach to international markets.[109]

According to *The Wall Street Journal*, Piedrahita bragged that his real job was "to live better than any of my clients,"[110] and he made this ethos a reality. Piedrahita lived lavishly. He had an apartment in Manhattan and a mansion in London, and then in Madrid, a butler, a chauffeured car, and a private jet. The native Colombian threw wild parties, assembled an impressive art collection, and held court from his Falcon yacht anchored off the Spanish island resort of Mallorca, where he had a hacienda. Friends he entertained included the Duke of Marlborough and Prince Felipe, the heir to Spain's throne, and top models such as Elle Macpherson.[111]

Once the Madoff criminal investigation broke, the Noel kingdom of wealth and excess came crumbling down in a rapid fall from grace. FGG was liquidated and Madoff Trustee Picard sought $3.6 billion in damages against 43 FGG defendants. As of the fall of 2012, Picard has recovered $1 billion from the FGG liquidators and another $212 million from the FGG Madoff feeder funds, Greenwich Sentry LP and Greenwich Sentry Partners LP.

Petters' Cast of Characters

How did Tom Petters go from selling overstocked warehouse electronic goods in his basement to one of the most prominent faux businessmen in American history? He needed help along the way from people in key places. Here is a list of the co-conspirators that made Petters a multi-millionaire and one of the most notorious financial criminals in history.

Larry Reynolds

Larry Reynolds was the ideal accomplice for Tom Petters. Like Petters, he had a checkered past and an uncontrollable criminal addiction for crime, fraud, and other illicit dealings.

Reynolds' real name was actually Larry Reservitz, a burnt-out, disbarred attorney and admitted swindler and drug trafficker who worked with the New England mafia in the 1980s and had to be placed in the witness protection program later in the decade.[112]

Reynolds grew up in Brockton, Massachusetts, became a lawyer, then perpetrated a phony accident scheme and was disbarred. He went to Europe but was extradited to face charges in a fraudulent check scam involving the Bank of New England, to which he pleaded guilty.[113]

Reynolds was then implicated in a marijuana smuggling case and began cooperating with federal authorities in 1984. He said he wore hidden tape recorders. In 1986, Reynolds testified that he was involved in a scheme to cash a bogus check for $2 million out of the account of L. Ron Hubbard, the late founder of the Church of Scientology.[114]

Reynolds said he met Petters in the mid-1990s in Los Angeles when they were both making shoe deals with the once-popular distributor LA

Gear. Reynolds said he never told Petters about his criminal past.[115] "We talked. We discussed things and got along pretty well," Reynolds said.[116]

Reynolds said he and Petters were both looking for merchandise such as footwear, golf bags, golf clubs, and a variety of other goods. He said at the Petters trial that they had a continuing "profitable relationship."[117]

Reynolds used a similar company to PCI, Nationwide International Resources (NIR), to move surplus goods. According to the transcript of the Petters trial, he said Petters called him in 2002 and asked if he could start parking money in the NIR bank account overnight for a small commission. This "small commission" eventually blossomed into nearly $10 million over time.[118]

Reynolds conspired with Petters to effectuate a gigantic Ponzi scheme fraud, ruining the lives of thousands of investors. Reynolds pled guilty to conspiracy to commit money laundering and was sentenced to 130 months in jail.

His role in the Petters Ponzi scheme was instrumental. Although Petters told his investors that their funds were used to purchase consumer electronics, it was Reynolds who siphoned off investor funds into a Petters shell company instead.[119]

Unlike the Madoff case, investors in Petters' electronics business believed that sending their money directly to the vendor that was supplying Petters with goods would protect them from potential fraud. Unfortunately, this was far from reality. Investors wired amounts ranging from $2 million to $25 million of funds to the accounts of supposed vendors Nationwide and Enchanted Family Buying Company, a shell company created by Reynolds and co-conspirator Michael Catain.[120] Catain and Reynolds both admitted that they knew these transactions were fraudulent.[121]

Reynolds also provided essential assistance to Petters in other ways. To deceptively show that Petters' company stored actual goods, Reynolds bought warehouse space in California, Nevada, and Kansas that held no inventory.[122] Reynolds duped institutional investors about the quantity and type of the little inventory that Petters actually did hold.[123] In one specific instance, Reynolds blatantly lied to a concerned investor that he was a legitimate supplier to Petters.[124]

Without Reynolds, there would be no Petters Ponzi scheme. He was the glue that kept the bogus investments operational and undetected by the many institutional investors that conveyed millions of dollars to Petters. Unlike the Madoff fraud, investors actually questioned the legitimacy of Petters' transactions.

Reynolds was the first line of defense to ensure that Petters' investors never got close to deciphering the true nature of Petters' dealings. Nonetheless, in the end, Reynolds betrayed Petters' trust. He testified against Petters during his trial and admitted to laundering $12 billion.

Just as critical as Reynolds was to the perpetuation of Petters' Ponzi scheme, he was just as crucial to the government's case against Tom Petters. Through his testimony against his former co-conspirator, Petters was sentenced to 50 years in prison.

"I regret the day I met Tom Petters," Reynolds admitted. "Greed and stupidity made me continue."[125]

Michael Catain

Michael Catain was another unsavory character associated with the Tom Petters Ponzi scheme. Catain's father, Jack Catain, was a reputed mob figure and loan shark.[126] Jack routinely engaged in activities similar to Tom Petters' fraud and was a career criminal.

Michael Catain followed in his father's footsteps. He was successful in the "liquidation" business and was also a music executive that touted close ties to Motown greats such as Smokey Robinson.[127] However, in 2002, working with Larry Reynolds, Catain created a sham business called Enchanted Family Buying, solely intended to siphon investor money to Tom Petters.[128] At Enchanted's principal place of business, FBI agents found only an empty office.

In his court confession, Catain apologized to his family and friends, saying, "I strayed off my path, and that was wrong." To explain his actions, Catain's attorney pleaded to the court that "he's a human being and he made a terrible mistake."[129]

This "terrible mistake" defrauded hundreds of investors of millions of dollars. On September 14, 2010, Catain was sentenced to 7.5 years in prison for his involvement in the Petters scam.

Robert White and Deanna Coleman

Internal personnel at PCI also assisted Petters in his criminal enterprise. PCI's two central figures that worked with Petters in defrauding investors were Robert White and eventual Petters whistleblower Deanna Coleman.

Prior to White's arrival at PCI, he was used as a marketer for Petters' Ponzi scheme.[130] He would target high-net-worth investors in the St. Paul, Minnesota, area and surrounding areas. In the late 1990s, Petters recruited White to join PCI for the sole purpose of fabricating bank records.[131] Day in and day out, White deceived and lied to investors by forging fake records of transactions that never occurred.

Over more than a 10-year period, White defrauded investors of $3.65 billion. In court, White issued an apology from "the depths of my soul" to family, friends, and other victims of the fraud.[132] White admitted that the guilt of perpetrating such a gigantic fraud was immense. According to White, he continually considered the prospect of turning himself in to authorities.[133] However, he never did.

Deanna Coleman was the whistleblower who brought down the Tom Petters empire. She joined PCI as an office manager in the early 1990s. Prior to turning on her former boss, Coleman was a loyal co-conspirator who assisted White in fabricating documents to induce third parties to provide PCI with billions of dollars in loans. Coleman specifically worked with White to fabricate the supposed supplier agreements with Larry Reynolds' company, NIR, and Michael Catain's company, Enchanted Family Buying.

"We didn't have any real deals at Petters that would generate revenue to repay investors," Coleman told jurors at the Petters trial.[134] Petters tried to assure Coleman that she wouldn't go to jail from his fraud, insisting that "if worst came to worst, you would not go to jail. I would."[135]

But unlike White, Coleman couldn't live with the guilt. Speaking publicly through her attorney, Coleman insisted, "She was deeply troubled by the scale [of the investment scheme]. She felt it had gotten out of hand. She lost her confidence in Petters' ability to ever pay back investors."[136]

Because she blew the whistle on PCI, saving future, current, and past investors millions of dollars, Coleman was sentenced to only one year and a day in jail on September 2, 2010.

Will We Witness Another Madoff?

The story of Madoff and Petters and the various persons and entities that aided and abetted their criminal enterprises is a disturbing tale of out-of-control lust and ambition. Both the Ponzi swindlers and their investors behaved symbiotically. Investors were perpetually addicted to the allure of consistent profits.

Madoff and Petters were transfixed with the premise that they were conducting a criminal enterprise and effectively getting away with it. Like an athlete pumping himself with performance-enhancing drugs to enhance his on-the-field performance, the Ponzi scheme framework was the proverbial "needle" for Madoff, Petters, and their investors.

In August and September of 2009, the SEC inspector general wrote a detailed report outlining the agency's extraordinary failures in investigating Madoff. Over the years, Madoff fostered very close relationships with the SEC and used high-level agency contacts to his advantage.

The SEC has dedicated an entire page on its website to detail the reforms undertaken since the Madoff scandal to ensure that such a heinous crime against the American investing public will never occur again.

Yet, are the SEC's reforms enough to stop a Madoff-style Ponzi scheme from reoccurring?

New regulations, astronomical settlements, damages, and jail sentences will not curb the perpetration of future Ponzi schemes. It is emblematic of the human condition. People are lured into deviance because of the promise and expectations of investor and conspirator utility. In Madoff's case, his conspirators not only enjoyed luxury lifestyles but also pleasured themselves with extreme drug use and sexual interactions.

Until the investing public evolves and becomes more educated and prudent about where they are sending their hard-earned money, the question will not be, "Will there be another Madoff?" but rather, "Who will be the next Madoff?"

Notes

1. Steve Fishman, "The Madoff Tapes," *New York Magazine*, February 27, 2011, available at: http://nymag.com/news/features/berniemadoff-2011–3/.

2. See generally, Erin Arvedlund, *Too Good to Be True, The Rise and Fall of Bernie Madoff* (New York: Portfolio, 2010) and David E. Y. Sarna, *The History of Greed, Financial Fraud from Tulip Mania to Bernie Madoff* (Hoboken, NJ: John Wiley & Sons, 2010).
3. Jerry Oppenheimer, *Madoff with the Money* (Hoboken, NJ: John Wiley & Sons, 2009), p. 24.
4. Ibid.
5. Ibid.
6. Ibid., p. 25.
7. Nicholas Varchaver, James Bandler, and Doris Burke, "Madoff's Mother Tangled with the Feds," *CNN Money*, January 16, 2009, money.cnn.com/2009/01/16/magazines/fortune/madoff_mother.fortune/index.htm.
8. See Ibid. It should be noted that a year later, Sylvia struck a deal with the SEC to avoid charges, so long as she agreed to stay out of business.
9. Oppenheimer, p. 43.
10. Ibid., p. 44.
11. Ibid.
12. Ibid.
13. Ibid., p. 54.
14. Ibid., p. 55.
15. Ibid.
16. Julie Creswell and Landon Thomas Jr., "The Talented Mr. Madoff," *The New York Times*, www.nytimes.com/2009/01/25/business/25bernie.html?pagewanted=all.
17. Ibid.
18. Fishman.
19. Ibid.
20. Ibid.
21. Ibid., p. 34.
22. Ibid.
23. Wexler Class Action, First Amended Complaint, N.Y. Supreme Court, October 21, 2009.
24. Ibid.
25. Ibid.
26. Ibid.
27. Ibid.
28. Ibid.
29. Ibid.
30. Ibid.
31. "Bernie Madoff's Secretary Spills His Secrets," *Vanity Fair*, May 5, 2009, www.vanityfair.com/online/daily/2009/05/bernie-madoffs-secretary-spills-his-secrets.
32. Ibid.

33. James L. Meriner, "Ponzi-Dot-Gov, Part One Personalities," 2011, www
.ponzidotgov.com/chapter.html.
34. David Phelps and Jon Tevlin, "The Collapse of the Petters Empire," *Minneapolis
Star-Tribune*, October 26, 2008.
35. Ibid.
36. Ibid.
37. Ibid.
38. Ibid.
39. Ibid.
40. Ibid.
41. Ibid.
42. Ibid.
43. Ibid.
44. Ibid.
45. Ibid.
46. Ibid.
47. In Re: *Petters Company, Inc.; Petters Group Worldwide, LLC; Pc v. Douglas
Arthur Kelley*, As Chapter 11 Trustee for Petters Company (8th Cir. 08/19/
2011).
48. Ibid.
49. Ibid.
50. Ibid.
51. *United States v. Tom Petters*, Defendant Sentencing Memoranda, http://www
.scribd.com/doc/29810748/Defendant-s-Sentencing-Memorandum-in-U-
S-v-Petters.
52. J. Wire Reports, "Investing With Madoff Leaves Jewish Community
Devastated," *J. Weekly*, www.jweekly.com/article/full/36426/investing-
with-madoff-leaves-jewish-community-devastated/.
53. Erin Arvedlund, "Too Good to Be True, The Rise and Fall of Bernie
Madoff," *Portfolio* (2009): 24.
54. Ibid., p. 21.
55. Ibid., p. 25.
56. Ibid.
57. Ibid.
58. Ibid.
59. Ibid.
60. Ibid.
61. Ibid.
62. Ibid., p. 31.
63. Ibid.
64. Ibid., p. 32.
65. Ibid., p. 24.
66. Ibid.

67. Nathan Vardi, "Carl Shapiro Could Still Go to Jail over Madoff Ponzi," *Forbes*, December 7, 2010, http://www.forbes.com/sites/nathanvardi/2010/12/07/carl-shapiro-could-still-go-to-jail-over-madoff-ponzi/.
68. Arvedlund, p. 65.
69. *S.E.C. v. Cohmad Securities Corporation, Maurice J. Cohn, Marcia B. Cohn, Robert M. Jaffe*. 09 Civ-5680 June 22, 2009 U.S.D.N.
70. Arvedlund, p. 57.
71. Kate McCarthy, "Bernard Madoff's 'Stealth Sales Force' Charged with Fraud," ABC News, June 22, 2009, abcnews.go.com/Blotter/story?id=7902259&page=1.
72. See generally, *S.E.C. v. Cohmad Securities Corporation, Maurice J. Cohn, Marcia B. Cohn, Robert M. Jaffe*. 09 Civ-5680 June 22, 2009 S.D.NY.
73. See *S.E.C. v. Cohmad Securities Corporation, Maurice J. Cohn, Marcia B. Cohn, Robert M. Jaffe*. 09 Civ-5680 June 22, 2009 S.D.NY, p. 10.
74. Ibid.
75. Arvedlund, p. 66.
76. See *S.E.C. v. Cohmad Securities Corporation, Maurice J. Cohn, Marcia B. Cohn, Robert M. Jaffe*. 09 Civ-5680 June 22, 2009 S.D.NY, p. 10.
77. Ibid.
78. See *S.E.C. v. Cohmad Securities Corporation, Maurice J. Cohn, Marcia B. Cohn, Robert M. Jaffe*. 09 Civ-5680 June 22, 2009 S.D.NY., p. 10.
79. Michele Dargan, "Financial Industry Regulatory Authority Orders Robert Jaffe to Pay Madoff Investors $1.1 M," *Palm Beach Daily*, March 30, 2011.
80. *S.E.C. v. Stanley Chais*, 09 Civ-5681 June 22, 2009 S.D.NY, p. 6.
81. Ibid.
82. Ibid., p. 8.
83. Ibid., p. 11.
84. Ibid., p. 12.
85. Ibid.
86. Arvedlund, p. 26.
87. Ibid.
88. Alex Berenson, "92 Ponzi Case Missed Signals about Madoff," *The New York Times*, January 16, 2009, www.nytimes.com/2009/01/17/business/17ponzi.html?pagewanted=all.
89. Ibid.
90. Ibid.
91. Ibid.
92. Ibid.
93. Ibid.
94. Ibid.
95. Ibid.
96. Ibid.
97. Ibid.

98. Ibid. (citing lawsuit against Avelino in Nantucket, Mass).

99. Ibid.

100. Michael Rothfeld and Chad Bray, "Madoff Trustee Targets Fairfield," *The Wall Street Journal*, July 22, 2010, online.wsj.com/article/SB100014240 52748704684604575381024250819284.html.

101. "Times Topics, People, Walter M. Noel, Jr." *The New York Times*, April 2, 2009, topics.nytimes.com/top/reference/timestopics/people/n/walter_m_ noel_jr/index.html.

102. PBS, "Frontline, The Madoff Affair," May 12, 2009, www.pbs.org/wgbh/ pages/frontline/madoff/etc/synopsis.html.

103. Vicky Ward, "Greenwich Mean Time," *Vanity Fair*, April 2009, http:// www.vanityfair.com/style/features/2009/04/noel200904.

104. Ibid.

105. Ibid.

106. Alex Berenson and Konigsberg, "Firm Built on Ties to Madoff Now Faces Tough Questions," *The New York Times*, December 22, 2008, query. nytimes.com/gst/fullpage.html?res=9C01E3DA1E3EF931A15751C1A96E9 C8B63&ref=waltermnoeljr.

107. Kristina Stewart, "Golden in Greenwich," *Vanity Fair*, October 2002, www .vanityfair.com/style/features/2002/10/noel200210.

108. Berenson and Konigsberg.

109. Jose De Cordoba and Tomas Catan, "The Charming Mr. Piedrahita Finds Himself Caught in the Madoff Storm," *The Wall Street Journal*, March 31, 2009, http://online.wsj.com/article/SB123845782470271683.html.

110. Ibid.

111. Ibid.

112. David Phelps and Jennifer Bjorhus, "Mystery Past of Petters Associate Unfolds," *Minneapolis Star-Tribune*, September 15, 2009, www.startribune .com/business/59288882.html.

113. David Phelps, "Petters Associate Reynolds Begins Testifying: Larry Reynolds Emerged From the Federal Witness Protection Program to Testify Against Tom Petters," *Minneapolis Star-Tribune*, Business News, November 9, 2009, www.startribune.com/business/69573442.html.

114. Ibid.

115. Ibid.

116. Ibid.

117. Ibid.

118. *U.S. v. Reynolds*, No. 10–3130, Eighth Circuit, June 24, 2011.

119. Ibid.

120. Ibid.

121. Ibid.

122. Ibid.

123. Ibid.

124. Ibid.

125. David Phelps, "Reynolds: I Regret the Day I Met Tom Petters," *Minneapolis Star-Tribune*, March 24, 2011, www.startribune.com/business/102889814 .html.

126. Jack Gordon, "The Family Business," *Twin Cities Business*, March 2009, www.tcbmag.com/peoplecompanies/peopleandcompanies/114053p1.aspx.

127. Trisha Volpe, "Michael Catain Gets 7½ years in Prison in Petters Case," KARE 11, September 14, 2010, www.kare11.com/news/news_article.aspx? storyid=871692.

128. Ibid.

129. Ibid.

130. *U.S. v. Robert White*, United States District Court District of Minnesota, No. 08–299.

131. Ibid.

132. David Phelps, "Petters Forger White Sentenced to 5 Years; He Also Apologizes," *Minneapolis Star-Tribune*, March 24, 2011, www.startribune.com/business/ 102959439.html.

133. Ibid.

134. Ashby Jones, "Deanna Coleman Takes the Stand: A Blue Monday for Tom Petters," *The Wall Street Journal*, November 2, 2009, blogs.wsj.com/law/2009/ 11/02/deanna-coleman-takes-the-stand-a-blue-monday-for-tom-petters/.

135. Ibid.

136. David Phelps and Jon Tevlin, "The Woman Who Brought Down Tom Petters," *Star Tribune*, November 2, 2008, www.startribune.com/printarticle/ ?id=33661359

Chapter 8

HealthSouth and WorldCom: How a Gluttonous Appetite for Expansion Resulted in Accounting Fraud and Failed Corporations

Gluttony denotes, not any desire of eating and drinking, but an inordinate desire . . . leaving the order of reason, wherein the good of moral virtue consists.

—*Thomas Aquinas*

M odern shareholders rarely demand temperance from their highly paid CEOs. The desired end for a company shareholder is usually consistent profits and high returns.

Company profits equal rises in the price of the company's shares, and accordingly, more money in a shareholder's bank account.

For public company CEOs, the devil is usually in the details in reaching the desired end of increased profits and prices per share. While many CEOs exercise virtue, diligence, and shrewd strategic planning to facilitate economic growth, there are many heinous examples of CEOs falling prey to the economic vice of gluttony.

Corporate gluttony is fatal. The popular definition of gluttony is "excess in eating or drinking" or "greedy or excessive indulgence."[1] Extended to the corporate world, gluttony is an inordinate desire to achieve the "indulgence" of quarterly profits, shareholder approval, and, in turn, the maintenance of extraordinary executive compensation. A lack of prudence and out-of-control corporate consumption, is of the one of the greatest sins a CEO can commit. Gluttony misleads shareholders, betrays market trust, and results in the evisceration of the corporate entity itself.

What actions define corporate gluttony? Think of the "food" of corporate consumption as the entities' balance sheet and assets. A healthy mix of diverse assets, appropriate leverage, and diligent accounting is critical for a corporation to survive on a day-to-day basis. Artificially inflating the value of a company's shares through unsustainable mergers and fraudulence results in its ruin.

Richard Scrushy and Bernie Ebbers, the former CEOs of Health-South Corporation and World Com, exemplify the fatality of corporate gluttony. Scrushy and Ebbers committed fraud because they refused to recognize inevitable balance sheet losses. They were obsessed with the continuance of their own personal pleasure, greed, and excess. Scrushy and Ebbers committed whatever fraud, misappropriation, and intimidation were necessary to artificially preserve profits for their own benefit.

The HealthSouth and WorldCom cases demonstrate gluttony in two different but equally heinous forms. HealthSouth, the largest US operator in rehabilitation hospitals as of 2004, overstated $2.7 billion in profits over a seven-year period to satisfy perceived shareholder and market expectations. "Scrushy was the CEO of the fraud," Judge Horn stated, after ordering Scrushy to repay $2.9 billion to company shareholders.[2]

Scrushy escaped jail time in 2005 after a bizarre trial in which the judge decided his fate, rather than a jury. He was charged with 36 criminal counts of fraud. "He was the orchestrator of this fraud," said Alice H. Martin, the US attorney who unsuccessfully prosecuted Mr. Scrushy.[3] After Scrushy was ordered to give back $2.9 billion, Martin stated, "That's what I'm calling my retirement gift."[4]

By all accounts, Scrushy was consumed by his own desire for endless material goods. Former HealthSouth CEO Aaron Beam stated that Scrushy was "one of the most enigmatic, nefarious, chilling, and truly fascinating human beings the state of Alabama has produced" and "one of the worst CEOs to emerge from the noted ranks of American business."[5]

In contrast, WorldCom was a story of one man's insatiable desire to grow his telecommunications company into an international conglomerate. Bernie Ebbers was an ambitious, self-made man to the extreme. He worked as a milkman, bouncer, basketball coach, and motel owner prior to founding Long Distance Discount Service on a cocktail napkin.[6] Long Distance Discount Service was the precursor to WorldCom.

Ebbers used close relationships with Salomon Smith Barney analysts to broker a series of telecommunications takeovers, including a massive $37 billion takeover of MCI Communications. Ebbers' rapid rise to fame, publicity, and fortune fed his desire to keep a wave of profits going.

HealthSouth employees called the organization "paramilitary" in nature. Many accountants literally feared for their life if they did not go along with the daily whims of Scrushy. Intimidation and fear defined the HealthSouth accounting department and followed the company to its own ruin.

Ebbers was addicted to generating profits through mergers and acquisitions. Scrushy's ravenous appetite resulted in one of the greatest accounting frauds of the modern era. The CEO's tremendous inordinate desire to consume for their own personal pleasure resulted in a complete hijacking of company balance sheets, artificial inflation of assets, and some of the greatest accounting frauds the world has ever known.

HealthSouth

This is the story of the rise of a small-town businessman, the birth of a health-care giant, and a massive accounting manipulation.

Scrushy's Idea

In 1952, Richard Scrushy was born in Selma, Alabama. Made famous as a civil rights battleground, Selma was a small town of 24,000 people. He was raised in a middle-class family, son of Gerald Scrushy, a cash register salesman, and Grace Scrushy, a nurse at a local hospital.[7]

Former HealthSouth CFO and friend of Scrushy's Aaron Beam said, "Richard was the quintessential American boy. He went by his middle name, Marin, attended a Methodist church with his family, was a Boy Scout, and played little league baseball."[8]

Scrushy was neither a stellar academic student nor a leader in high school social circles. His friends were in the high school band the "Born Losers," and he was an admitted follower of the group's lead singer, Fielding Pierce.[9]

The future HealthSouth CEO was carefree. Because of an accidental pregnancy with his girlfriend he decided to get married and support his new family as a bricklayer.[10] Scrushy made a home in a local trailer park, where he made quite the impression on his neighbors: "You went over to Marin's trailer," trailer resident Gary West recalls, "and he didn't serve Pabst; he served wine and cheese."[11]

Scrushy had ideas of a life beyond laying bricks and living in a Selma trailer park. According to a tale Scrushy told his friends, he ceased work as a bricklayer when one day he had trouble hauling a load of cement up a ladder. A fellow worker berated him and snarled for him to hurry up. The guy yelled, "Now go get another one."[12] Scrushy had had enough; he walked off the job and never came back.

Community College to Health Care Mogul

Scrushy was married with a child at the young age of 20. However, despite these obligations, the future health-care titan chose to invest in his education. Scrushy briefly attended Wallace Community College in Selma and then enrolled at Jefferson State College in Birmingham.[13] He worked nights in a local hospital's respiratory therapy program.[14]

"Jefferson State allowed me the flexibility to go to school and work. Plus, it was affordable," Scrushy later said.[15] After spending a year at

Jefferson State and then a year of clinical training at the University of Alabama at Birmingham, he graduated in 1974 and became a UAB teacher in respiratory therapy.[16]

Scrushy spent two and a half years teaching at UAB and paid his bills by working in the evenings as a respiratory therapist at local hospitals.[17] At this time, Scrushy decided to look into a career in private practice. He divorced his young wife, cut his long hair, and began going by his first name, Richard. Scrushy was offered a position in the respiratory care unit at LifeMark, a Houston-based for-profit hospital chain. Scrushy worked to build up the respiratory department and became a prominent manager within the company.[18]

First Signs of Deceit: Scrushy and LifeMark

In his memoir, Aaron Beam, Scrushy's future prized HealthSouth CFO, describes that he observed Scrushy's true colors on his first day on the job at LifeMark. For example, Scrushy utilized whatever means necessary to make a positive impression on his superiors. Beam recounts the first time he saw Scrushy lie to his boss:

> He told me that he wanted me to go with him to present a proposal for signing a new contract to his boss. I said sure. We went to his boss's office and Richard introduced us. We sat and Richard said, "Aaron and I stayed up late last night working on these numbers and we think we need to sign this contract." I was stunned. I hadn't worked with Richard 30 minutes and he'd already told a lie.[19]

It was these sorts of deceitful tactics that enabled Scrushy to move up quickly within the LifeMark ranks. Two years later, in 1980, Scrushy was promoted to vice president of the respiratory, physical, and pharmacy divisions. Despite this new leadership role, Scrushy was significantly overweight and an avid cigarette smoker.[20]

Status meant everything to Scrushy. In 1983, he saved up enough money to afford a used Mercedes Benz. Scrushy "loved being the focus" and "the show," Beam recounted.[21] He expensed department-wide visits to gentlemen's clubs and tried to deceive company auditors of such trips.[22]

Luckily for Scrushy, he would soon not have to answer to company auditors—or anyone else. Scrushy and Beam left LifeMark in 1983 after the company merged with American Medical International. Scrushy left with the idea of a new nationwide outpatient facility; it would be called "HealthSouth."

During the LifeMark merger, Scrushy began telling his top managers of his new idea, a rehabilitation company that would provide high-quality, low-cost health care. Scrushy worked to secure a $1,000,000 line of credit from Citicorp venture capitalists.[23] Within days, Scrushy had recruited Beam and other top LifeMark talent to join his cause. Scrushy and Beam completed a five-year business plan, relocated to Birmingham, and opened up their first office.

Looking back, Beam recounts that this idea was extremely new to the market. "It is important to understand that this outpatient approach to health care was extremely cutting edge. Outpatient surgery and diagnostic centers were just beginning to appear."[24] Scrushy and Beam fantasized about becoming millionaires.[25]

To achieve these ends, in 1984, Scrushy and his fellow managers invested $55,000 in a new company called "AmCare."[26] AmCare eventually changed its name to HealthSouth in 1985. Scrushy poached various clients from his former company, LifeMark, and as a result, he was able to make a profit in his very first month of doing business. By 1986, Scrushy had $20 million in profits, and HealthSouth became a publicly traded company.

As Beam indicates, Scrushy's path to tremendous profits within two years was due to massive risk taking and expansion. Scrushy built many new rehab hospitals and outpatient centers in new locations in Alabama, costing phenomenal amounts of capital.[27] While start-up costs were great, at this time, outpatient facilities could generate $1 million to $2 million annually and in-patient hospital facilities could generate $10 million annually, providing incentive for the growth.[28]

A Gluttonous Appetite for More

In leading HealthSouth, Scrushy motivated his employees by comparing their work to pulling a heavy wagon for the benefit of the team. In fact, t-shirts were made with stick figures pulling the HealthSouth "wagon."

Employees at HealthSouth were aware that they had to do whatever was necessary to pull their share of the HealthSouth wagon.[29]

Scrushy would not accept failure—not personal failure, and not failure from any of his employees. After the public offering, Health-South stock soared, and Scrushy quickly capitalized on his newfound success. In October 1987, HealthSouth stock was trading at $16, up from $6.50 from a year prior.[30] This jump in company stock fueled Scrushy's taste for lavish goods. Even in the early stages of the company, Scrushy had an insatiable desire for personal wealth and power. Beam states:

> Richard loved nice things, and as his wealth quickly accumu-
> lated as a result of his business success, so did his playthings.
> Richard loved fast cars and airplanes. At one time, he had nearly
> forty automobiles, including a $250,000 Lamborghini, and ten
> homes, including a $10 million, 11,000 square foot Palm Beach,
> Florida mansion.[31]

Scrushy became an expert in facilitating corporate waste with his newfound company profits. By 1995, he had purchased a "fleet" of ten private jets valued at $25 million apiece, complete with stewardesses and chefs.[32] When he wasn't in his jets navigating the friendly skies, Scrushy would race his Lamborghini on local highways.[33]

Tasting the fruits of what money, success, and power could buy in a very short period of time, Scrushy became insatiable. He wanted more—and no merger, quarterly profit, or new hospital could satisfy his gluttonous urges. Beam said, "In my estimation with all of this compensation, Richard was worth $100,000,000 by the early 1990s. But he became greedy. Even with all of this wealth, he still wanted more, he was never satisfied."[34]

The "wagon" had to be pulled to the brink.

The Rapid Expansion of HealthSouth

In the early days of HealthSouth, venture capitalists helped finance the company's operations. As time wore on, these same venture capitalists helped fuel HealthSouth's extraordinary growth by finding Scrushy deals at "ground floor company prices."[35]

Scrushy learned fast. Soon, he was finding companies like Capstone Capital & Med partners for pennies on the dollar.[36] In September 1989, he bought another young hospital with lots of upside: South Highlands Hospital in Birmingham, Alabama.[37] The famous and respected doctors Larry Lemark and James Andrews practiced out of this hospital, which increased HealthSouth's visibility and respect in the community.

From 1989 to 1997, HealthSouth grew exponentially. In 1989, the company owned 8 inpatient rehabilitation hospitals, and by 1997, this number reached 104.[38]

HealthSouth first focused on expanding its existing hospitals, starting new facilities, or buying small hospitals on the cheap. This strategy resulted in $500,000,000 in profits by 1994. Yet Scrushy was not satisfied with this terrific growth and he continued to want more.

Beginning in 1994, Scrushy pushed the HealthSouth wagon forward on a groundbreaking, rapid, expansion scheme. In January 1994, he purchased 73 facilities from National Medical Enterprises. This nearly doubled the size of HealthSouth and, in turn, its revenue. Later, in 1994, the company bought out the company Relife for $220 million, and only one year later, HealthSouth acquired Surgical Health Corporation for $155 million.

Then, on February 7, 1995, Scrushy announced that HealthSouth was buying NovaCare's entire rehabilitation hospital division for $235 million. NovaCare consisted of 11 rehabilitation hospitals in seven different states and 12 other rehabilitation facilities. The NovaCare deal increased HealthSouth's operations to over 450 sites.[39]

HealthSouth was growing rapidly and soon dominated its industry. The company was entering new business sectors and locations, and revenue. In 1995, HealthSouth was now grossing $1.6 billion annually. "We were devouring our competition at an alarming rate," Beam stated. "However, digesting them was another story."[40]

HealthSouth's business strategy was to buy out their competition to drive up revenue as quickly as possible. Scrushy's ravenous appetite for excess was driving the company's wagon of growth and profits. Nonetheless, the firm failed to efficiently consolidate, maintain internal controls, and have any semblance of risk management.

A man who was serving wine and cheese out of his trailer only ten years ago, with no business experience, was now leading a $1.6 billion company on a path to destruction. Scrushy was firmly committed to taking whatever actions were necessary, legal or not, to maintain the firm's profits, meet industry expectations, and satisfy his own insatiable appetite for private jets, expensive sports cars, and other material goods.

Fraud, Intimidation, and Corruption to Meet Expectations

Scrushy failed to concern himself with the logistics of accounting for HealthSouth's rapid and exponential growth. In 1990, the firm had 3,500 employees; by the end of 1995, HealthSouth had over 22,500.[41] Beam stated that during this period, the assimilation of all of these companies from an accounting point of view was "horrendous. However, you would have been considered out of your mind to suggest to Richard that the company should slow its growth for accounting purposes."[42]

Scrushy was still the trailer park student living his well-crafted dream. He did not want to wake up, ever. Accordingly, as the SEC concluded in its complaint against HealthSouth, "Shortly after HRC became publicly traded in 1986, and at Scrushy's instruction, the company began to artificially inflate its earnings to match Wall Street analysts' expectations and maintain the market price for HRC's [HealthSouth's] stock."[43]

"Richard simply could not bear the thought of the stock dropping significantly," Beam explained. "Our same store growth was not as good as we were leading people to believe . . . This happened because we were making our core business with these mergers . . . Some might say it was like putting lipstick on a pig . . . "[44] Beam further stated that he "sincerely believed" investors knew what was going on, as did the "Street."[45]

To effectuate this accounting fraud, HealthSouth senior officers met on a quarterly basis and presented Scrushy with an earnings report. The officers would then compare these earnings to Wall Street's expectations.[46]

If HealthSouth earnings fell short of Wall Street expectations, Scrushy would demand his accounting personnel "fix" the problem by fudging the company's earnings to investors.[47] By 1997, accounting personnel referred to these meetings as "family meetings" amongst "family members."[48]

Under the direction of Scrushy, in these meetings HealthSouth accounting personnel conspired to falsify accounting entries for the purpose of matching Wall Street analyst expectations.[49] The SEC explains that these entries usually included reducing a contra revenue account, called "contractual adjustment," or deceptively decreasing expenses and correspondingly increasing assets or decreasing liabilities.[50]

The "contractual adjustment account" was a revenue allowance account that HealthSouth used to estimate the difference between the gross amounts billed to a specific patient and the amount that an insurance company would pay for the service. HealthSouth accountants were masterful at deducting this account from gross revenues, to derive "net revenues," which eventually became the improper amounts disclosed to the SEC and markets.[51]

Moreover, HealthSouth senior accounting personnel knowingly recorded false accounting statements to the "fixed asset" books of its numerous subsidiaries under pressure from Scrushy himself.[52] Scrushy pressured his most senior accountants to continually fabricate records. By 2002, the fraud had reached extraordinary levels. In the third quarter alone of 2002, HealthSouth allegedly overstated company income by $800 million.[53]

Intimidation, Suicide, Guns, and Grenades: All Part of the HealthSouth Wagon

On November 5, 2003, Scrushy was arrested on 85 different charges of falsifying the HealthSouth books of over $2.7 billion in assets. Scrushy was the first CEO to be charged under the new Sarbanes–Oxley legislation, which requires CEOs and CFOs to certify company financial statements as accurate and holds them criminally liable for any falsehoods within the documents.

Only a week after Scrushy's arrest, government witnesses came forward in sentencing testimony suggesting that HealthSouth was run similar to a paramilitary organization replete with expensive guns, grenades, and spy equipment.[54]

Government witness Emery Harris, a former assistant controller at HealthSouth, indicated that he was afraid to report the ongoing accounting fraud because of massive invoices he saw for weapons, small cameras hidden in plants, car-tracking devices, and disguises with wigs.[55]

"There was a tremendous amount of intimidation," he said.

With orders from senior managers who were taking their marching orders from Scrushy, Harris said he told the others to make bogus entries on accounting ledgers on orders from senior managers.[56]

Harris testified he approached two superiors in August 2002 on behalf of himself and the four women. His major concern was over the passage of Sarbanes–Oxley. He no longer wanted to participate in the knowing fraud, despite the obvious fear over the potential consequences.[57]

"It became apparent to us that anyone who participated in any fraud . . . could be held liable," said Harris.[58] Subsequent to Harris's meetings, Scrushy and other top HealthSouth officers sought to clean up the books without detection, yet at this point it was too late.

FBI personnel investigated the suicide of William Massey Jr., Scrushy's personal accountant. Shortly after Scrushy's arrest, Massey managed Marin Inc., an umbrella company for Scrushy's financial interests.[59]

Coincidence or not, the day after Massey's suicide, Scrushy sold $25 million of his shares in HealthSouth.[60]

From the Trailer Park to Corporate Jet to Jail

In 2004, Scrushy was charged with 36 of the original 85 counts brought against him. However, a jury later acquitted him of all criminal charges on June 28, 2005.

This was a major failure for prosecutors, and the first time the defense of "I didn't know" worked in a major securities fraud case. Nonetheless, on June 29, 2007, Scrushy was sentenced to seven years in prison for bribing the governor of Alabama for a seat on the state's hospital regulatory board.

Scrushy is currently serving the rest of his seven-year sentence. Countless other HealthSouth officials, including former CFO Aaron Beam, were jailed to various sentences pertaining to the fraud.

Today, HealthSouth is an operating company and is composed of over 1,800 facilities in all 50 states, the United Kingdom, Australia, Saudi Arabia, and Puerto Rico.

Bernie Ebbers and WorldCom

On August 27, 1941, Bernard Ebbers was born in Alberta, Canada, the second of five children. In the late 1940s, his family moved to California, where his father got a job as an auto mechanic. Soon after, the Ebbers family moved to New Mexico, where Ebbers attended school on a Navajo Indian reservation while his father worked as a mechanic.[61]

Ebbers' father's career took the family back to Edmonton, and Ebbers enrolled in the University of Alberta. By his own admission, Ebbers was a very poor student. He dropped out of Alberta because his "marks weren't good" and thereafter transferred to Calvin College.[62] But Ebbers lasted only two years there because "My marks were not as good as they should have been, and I didn't know exactly what I wanted to do at that time, or just a little confused about my major."[63]

After dropping out of college twice, Ebbers was recruited to play basketball at Mississippi College, a small Baptist school in Jackson. In between schools, Ebbers worked as a milkman and a bar bouncer. He eventually graduated with a degree in physical education. Ebbers did not take any advanced classes in economics, business, or accounting, only a preliminary course in economics.[64] His first jobs out of college were a basketball coach at Mississippi and a local hotel owner and investor.[65]

Ebbers' Big Break in Telecom

In 1983, by chance, Ebbers met a group of investors who came to central Mississippi to cash in on the federally mandated breakup of AT&T.[66] By this time, Ebbers had made some impact as a hotel investor as he grew his hotel management work into a collection of Best Westerns throughout Mississippi and Texas. Working out of a company called the Master Corporation, Ebbers acquired local car dealerships, seeking profits.[67]

In a quiet restaurant in Hattiesburg, Mississippi, Ebbers and the group of investors drew up plans for a new telecom company, to be called Long Distance Discount Services (LDDS), on a napkin.

This chance meeting was the switch that turned on Ebbers' insatiable greed. "He was the most focused leader I'd ever seen," said Murray Waldron, one of Ebbers' original LDDS partners.[68]

LDDS did not fare well in 1984, its first year of operations. The company began with 200 customers but lacked institutional telecom knowledge, expertise, and equipment. Accordingly, LDDS decided to invest in enhanced infrastructure, equipment, and training services for its personnel. By the end of 1984, the company was in debt of $1.5 million.

To reverse the company's fortunes, LDDS turned to Ebbers. Ebbers swiftly made the company profitable through cost-saving initiatives and smart strategic planning. Ebbers focused LDDS on the small business customers neglected by the telecom giants AT&T and MCI.[69]

Like Scrushy, Ebbers was not content to manage a small southern company. He had a never-ending desire for more. Around 1987, Ebbers embarked on a bold expansion strategy where LDDS bought other small, competing telecom companies, absorbed their customers, and used LDDS's cheap infrastructure to please its customers.[70]

The Beginning of Ebbers' Telecom Universe

Scott D. Sullivan was Ebbers' righthand man until the end. He was the prototypical behind-the-scenes guy—the technical CFO who helped Ebbers expand, grow, and reach heights he had never dreamed of as a physical education teacher and hotel operator in a sleepy small town in Mississippi.

A former General Electric executive and KPMG accountant, Sullivan was astute with numbers, and a counter to Ebbers slick-talking, in-your-face personality.[71] Sullivan not only developed the accounting fraud with Ebbers side by side, he helped sell LDDS and, thereafter, WorldCom's rapid acquisitions to clients, and future shareholders of the company.

In 1987, Ebbers made his first major acquisition with an aim to gain credibility to bring the rising telecom company public. Ebbers bought Telemarketing Communications of Mississippi Inc. (TMC) for

$2 million in March of 1987, which was a major provider of long-distance services with locations in Indiana, Kentucky, and Alabama. It was the perfect strategic decision to build LDDS's capabilities and market power.

Ebbers used extreme leverage and debt financing to make these deals work. This would be a pattern. Ebbers was fully committed to financing his gluttonous appetite by whatever means necessary. Ebbers consummated 75 acquisitions in 15 years.

"Nobody wanted to borrow more money or encourage more debt," said Danny M. Dunnaway, a top executive at LDDS at the time. "Bernie took a big risk and mortgaged everything he had to buy TMC outright."[72]

Ebbers used the same debt-financing firm he had used to finance his hotel deals. Through these transactions he increased his shares and control of the company, which went hand in hand with his own profits.

In June 1987, LDDS acquired Southland System of Mississippi Inc., a long-distance telecommunications reseller in Jackson, Mississippi, to increase the companies' dominance in the South and Midwest.[73] To finance this deal and others, Chicago-based Heller Financial provided more debt financing in the form of $50 million.[74]

With this massive injection of capital, LDDS had the necessary funds to facilitate the company's breadth of services and, in turn, increase revenue. By 1989, the growing number of LDDS subsidiaries provided long-distance telecommunications services in nine states in the South and Midwest. Yet, Ebbers grew even more gluttonous in his pursuit of corporate expansion.

In 1989, LDDS bought the public company Advantage Companies, Inc., which was on the brink of massive bankruptcy. Advantage was known more for its publishing and hotel business than its telecom divisions. For Ebbers, it was a quick and easy way to go public and spend the extraordinary money loaned to him.[75]

From Regional to International Telecom Powerhouse

Under the control of Ebbers, LDDS grew at an extremely rapid pace during the early 1990s. In 1992, it was one of the largest regional long-distance companies in the United States and had increased its scope to

27 states. The company reported annual revenues of $948 million in 1992.[76]

Scott Sullivan, a future CFO of WorldCom and confidant of Ebbers, became an assistant treasurer with LDDS at this time.

In 1993, LDDS became a national provider of long-distance telecommunication services by means of a three-way merger between LDDS, Metromedia Communications Corp (MCC), and Resurgens Communications Group, Inc.[77] Purchasing MCC provided LDDS with a national long-distance provider that increased its customer base dramatically.

Only a year later, LDDS acquired the company IDB Communications Group (IDB), the fourth-largest international telecommunications provider at the time, which provided the firm with even greater exposure. The transaction was valued at $936 million.

Like Scrushy, Ebbers cared only about expansion, completely disregarding the complex and intricate accounting necessary to manage billion-dollar deals that were drastically changing the face of the company. In fact, after changing its name to WorldCom, LDDS next bought Williams Technology Group for $2.5 billion.[78] At the end of 1995, newly minted WorldCom reported $3.8 billion in total revenue.

In 1997 and 1998, WorldCom completed its most famous acquisition. Ebbers was proud to consummate a $40 billion merger with MCI, which was the largest ever of its kind. The company changed its name to MCI WorldCom, increasing its local services to over 100 domestic markets.

In October 1999, WorldCom and Ebbers continued their push for more. The company announced another landmark deal with its chief competitor, Sprint. The regulatory community finally took notice. Eyebrows were raised. Ebbers' passion for eating up rival companies had reached its limits. The US Department of Justice blocked the merger and launched an investigation into the financial accounting carnival that was Ebbers' WorldCom.

Culture of Fraud, Negligence, and Insatiable Greed

The telecommunications industry on the whole suffered significant downturns at the turn of the century because of the dot-com bubble.

WorldCom was not spared. Its stock dropped from $96 on June 30, 1999, to $46 on June 30, 2000.[79] By the end of the third quarter 2000, WorldCom's revenue had decreased dramatically while its expenses had increased. Ebbers' ravenous personal growth agenda was uncompromising, and it resulted in the downfall of WorldCom.

To fuel his expensive tastes and insatiable desire for personal goods, Ebbers took the only strategy he knew to accumulate wealth—borrow. Ebbers borrowed over $400 million from banks as of 2000 and used his WorldCom stock as the collateral to secure these loans.[80] He purchased a ranch, timberlands, and a yacht-building company.

Unconscionably, Ebbers directed WorldCom to be the entity liable for these personal debts, resulting in massive exposure for the company.[81] This transaction breached his fiduciary duties as CEO to protect the property of WorldCom's shareholders. It would soon get worse.

After poor third-quarter results, CFO Scott Sullivan advised Ebbers that the company had failed to meet Wall Street's quarterly expectations and, accordingly, Ebbers should preemptively issue a warning to investors.

Ebbers refused. "We have to hit our numbers," he sternly advised Sullivan. To meet his CEO's desires, Sullivan instructed other accountants to increase the publicly reported revenues by adding $133 million in anticipated "underusage penalties" to the revenue calculation, even though he knew these millions of dollars were nonexistent.[82]

Sullivan then advised Ebbers that the company's line cost expenses would be $1 billion more than expected. Ebbers maintained that the company had no other option other than to hit its quarterly earnings estimates, and that this number was unacceptable. Accordingly, Sullivan fabricated line cost expenses' reserve numbers, which lowered the line costs by $828 million. This overstated the company's earnings by that amount.[83]

In the fourth quarter, WorldCom suffered from similar financial performance declines. Ebbers again refused to release the true financial results of the company. Sullivan conspired with other accountants to hide over $800 million in quarterly losses. The WorldCom 2000 annual report and 10-k included this false and deceitful financial information.[84]

Ebbers steadfastly refused to recognize company losses. He did not want his gravy train of profits to dissipate. Nonetheless, in the first quarter of 2001, WorldCom's fortunes continued to dwindle. At quarter end, Ebbers told Sullivan once again that "we have to grow our revenue and we have to cut our expenses, but we have to hit our numbers this quarter."[85] Ebbers demanded that Sullivan change the format of line cost figures to hide continuing losses.

Notably, in Ebbers' first-quarter conference call of 2001, the CEO, consumed by his own insatiable desire, stated that there were no storms on the horizon and urged his investors to "go out and buy stock."[86]

To continue the accounting fraud, Sullivan, Ebbers, and a handful of other executives created a new program called "Close the Gap" to "get [the] operating performance . . . up to the market guidance expectations" by finding new items to include in revenue.[87]

Sullivan informed Ebbers that there was no proper means for including many of the ideas expressed in the "Close the Gap" program in reported revenues. In a voicemail to Ebbers, Sullivan described some of the items eventually included in reported revenues as "accounting fluff," "one-time stuff," and "junk."[88]

Yet, Ebbers did nothing to assuage his concerns. He was dedicated to taking whatever action, no matter how fraudulent and illegal, to keep his company's profits, revenue, and personal desires afloat.

The Fraud Continues—and Then Unravels

In the third quarter of 2001, WorldCom's revenue growth rate had diminished to around 5.5 percent. Yet, again, Ebbers issued false information to markets, representing that the revenue growth rate was 12 percent. Hiding the downturn, Ebbers stated that WorldCom had delivered "excellent growth this quarter," despite that he had internally missed expectations by hundreds of millions over the past year.[89]

At this point, Ebbers was desperate and looking for a way out. He engaged Verizon in merger negotiations but grew concerned that Verizon would uncover his accounting fraud. He immediately called off discussions in the summer of 2001.

Similarly, Ebbers kept his own board in the dark. Despite calls for transparency, Ebbers ensured that the board members were unaware of his massive accounting fraud, until it was too late. For instance, the

"Close the Gap" program was never included in any board of director meetings while Ebbers was CEO.[90]

At the end of the fourth quarter of 2001, Ebbers and Sullivan hid $1 billion in costs. On the fourth-quarter earnings conference call, Ebbers assured investors that "[w]e stand by our accounting," and later said in a CNBC interview that "[w]e've been very conservative on our accounting."[91]

Finally, Ebbers' scheme to deceive shareholders, markets, and himself unraveled. In the first quarter of 2002, his accountants could no longer fraudulently adjust revenue expectations to meet investor expectations. WorldCom for first time announced its results fell short of Wall Street expectations.[92]

In March 2002, the SEC was quickly learning about Ebbers' fraudulent activities, and word began to spread on the Street that WorldCom was an accounting mess. At the end of April 2002, WorldCom's board asked Ebbers to resign, which he did on April 29, 2002.

Only a month after his departure, WorldCom's internal audit department learned of the accounting fraud. Sullivan was thereafter fired, and WorldCom disclosed the fraud to the public on June 25, 2002. Subsequently, WorldCom's stock collapsed, losing 90 percent of its value, and the company filed for bankruptcy.[93]

Ebbers was eventually convicted in March 2005 of $11 billion worth of criminal accounting fraud. He was sentenced to 25 years in jail. WorldCom was the biggest accounting fraud of a decade defined by Enron, Tyco, Adelphia, and other corporate scandals.

Still, despite his obvious criminality in orchestrating the accounting fraudulence, Ebbers remained unrepentant. At the time, he told CNN he thinks he was treated unfairly and that his situation was "completely bizarre."[94]

Blunting Future Accounting Fraud

The cases of HealthSouth and WorldCom are illustrative of the human condition overtaken by insatiable greed and an overwhelming desire to commit illegality for personal gain. This correlates with the loss of virtue espoused by theologian Thomas Aquinas.

Richard Scrushy's and Bernie Ebbers' rise to power was categorized by rapid expansion. The CEOs ate up companies through mergers without due diligence or long-term strategic planning. By merging with companies to boost profits rather than to benefit their firm's long-term value, the CEOs abused their fiduciary duties to shareholders.

This expansion resulted in accounting chaos, but this did not matter to Scrushy and Ebbers. The end game was stock price, appeasing Wall Street expectations through fraud, and deceiving shareholders of the overall performance of the company. Company funds were used as backstops to personal loans in order to please the inordinate wants of these all-powerful CEOs. The corporate ownership structure held no credibility.

In looking back on what we can learn from the two most heinous accounting frauds in the modern era, it is clear that governance, internal controls, and whistleblower incentives are critical tools to fight against out-of-control, gluttonous CEOs. Corporate gluttony is a dangerous problem, and it is up to our public and private institutions to mount proper defenses.

Notes

1. See *Merriam-Webster* Dictionary.
2. Jack Healy, "Richard Scrushy, Ex-Chief of Health South, Loses Civil Suit," *The New York Times,* June 18, 2009, www.nytimes.com/2009/06/19/business/ 19scrushy.html.
3. Ibid.
4. Ibid.
5. Aaron Beam, *HealthSouth: The Wagon to Disaster* (Fairhope, AL: Wagon Publishing, 2009), p. 12.
6. Marin Wolk, "From Bouncer to Billionaire Ebbers took unorthodox path," MSNBC, www.msnbc.msn.com/id/7080668/ns/business-corporate_scandals/t/ bouncer-billionaire-ebbers-took-unorthodox-path/#.TrbbE0-nRQk.
7. John Helyar, "The Insatiable King Richard," *Fortune,* July 7, 2003, money.cnn .com/magazines/fortune/fortune_archive/2003/07/07/345534/index.htm.
8. Beam, p. 17.
9. Helyar.
10. Ibid.
11. Ibid.

12. Ibid.
13. "Richard M. Scrushy, Outstanding Alumni Award," American Association of Community Colleges, http://www.aacc.nche.edu/About/Awards/oaa/Pages/rmscrushy.aspx.
14. Beam, p. 17.
15. Ibid.
16. Helyar.
17. Beam, p. 18.
18. Helyar.
19. Beam, p. 19.
20. Ibid.
21. Ibid.
22. Ibid., p. 21.
23. Ibid., p. 31.
24. Ibid., p. 30.
25. Ibid., p. 34.
26. Serge Matulich and David M. Currie, *Handbook of Frauds, Scams, and Swindles, Failures of Ethics in Leadership* (CRC Press, Boca Raton 2008), p. 339.
27. Beam, p. 38.
28. Ibid.
29. Ibid.
30. Ibid., p. 53.
31. Ibid., p. 51.
32. Ibid.
33. Ibid.
34. Ibid., p. 54.
35. Ibid., p. 53.
36. Ibid., p. 54.
37. Ibid.
38. B. Wheatley, G. De Jong, and J. Sutton, "Consolidation of the Inpatient Medical Rehabilitation Industry, *Health Affairs*, 17, no. 3 (1998): 209–215.
39. "Company News, HealthSouth to Acquire NovaCare Unit," *The New York Times*, February 7, 1995.
40. Beam, p. 53.
41. Ibid., p. 56.
42. Ibid.
43. *SEC v. HealthSouth Corporation & Richard Scrushy*, CV-03-J-0615-S, U.S. District Court of Alabama, 2003.
44. Beam, p. 58.
45. Ibid.
46. Ibid.
47. Ibid.
48. Ibid.

49. Ibid.
50. Ibid.
51. Ibid.
52. Ibid.
53. Ibid.
54. Associated Press, "HealthSouth Staff Claims Intimidation," *St. Petersburg Times*, November, 13, 2003, www.sptimes.com/2003/11/13/Business/HealthSouth_staff_cla.shtml.
55. Ibid.
56. Ibid.
57. Ibid.
58. Ibid.
59. Milt Freudenheim, "HealthSouth Inquiry Looks For Accounts Held Offshore," *The New York Times*, March 31, 2003.
60. Helyar.
61. "Bernard Ebbers," *The Wall Street Journal*, online.wsj.com/public/resources/documents/info-life-bebbers-frame.html.
62. "In His Own Words: Ebbers Takes the Stand," *The Wall Street Journal*, March 2, 2005 http://online.wsj.com/article/0,,SB110970605076867314,00.html.
63. Ibid.
64. Ibid.
65. Ibid.
66. Tim Padgett, "The Rise and Fall of Bernie Ebbers," *Time*, May 5, 2002.
67. Om Malik, *Broadbandits: Inside the $750 billion Telecom Heist* (Hoboken, NJ: John Wiley & Sons, 2003).
68. Padgett.
69. Malik, p. 5.
70. Ibid., p. 6.
71. Ibid., p. 7.
72. Lynne W. Jeter, *Disconnected: Deceit and Betrayal at WorldCom* (Hoboken, NJ: John Wiley & Sons, 2003), p. 36.
73. Ibid., p. 39.
74. Ibid., p. 39.
75. Ibid., p. 43.
76. In *Re World Com, Southern District of New York*, United States Bankruptcy Court, Chapter 11 Case No. 02–155533.
77. Ibid.
78. Ibid.
79. Ibid.
80. *U.S. v. Bernie Ebbers, United States Court of Appeals*, Second Circuit. July 28, 2006 Docket No. 05–4059 CR.
81. Ibid.
82. Ibid.

83. Ibid.
84. Ibid.
85. Ibid.
86. Ibid.
87. Ibid.
88. Ibid.
89. Ibid.
90. Ibid.
91. Ibid.
92. Ibid.
93. Ibid.
94. Krysten Crawford, "Ebbers Gets 25 Years," CNN, September 23, 2005, money.cnn.com/2005/07/13/news/newsmakers/ebbers_sentence/.

Part Two

RECOMMENDATIONS

*T*his section of the book identifies solutions to problems deeply embedded in global markets, corporate cultures, and interpersonal business dealings. The recommendations are designed to provide a roadmap for an essential return to ethics, virtue, trust, and sustainable global economic growth. They are market based but require major changes on all fronts.

The targeted goal must be to rebuild the international bridges of economic vitality, increase competition, develop investor trust in the banking system, and focus on our own ethical awareness as citizens.

There exists an overwhelming and systemic need to overcome economic vice with virtue. Restoration of shareholder trust in the corporate modality is imperative so that free markets and people everywhere can prosper.

Chapter 9

Why Financial Regulation Has Failed, and What to Do about It

D etailed below are various shortcomings of recent financial regulation, with recommended solutions to make the global financial system safer for investors and other market participants.

The Failed Promises of Dodd–Frank

July 21, 2010, was the day of a supposed new order.

A new era of progressive Dodd–Frank legislation intended to prevent financial crisis, fraud, and the collapse of global economic institutions. Upon signing the legislation, President Barack Obama's comments were exceedingly rosy.

The president envisioned the statute as the cure for all of Wall Street's perceived ills:

> This reform will help foster innovation, not hamper it. It is designed to make sure that everybody follows the same set of rules, so that firms compete on price and quality, not on tricks and not on traps. It demands accountability and responsibility from everyone. It provides certainty to everybody, from bankers to farmers to business owners to consumers . . .
>
> So, all told, these reforms represent the strongest consumer financial protections in history. (Applause.) In history. And these protections will be enforced by a new consumer watchdog with just one job: looking out for people—not big banks, not lenders, not investment houses—looking out for people as they interact with the financial system.[1]

Unfortunately for President Obama, Congress, economists, and others who helped draft the bill, Dodd–Frank has done little to shun the interests of "big banks" and look out for "people." So far, the legislation has not enhanced the way business is conducted on a global scale. Dodd–Frank's solutions fail to develop pragmatic and expedient solutions for tangible reform, better regulation, and governance.

Contrary to the signing statement and subsequent political "spin," the legislation provides no means to salvage long-forgotten economic virtues, foster competition and growth, and build personal bonds of trust international markets rest upon.

Examples abound as to why Dodd–Frank regulations have not yet met their lofty purpose. For instance, where were its proverbial teeth when Jon Corzine lost many billions of customer and shareholder capital?

Similarly, how did it protect against a mini MF Global in the collapse of Peregrine Financial? What risk mitigation strategies were in place to curtail JP Morgan's billions of trading losses in the spring of 2012? How did Dodd–Frank change the executive-fueled greed that allowed Libor manipulation to exist and prosper to the detriment of investors all around the world?

Certainly, Dodd–Frank has not been fully implemented as we write this book in the fall of 2012. The full effect is not yet known. However, one thing is known. In the past two years, nothing has been done to materially alter a dysfunctional corporate culture of systemic vice.

Indeed, profits continue to be made on risky bets, gambling mentalities, and exotic synthetic derivative products. Worse, jumbo banks still enjoy the promise of "too big to fail." There is no risk or threat of capitulation.

As will be explained in this chapter, Dodd–Frank's provisions only cement the guarantee that "big banks" will always prosper and exist, regardless of the harm they inflict on their shareholders and international markets.

Alarmingly, there is no competition. Remember Bear Stearns? Remember Lehman Brothers? These investment banks were strong competitors to JP Morgan and Goldman Sachs. Now, they no longer exist. Supercharged banks enjoy a heavily consolidated market where only a small handful of firms can operate. These banks, "too big to fail," operate undisturbed, without the threat of intense competition from upstart rivals.

In any relevant market, competition is essential to push companies toward innovation, shareholder-friendly policies, and continued prosperity. Today, only a select few banks can offer commercial and investment services on an international scale. This blunts competition.

In fact, massive banking institutions conduct business similar to the oil trusts of the early 1900s. There is little (if anything) to prevent them from being unethical, falling prey to economic vice, and ultimately losing money. They are simply too big to fail.

The Libor scandal, JP Morgan "whale trading loss," MF Global bankruptcy, and the many disasters of the credit crisis show that it is almost a near certainty that international jumbo banks cannot and will not rein themselves in when there is money to be made or illustrious careers to be forged. Personal egos, greed, envy, and a gluttonous appetite for more—regardless of the price to shareholders, investors, and society as a whole—provide irresistible temptations.

Today, markets remain a very scary place for institutional investors, shareholders, brokers, and other market participants. As a more international, globalized society, we have become immunized to fraud. We can only ask ourselves, when will be the next Libor? When will be the next collapse? This dismal attitude has been the result of out-of-control greed, as has been popularly documented by a slew of authors, academics, and analysts.

In layman's terms, there exists a lack of guts among anyone with the power to make a difference, including global leaders, parliaments, and administrative agencies.

Our politicians lack the conviction to truly rid our markets of economic vice. In many instances, they are part of the problem. For example, during the 2012 Republican primary, Former Governor Tim Pawlenty proudly emphasized, "I went to Wall Street and told them to get their snout out of the trough because they are some of the worst offenders when it comes to bailouts and carve-outs and special deals."[2] Incredibly, financial journalist Andrew Ross Sorkin reported in the fall of 2012 that Pawlenty accepted a position as president of the Financial Services Roundtable, one of Wall Street's most influential lobbying organizations.[3] The self-professed enemy of Wall Street will now potentially earn $1.8 million annually trying to convince lawmakers that those "carve-outs and special deals" really are beneficial for the nation's banking system.[4]

Globally, regulators have failed to acknowledge that Wall Street (i.e., investment banking) has morphed into a vast Las Vegas–style casino. Except in this dysfunctional casino of unbridled risk and excess, there are no friends looking over your shoulder telling you to "tap out," and no "pit bosses" regulating the hubris and greed of its players.

The cases presented in this book show that the "pit bosses" (i.e., the federal government and regulators) have stood idly by while Wall Street has continued its diseased casino culture of economic vice. No "pit boss" has had the fortitude to force a Wall Street high roller to fold his hand.

We find an elixir to our culture of economic vice in a distant relative of the co-author of this book. Indeed, President Theodore Roosevelt is an excellent example of how virtue, passion, and an intense desire to reform a broken system can fundamentally change international business for the better.

Roosevelt became president in September 1901. Similar to now, the nation was rebounding from an intense depression, "The Panic of 1893," which lingered for four long years. Despite the nation's depression, this was an era in which gigantic business trusts virtually controlled the entire global economy. The divide between rich and poor was deep. Exploitation, greed, and hubris were at an all-time high. Rather than believing that virtue, ethics, and reform were unattainable goals, Roosevelt's conviction moved him to emphasize that there are "real and grave evils" in need of correction.

To the shock of the business community, Roosevelt did not play by pre-established rules. A famous example is Roosevelt's suit against J. P. Morgan. J. P. Morgan was one of Roosevelt's most generous donors. The president let his ethical compass control policy. J. P. Morgan controlled an empire. In addition to U.S. Steel, Morgan controlled General Electric, Western Union, Aetna, the Pullman Car Company, the British Leyland Steamship lines, and some 21 railroads. The US government filed suit against Morgan's Northern Securities Corporation for anti-competitive behavior in 1902.

Legend has it that Morgan pleaded with Roosevelt late one night to renege on his lawsuit to break up his business empire based on trust conglomerates. "If we have done anything wrong," Morgan said, "send your man to my man and we can fix it up." Roosevelt replied, "that can't be done."[5]

In addition to the J. P. Morgan lawsuit, Roosevelt's administration brought 44 actions against trusts to enforce the terms of the Sherman Antitrust Act, which had previously been laxly enforced. These lawsuits, in conjunction with reform-minded legislation, harnessed the vice of an era, created distinct rules of the game, and reenergized the American economy through competition and virtue-based capitalism.

In our new era of diseased corporate culture, the world is in need of a new-styled Roosevelt.

The New Rules of the Game that Reinforce Vice

Boom and bust economic cycles are typical to free markets. They always have been and always will be.

However, what makes this bust cycle different from all others is that federal and state corporate regulations, including Dodd–Frank, have only worked to encourage greed, the moral hazard mentality, "too big to fail," and inefficient capital markets. In fact, the International Monetary Fund (IMF) wrote in September 2012, as part of its Global

Financial Stability report, that the aftermath of the financial crisis has only resulted in even bigger and more interconnected banking groups and financial institutions.[6]

The failure of anyone with power to enact any meaningful reform was emphasized in the IMF report. "Overall, risks in the financial system remain. Of particular concern are the larger size of financial institutions, the greater concentration and domestic interconnectedness of financial systems, and the continued importance of non-banks in overall intermediation."

July 22, 2012, marked the two-year anniversary of Dodd–Frank legislation. Over the two-year period of its existence, the legislation can only hang its hat on governmental delay, obstruction, and marginal change.

The stated purpose of Dodd–Frank was to "promote the financial stability of the United States by improving accountability and transparency in the financial system, to end 'too big to fail,' to protect the American taxpayer by ending bailouts and to protect consumers from abusive financial services."[7]

This was a very noble cause indeed. However, there are few if any provisions of this legislation that have actually enacted any measures to tackle the root problems of the great credit crisis. The bill sponsors would be hard pressed to present a handful of solutions that have fundamentally changed Wall Street culture for the better. Instead, the legislation only demonstrates the power that lobbying and government can inflict to the detriment of global investors, shareholders, and market participants.

In the summer of 2011, SEC Chairman Mary Schapiro proudly announced that the agency completed "the first stage" of Dodd–Frank implementation. Yet, she also emphasized that the agency needed increased funding to perform its obligations under law. According to Chairman Schapiro's congressional testimony, the SEC's responsibilities are "so significant that they cannot be achieved solely by wringing efficiencies out of the existing budget without also severely hampering our ability to meet our existing responsibilities."[8]

Notably, Dodd–Frank deferred a considerable amount of power to administrative agencies like the SEC and CFTC rather than establishing many private causes of action, "per se" rules of fraud, and straightforward rules of the game, immune from the interpretation of unelected administrative officials.

In practice, delegating authority to governmental agencies has resulted in an extraordinary amount of lobbying to create exemptions, soft rules, and other loopholes to any teeth the regulation has.

Consider the CFTC's announcement of its final vote approving Dodd–Frank definitions and exemptions for the swap market on July 10, 2012. Aside from the fact that it took the agency two years to craft only definitions, the CFTC reported that it estimated 30,000 companies will have an exemption from the rules.[9]

When inactive regulators were part and parcel of the causes of the financial crisis, it seems axiomatic that Dodd–Frank defers to them the power to create rules designed to make our markets safe again. This is a common criticism of the legislation. For example, former FDIC Chairman Bill Isaac explained in a 2012 interview with CNBC:

> I will you that this crisis we went through, financial crisis, did not have to happen. The regulators had every power to deal with institutions that were getting out of line and taking excessive risks. The only issue is, do you have the political will to take action?[10]

Isaac doubts regulators have the political will, conviction, and guts to make a difference—and for good reason. The historical blunders of the SEC provide a window into the world of administrative delays, obstructions, and inaction resulting in investor harm.

The SEC has been the subject of many internal investigations by its own Office of Inspector General (OIG). The OIG has repeatedly uncovered inaction in the face of fraud, in-house pornography scandals, and lack of sophistication to understand complex derivative securities.

Worse, the SEC has historically targeted smaller banks, rather than ambitiously investigating larger institutions that are far more integral to market liquidity. For example, Berkeley Professor Stavros Gadinis published a study in 2012 indicating that the SEC targets smaller broker-dealers instead of bigger banks that hold more money.[11]

"Big firms get different treatment," Gadinis said in an interview. "That could be for many reasons (but) it's not a nice result for the

SEC, which is supposed to be an unbiased regulator of markets . . . Historically, [the SEC] is reluctant to bring cases against individuals connected with big firms. . . ."[12]

Aside from its biases, the SEC has struggled to meet its regulatory purpose and enforce existing rules over the past ten years. Therefore, it remains questionable how the SEC, because of its track record, can be asked to enforce existing rules and new ones with needed voracity.

As explained in the first half of this book, the SEC continually failed to investigate Bernie Madoff. This was despite having repeated warnings of his Ponzi scheme going back for many years. Most agree that apart from Madoff and his accomplices, the SEC shoulders considerable blame for allowing the Ponzi scheme to continue since 1992.

While Madoff is the most famous case of SEC inaction, the OIG in 2010 set forth a report on unconscionable delays in investigating Metromedia International Group, Inc. The OIG investigation revealed that the SEC ignored whistleblower Kevin McLaughlin's complaints over 20 times of false financial reporting, self-dealing, and accounting fraud.[13] The SEC never took any action against Metromedia because the company was later sold and no longer existed as a stand-alone public company.

Another 2010 OIG investigation found that the SEC failed to take action against Westridge Capital Management for fraud, despite "numerous red flags" and warnings.[14] The Westridge fraud resulted in an $815 million loss for the firm's investors, that were mostly institutional pension plans.[15]

The OIG's identification of the SEC's various failures to act when confronted with obvious evidence of fraud is troubling news for the protection of American investors, shareholders, and the implementation and enforcement of Dodd–Frank.

The OIG can investigate and numerous academic papers can be written about their inaction, yet, until the SEC is reformed to achieve its stated purpose of protecting investors, it is difficult to imagine the agency providing a beacon of hope.

To its credit, Dodd–Frank called for the SEC to retain an independent consultant to reform its operations and improve efficiency. Accordingly, the Boston Consulting Group (BCG) has provided 16 "optimization initiative recommendations" designed to change the SEC for the better. The BCG Report urged the SEC to reprioritize its activities, reshape the organization, invest in better infrastructure, and bolster its relationship with self-regulating organizations.[16] Apparently unhappy with BCG, the SEC has engaged the firm Booz Allen Hamilton to do similar work. This additional consulting work has cost $100 to $300 an hour and upward of $1.4 million a month.[17]

How many expensive consultants are needed to develop a path to the agency's necessary reform? Moreover, if the agency needs consultant services of $1.4 million a month, how can it be relied on to efficiently implement Dodd–Frank, safeguard investors, and be the vigilant watchdog that international markets need it to be?

The SEC is not just a government entity suffering from narcolepsy at the wheel. At its core, the organization is ineffectual from top to bottom. For example, *The Wall Street Journal* reported on December 2, 2012, that former SEC Chairman Mary Schapiro obstructed the implementation of the Jumpstart Our Business Startups (JOBS) Act. The legislation is intended to make it easier on smaller businesses to raise much needed capital in a difficult economic climate.[18] According to the *Wall Street Journal*, Schapiro was persuaded by a consumer lobbyist to delay lifting the general solicitation ban called for in the JOBS Act because she did not want to be "tagged with an anti-investor legacy."

Perhaps even worse for the government agency, David Weber, the former chief investigator of the OIG brought a lawsuit against the SEC in November 2012, claiming the SEC retaliated against its own whistleblowers.[19] Weber claims that the former inspector general and his successor Noelle Maloney were sleeping together and that Kotz was also having an affair with victims of the Stanford Financial Ponzi scheme (that the SEC was prosecuting at the time).

These allegations come in the wake of a 2010 study conducted at the request of Sen. Chuck Grassley which found at least 31 SEC employees surfing pornography at work, including one senior attorney who spent up to *eight hours a day* accessing Internet porn.[20] American investors and taxpayers deserve those possibly thousands of hours back. The SEC is not only ineffectual. It is a government bureaucracy awash with selfish motives, obstructionist policies, and out-of-control, knowing, complacency. The SEC's embarrassing scandals and glaring failures during a time of extraordinary financial fraud are a colossal disservice to the American investors the agency is charged to protect by regulatory mandate.

A Dummies' Guide to Save the SEC

The following are some solutions that will cost the SEC far less than expensive consultants.

Like a failed private company, the SEC and CFTC should be fundamentally reorganized. Talent should be retained. Focuses on new employment should be based on passion, conviction, virtue, and broad-based knowledge. The SEC should recruit from global business schools and attract the best talent from private industry. Offering competitive and attractive compensation to new employees rather than wasting millions of dollars on consulting advice that may never be implemented is a must. Investing in the SEC's human capital is paramount.

Additionally, the SEC should form new programs, partnerships, and affiliations with private companies that will encourage the sharing of information on a confidential basis. The agency should create an active, confidential "ethics hotline" straight to the SEC Enforcement division. Think of this as a financial fraud 911 call. Upon receiving whistleblower knowledge, this information should be seriously considered by an enforcement committee.

Any failure to act on whistleblowing information should be documented. An explanation as to the reasons why an investigation was unnecessary will be required. These recommendations are simple and easy, and will improve the agency's operating efficiency.

Moreover, the very will of the SEC must be transformed. Working for the agency must inspire a source of awesome pride and responsibility. Employees must exude the passion in meeting the SEC's purpose to "protect investors and maintain fair, orderly and efficient markets."[21]

The Regulatory Reforms Necessary to Reverse the End of Ethics

The SEC is not alone. The malaise and confusion of financial regulators is an unfortunate pattern in international business. Consider the US Federal Reserve's conference on June 7, 2011. In one of the most glaring examples of governance and regulatory failures, JP Morgan CEO Jamie Dimon asked Ben Bernanke, chairman of the Federal Reserve if the Federal Reserve had considered the cumulative effect of Dodd–Frank rules and regulation on available credit in US markets.

Certainly, this was a fair question to the chairman of the Federal Reserve, Dimon's chief regulator. However, Bernanke's response was startling, to say the least: "Has anybody done a comprehensive analysis of the impact on credit?" Bernanke said. "I can't pretend that anybody really has. You know, it's just too complicated. We don't really have the quantitative tools to do that . . . We are trying to develop rules that make sense, that are consistent with good practice, but which do not unnecessarily impose costs, or unnecessarily constrict credit."[22]

According to Bernanke, the Federal Reserve does not have quantitative tools at his disposal, nor is he able to decide "complicated" issues.

The failure of US financial regulation is not a new phenomenon. The SEC, Congress, and President Clinton succumbed to lobbying pressure and repealed the Glass–Steagall Act in 1999.

Glass–Steagall was a shrewd Great Depression piece of legislation that put in place the famous Chinese wall between US investment banks and traditional depository institutions. The idea was to ensure that super-charged monster bank failure would not cripple US and international markets.

During the latter half of the twenty-first century, Glass–Steagall was continually weakened. The greed of commercial banks drove them to tap into investment bank revenues, profits, and clients. When Glass–Steagall was finally repealed in 1999 by the Gramm–Leach–Biley Act, it set the stage for commercial and investment banks to merge, creating massive banking institutions that were simply "too big to fail"—but when they did, the government and the taxpayers were there to bail them out.

Fast forwarding to 2010, when US regulators were picking up the pieces from the last ten years of failed policies, regulations, and the public's distaste for taxpayer bailouts, one would think that US regulators and legislators would reinstitute the investment and commercial bank Chinese wall and, in the process, safeguard the American public from future systemic risk calamity. Instead, Dodd–Frank abused its own stated purpose of ensuring "too big to fail" was a phenomenon of a lost, bygone era.

Under the guise of financial stability, the US Congress continued the bank holding company model that allows institutions like JP Morgan and Citigroup to operate as gigantic commercial and investment banks regulated by the Fed—an organization that, by its own admission, is unable to quantitatively analyze the consequences of government regulation on available credit.

Dodd–Frank's supposed greatest coup, to protect the American public from bailouts of massive institutions, is the establishment of the Orderly Liquidation Authority (OLA). This Orwellian government bureau is a "bankruptcy alternative" and has the power to seize and dismantle financial institutions that threaten the stability of US and international markets.[23]

The OLA is intended to ensure US financial stability; however, the organization will have little tangible impact on investor security, market chaos, or any eventual bailout. Instead of targeting the real evils of finance today, off-balance-sheet accounting gimmicks, excessive speculation, lack of effective risk management, ethics, and independent governance failures (like rating agencies), the OLA is merely an all-powerful governmental bureau that allows regulators to take over failed companies and put them in receivership for efficient wind-downs.

In deciding whether to appoint the FDIC as receiver through the OLA, the Secretary of the Treasury must determine:

1. that the financial company is in default or in danger of default;
2. that the failure of the financial company and its resolution under otherwise applicable federal or state law (likely referring to the Code) would have serious adverse effects on financial stability in the United States;

3. no viable private sector alternative is available to prevent the default of the financial company;

4. any effect on the claims or interests of creditors, counterparties and shareholders is appropriate;

5. any action under the liquidation authority would avoid or mitigate such adverse effects on the financial system, the cost to the general fund of the Treasury, and the potential to increase excessive risk taking on the part of creditors, counterparties and shareholders;

6. a federal regulatory agency has ordered the financial company to convert all of its convertible debt instruments that are subject to a regulatory order; and

7. the company satisfies the definition of a financial company under the Dodd–Frank Act.[24]

Think about these words. They are scary powers granted to an unelected official (the Secretary of the Treasury) to take over a private entity. Yet, perhaps most strikingly, the legislation seeks to attack economic vice only after the fact.

The legislation assumes that the vices set forth earlier in the book will occur—that businesses are, in fact, bound to fail. What happened to tightening risk controls and governance? Accordingly, the OLA seeks to deal with failed companies that have been the victims of bad corporate behavior. It is dubious whether this organization can even accomplish that.

For example, in a 2012 story in *The New York Times*, Stephen J. Lubben doubts that the Dodd–Frank perceived sword can in reality do any good in winding up bad companies:

> My key concern with O.L.A. is the many ways it pulls a large financial institution apart. Congress could have enacted an insolvency process that was comprehensive, but instead the authority still does not cover key parts of the financial institution. Insurance companies will go into state receiverships, and banks are still subject to separate receiverships under the banking laws.
>
> While these are most often run by the F.D.I.C., they are governed by a distinct set of legal rules. And broker-dealers are subject to a very odd version of the normal Securities

Investor Protection Act process, where the Securities Investor Protection Corporation gets to be trustee of what will likely amount to a bunch of scraps.[25]

Why should the government, through one person, have the power to decide "good and bad" parts of a bank? Moreover, how on earth will a government takeover of a massive company boost market confidence? How will it even prevent the "too big to fail" mindset?

Standard & Poor's provided the answer. On July 13, 2011, the rating agency published a report stating that the OLA will likely not reverse the modern trend of "too big to fail."[26]

The solution to these banks continuing to commit fraud is not to create a Dodd–Frank comfortable safety net for them to lounge in whenever they fall from their cliff of unsustainable risk. Instead, the solution should be to create new rules of the game that inspire market competition, innovation, virtue, and long-term growth.

This is why any new rules of the game or solutions must include the reinstitution of Glass–Steagall. There is no benefit to the American economy when a small handful of banks with a plethora of subsidiaries, all dominated by the same persons. Like the time of Theodore Roosevelt, these jumbo corporations must be intelligently broken up for the betterment of the global economy.

Take the perceived ills of proprietary trading as an example. Proprietary trading is when a company trades on its own account (not that of its clients).

In-house trading was a major cause of the financial crisis because it allowed banks to take on tremendous risk and leverage (sometimes over 40 or 50 times). When trades went bad, firmwide liquidity suffered. Reputations were damaged, shareholders lost money, and investors lost confidence. However, if bank sizes were reduced, proprietary trading would be substantially limited because banks would have less house money to play with.

Like the railroad and oil trusts of the early twentieth century, it only serves the interests of the few to conduct such proprietary trading. It does not benefit the larger economy. In many ways, the gambles of proprietary trading are synonymous with our era of economic vice.

While "busting" the jumbo banks provides a solution, reform of the exotic derivative market is another.

In the private sector, the use of credit default swaps (CDS) have yielded destruction in global markets. If you are not a Wall Street trader, in layman's terms, these instruments are used to provide insurance on deals that have the potential to go sour.

CDS instruments were created by JP Morgan in the late 1990s and are used to hedge risk of default with a counterparty. The CDS demonstrates everything that is wrong in today's capital markets and corporate casino culture.

Capital markets are most efficient when they are based on trust, confidence, and diligence. Longstanding Judeo-Christian values of thrift, responsibility, and good/honest governance have led this country through the Industrial Revolution, Roosevelt's Progressive Era, and the post–World War II economic boom.

However, the CDS itself is essentially an instrument of mistrust. It operates as insurance against a default; a wager that another company will fail. Is this Adam Smith's vision of virtuous business?

Think of the CDS market today as high-rolling gamblers who sit across a table betting on financial destruction. If you need "insurance" on a deal, why agree to do the transaction in the first place? Unfortunately, today's Wall Streeters do not play with fake monopoly money. When the bets go bad, the outcome can be an outright disaster for the market, shareholders, and all global investors.

For instance, in the spring of 2012, Jamie Dimon's JP Morgan, supposedly one of the best-run shops on Wall Street, suffered billions of CDS losses. Because the CDS is a default speculation product, when the gamble proves to be wrong, shareholders are victimized to the tune of dramatic stock drops and exponential losses. JP Morgan's stock lost 24 percent of its value in the month after Dimon disclosed the CDS-related trading loss.[27]

Dodd–Frank could have come out swinging against the CDS product and limited its use in global markets. It could have set in place specific, nonexempt rules that reduced the negative effects CDS can have in reducing market value and liquidity.

However, the regulation only calls for formalistic definitions that mandate some CDS to be centrally "cleared" and traded on an exchange and for other CDS counterparties to post margin and capital requirements.[28] The new CDS regulations are highly beholden to formalistic agency definitions and exemptions.

An estimated 30,000 companies will be exempt from the CFTC Dodd–Frank swap rules.[29]

It is time that financial rules were readable, fair, and universal. CDS rules should not depend on small categories, complex definitions, and exemptions.

In fact, prominent persons in the banking regulatory sector believe that CDS regulations need to be more aggressive. Shelia Bair, former chairperson of the FDIC, recently remarked, "I'd push them [CDS] off the planet. The CDS market is very volatile and very opaque, from a safety and soundness point of view. I'm very uncomfortable with that."[30]

One possible universal solution is to force banks to use CDS at their own peril. For example, mandate a minimum reserve to be taken as a hedge against all potential losses from CDS investments.

Why should there be any exemptions? Regardless of institution size, all investors suffer from CDS risk. Institutions should be required to update their CDS reserve whenever there exists a material change in the bank's CDS investment. This hedge could be monitored, maintained, and audited similar to current rules governing minimum firm-capital requirements.

By taking a mandatory reserve only against CDS, banks would be required to use the speculative product wisely, rather than stubbornly gambling on the risks of default without fear of reprisal. This solution is simple and effective, rather than following the formalistic and exemption-riddled rules of Dodd–Frank.

In the past, financial transactions took place without these complex tools of synthetic insurance. Without the prevalence of the CDS in the market, deals will be more thoughtful, deliberated, and virtuous.

Shares of JP Morgan declined more than 24 percent the month after announcing their CDS losses.[31] Because of CEO Jamie Dimon's disgust with these losses and his own shrewd loss mitigation policies, he enabled the firm to reverse these losses in September 2012.

However, other firms do not enjoy Dimon's judgment. They will not be as fortunate. A universal mandatory CDS reserve should be required.

Next, we must address another failure of Dodd–Frank, the inability to curtail gimmicky or false accounting and "shadow banking" resulting in off-balance-sheet risk. Off-balance-sheet risk can doom an entire company's future and liquidity.

Indeed, Lehman Brothers is the perfect example of how hiding a company's illiquid assets off-balance-sheet will eventually have devastating consequences. Lehman's duplicitous "Repo 105" transactions could not dupe the market forever. As Lehman's bankruptcy examiner explained, "Repo 105 transactions were nearly identical to standard repurchase and resale transactions . . . with a critical difference . . . by re-characterizing the transaction as a "sale," removing the inventory from its balance sheet."[32]

The deception ran deep. For numerous required quarterly reports from 2007 to 2008, Lehman conducted Repo 105 transactions to reduce its reported leverage and balance sheet. The public, investors, and the market were entirely unaware of these transactions that, in effect, borrowed tens of billions of dollars. A few days after the new quarter began, Lehman would borrow the necessary funds to repay the deceptive cash borrowing plus interest, repurchase the securities, and restore the illiquid assets to its balance sheet.

Fuld failed to disclose the Repo 105 practice. Martin Kelly, Lehman's former Global Financial controller, explained that a careful review of Lehman's annual Forms 10k and quarterly 10-Q would not reveal Lehman's use of Repo 105 transactions.[33]

Kelly repeatedly contested the validity of Repo 105 transactions to two Lehman CFOs Erin Callan and Ian Lowitt. He felt there was no substance to the Repo 105 deals and advised Callan and Lowitt that the transactions meant reputational risk to Lehman.[34]

Rather than weakly admonishing the use of Repo 105 and other accounting tricks to hide risk, we must enact new rules of the game to ensure that financial wizardry can never again doom a proud centuries-old company like Lehman.

The "shadow banking" system is also used to hide losses and provide liquidity in off-balance-sheet entities. Shadow banks are small institutions, often unregulated, that provide credit on an international scale. Although many forms of shadow banking are beyond the scope of this book, think of the industry as small, special purposes entities, hedge funds, and other financial intermediaries designed to offload money, enhance liquidity, and make balance sheets look better than reality.

The Financial Stability Board estimated in October 2011 that shadow banking is a $60 trillion off-balance-sheet business that is largely unregulated.[35]

The solution to shadow banking enterprises and Repo 105 accounting is transparency. Balance sheets must include fewer asterisks, exceptions, and GAAP acrobatics. Regulations and rules must be introduced that allow only a certain amount of money to be maintained off balance sheet. This amount should be a small fraction of the company's overall capital to ensure adequate liquidity.

This off-balance-sheet capital should also have its own balance sheet disclosed to investors, rather than just appear as a footnote buried away in an SEC disclosure. If a bank wishes to use a GAAP loophole to make its SEC disclosures look better, it needs to provide justification through transparency to the market and shareholders.

Too often, banks operate out of fear—fear that disclosing lack of liquidity and losses can be a crisis for their short-term price per share.

Yet, take Dimon's massive public disclosure of his CDS loss as an example. Sure, the transparency and disclosure had an effect on the JP Morgan share price. But, through remedial policies aimed at reform and sustainable growth, the bank recovered in a matter of months.

CEOs, CFOs, and risk management personnel who run banks based on fear will pay the ultimate price eventually. Relying on shadows to be successful in the short-term is unsustainable.

New policies must shed light on the shadows that pervade our economic system corrupted in vice. Transparency and mandatory detail of all off-balance-sheet dealings must be required, as should be a minimum amount of assets that can be placed off balance sheet.

Reforms Needed for the Commodities Market

The commodities market is another area in need of urgent reform. No other event indicates this is a necessity more than the fall of MF Global and Peregrine Financial, two prominent commodities dealers. MF Global's and Peregrine's demise suggests that many of the same practices that led to the demise of Bear Stearns, Lehman Brothers, and Merrill Lynch still plague the financial system today. Little has changed.

In the case of MF Global, the story of the firm's fast track to bankruptcy includes the firing of whistleblower risk personnel, ineffectual government regulations, repeated failures to act, extraordinary off-balance-sheet leverage, and a stubborn resistance to deleverage amidst turbulent market conditions.

The underlying causes of MF Global's bankruptcy were supposedly vanquished by new legislation, investor protections, and government activism. Yet, the recent crisis only provides more reason to hasten reforms of the current system that create enhanced governance structures, more effective derivative regulation, and ethical imperatives designed to change Wall Street culture and protect investors.

The following solutions are some of those necessary to tame the wild-west commodities market.

Better and More Frequent Regulatory Audits

Because MF Global operated as an FCM and a broker dealer, the SEC and CFTC regulated it along with multiple self-regulating organizations, including The Chicago Mercantile Exchange (CME Group) and FINRA.

According to CME Executive Chairman Terrance Duffy, CME Group regulations worked flawlessly in the MF Global crisis. "CME was the only one that gave a very detailed outline of what we did minute-by-minute to show that our [self-regulatory organization] worked flawlessly," Duffy said. "You cannot prevent against fraud."[36]

Nonetheless, CME was responsible for conducting audits of MF Global books—namely, ensuring that customer capital was not commingled with the firm's proprietary interests. Duffy testified to Congress on December 8, 2011, notably stating, "Our clearinghouse rules require that money and other customer property must be separately accounted for and may not be commingled with the Funds of the FCM or be used to margin, secure, or guarantee any trades or contracts."[37]

Why couldn't CME enforce these rules in their audits and investigations of MF Global?

It is simply because CME didn't regularly audit MF Global. Its last official audit of the firm was January 31, 2011.[38] CME Group, along with the SEC and FINRA, only stormed into the MF Global offices the week of October 24, 2011, when it became obvious that MF Global could no longer function as a stand-alone business.[39]

Higher frequencies of on-site audits and controls are necessary, not just by the CME, but by the CFTC and SEC. Audits should accelerate once a firm is placed on credit watch or is downgraded.

Smarter Corporate Governance

Moreover, as demonstrated by the marginalization of MF Global's risk personnel, independence among the board of directors and risk management is paramount. There must be appropriate governance checks and balances in which the board, risk managers, and other important officers and senior executives have authority and independence.

Dodd–Frank has made certain modest structural improvements, but these regulations can be enhanced to curtail powerful CEOs (like Corzine) from employing excessive leverage, marginalizing risk personnel, and employing complex off-balance-sheet arrangements to camouflage increased market risk. Possible improvements include an enhanced shareholder role, stricter fiduciary standards, and mandatory risk thresholds for enumerated classes of assets.

The success of the investment banking system rests on the bedrock of investor trust and confidence. The MF Global crisis is yet another example of private and public institutions with a short memory. Private investment banks are stewards of investor capital and have a fiduciary duty to protect client interests above all other interests. MF Global is a sign that the premise of restoring investor faith, prudence, and ethics to Wall Street may have been lost in the rubble of 2008 and replaced with a stubborn, obsessive gambler mentality.

Now must not be the time to double-down. We can no longer cling to the myth that excessive risk, plastic leverage ratios, and exotic derivative transactions result in efficient capital markets. Regulators must take a defiant stand.

The SEC must defend its mission statement of "protecting investors" and "maintaining fair and orderly markets" through smarter, tough new rules of the game. Likewise, the CFTC must ensure it adopts new governance and oversight measures that mirror its regulatory objective of protecting "market users and the public from fraud, manipulation, abusive practices and systemic risk related to derivatives."

The promise of these agencies must be renewed. We can become accustomed to failures like MF Global or take decisive action to facilitate the restoration of investor trust and confidence in our banking system.

The Need for Heightened and Streamlined Fiduciary Rules

In addition to the above provisions of Dodd–Frank, another important element of the regulation was reform of the broker-dealer industry, the implementation of strong new fiduciary standards, and enhanced transparency for retail investors.[40]

Publicly, the SEC has represented that Dodd–Frank rules and studies have remained true to the central purpose of the legislation through protecting investors and encouraging issuance of strong fiduciary standards. The SEC has assured investors that the new retail rules of the game are fair, transparent, ethical, and founded on good governance.

Section 913 of the Dodd–Frank Act required the SEC to conduct a study on the effectiveness of existing fiduciary standards regulating the conduct of broker-dealers and investment advisers that provide personalized advice to retail customers.[41]

On January 21, 2011, the SEC issued its published "913" Study On Investment Advisers and Broker-Dealers. Specifically, the SEC recommended adoption of a new "uniform" fiduciary standard that would apply to both broker dealers and investment advisers. The proposed standard is intended to supplement existing fiduciary standards under the Investment Advisers Act of 1940 and would read as follows:

> The standard of conduct for all brokers, dealers and investment advisers, when providing personalized investment advice about securities to retail customers . . . shall be to act in the best interest of the customer without regard to the financial or other interest of the broker, dealer or investment adviser providing the advice.[42]

The 913 Study explained that the components of this new fiduciary standard would include a duty of loyalty and a duty of care pursuant to the current standard under Section 206 of the Investment Advisers Act. Notably, the standard would not require a continuing duty of care or loyalty to a retail customer after personalized investment advice has been rendered.

To implement the report's recommendations, the document called for rulemaking, the identification of specific examples of material conflicts, and consistent interpretations for broker-dealers and investment advisers.

The 913 Study does not provide guidance as to the most important element of the new standard, "the best interest of the customer." The proposed "best interest of the customer" is a highly subjective standard for broker-dealers and at the heart of the new uniform fiduciary standard.

Who is to decide what is in a retail investor's best interest?

Carlo V. Di Florio, director of the SEC Office of Compliance, Inspections, and Examinations (OCIE), explained in a speech titled "The Role of Compliance and Ethics in Risk Management" that the Dodd–Frank mandated "913" broker-dealer study is emblematic of how ethics can shape the new securities legislation and fiduciary standards in general. "The manner in which the federal securities laws are illuminated by ethical principles was well illustrated by the Study on Investment Advisers and Broker-Dealers that the Commission staff submitted to Congress earlier this year pursuant to Section 913 of the Dodd-Frank Act," Florio remarked.[43]

However, contrary to Florio's statements, the 913 study fails to adequately address key underlying issues surrounding broker-dealer fiduciary standards. It does not call for greater ethical mandates for broker-dealers and misses the critical issue of regulating market makers and their duties to retail customers.

Sophistication is clearly not universal for retail investors. The 913 Study concedes that "retail customers do not understand the roles of broker-dealers and investment advisers."[44] Therefore, it is unrealistic to conclude that all retail investors will understand what sort of trades and securities are most suitable for them. While broker-dealers are currently guided by case law suitability rules, it is unclear if the subjective "best interest" determination should fall within this determination or whether a higher standard should be established.

Rather than subjective suitability and best interest determinations, broker-dealer conduct should be regulated by bright-line, objective rules that make clear which interests of retail investors should be fundamentally protected. The study fails to elucidate any such standards and, as a result, makes the broker-dealer regulatory landscape even more confusing.

The 913 Study maintains that the duty of loyalty under the Advisers Act, incorporated into the Uniform Fiduciary Standard, would mandate "full and fair disclosure of all material conflicts of interest."[45] Nonetheless, the 913 Study states that this duty "is not continuing" and only "requires a firm to eliminate or disclose material conflicts of interest, it does not mandate the absolute elimination of any particular conflict."[46] The document defers to the SEC rulemaking process in deciding what conflicts are "material" and require disclosure.

These recommendations fail to elucidate objective standards that broker-dealers can apply in realistic transactions. Broker-dealer interests may undeniably conflict with retail customers when the dealer engages in proprietary trading. In these instances, what sort of information should broker-dealers disclose? Even when appropriate disclosure occurs, how will retail investors know the true nature of "material" conflicts when the SEC itself acknowledges that their education and knowledge are inadequate?

Perhaps most troubling is the absence of the market maker issue in the 913 Study. Market makers are critical components of the financial system because they receive buy and sell offers for the asset inventory they hold. They buy and sell their own inventory for profit and often reject lower prices to receive a greater return.

As a result, retail investors purchasing securities priced by market makers likely do not buy such assets at the best possible market price. Retail investors may be receiving overpriced securities from their own broker-dealers and other market makers because of conflicts of interest in the current system.

Because of this situation, there should be rules governing the duties and appropriate disclosures from market makers and broker-dealers. Particularly, market makers should be compelled to disclose the price quotes they receive for their own inventory, bought and sold, that end up in the accounts of retail investors.

This should especially be an issue front and center for the SEC because of the role of market makers in the financial crisis. Market maker banks and broker-dealers sold assets at levels higher than their true value to realize greater profits when it was known that such prices were inflated representations of market value. The 913 Report suggests no solution or specific disclosure to this problem.

The SEC has proclaimed that the 913 Study and the proposed uniform fiduciary standard are a major triumph for the agency and a win for governance and better business ethics. Yet, the standard suggests nothing new other than to propose an open-ended universal fiduciary standard that is overly ambiguous and dependent on future SEC rulemaking.

Most troubling is that the 913 Study dodged the most critical issue of market-maker trading. Market makers owe a greater duty to retail investors because they price the assets received from broker-dealers. Retail investors deserve investments that are priced fairly and in their best interest, not in the best interest of a market-maker bank.

In a free market, investors should, at the very least, be aware of all quotes received for market-maker inventory to evaluate (along with their broker-dealer) if the asset is a fair price and in their best interest. This would be a clear rule that would forward the key principles of Dodd–Frank: transparency, good governance, ethics, and better fiduciary standards.

The 913 rules have still not been issued in the fall of 2012. It remains to be seen what elements will be implemented. However, based on the language of the study itself, the SEC seems to be on the wrong track. The agency must be willing to take a stand on enhancing broker-dealer and investment adviser regulation when markets, investors, and the general public need them most. These changes are honest market measures and expected in an optimal free market system.

Notes

1. Jesse Lee, "President Obama Signs Wall Street Reform: No Easy Task," White House blog, July 21, 2010, www.whitehouse.gov/blog/2010/07/21/president-obama-signs-wall-street-reform-no-easy-task.
2. Andrew Ross Sorkin, "About Face For Bankers' New Lobbyist," *The New York Times*, September 24, 2012, dealbook.nytimes.com/2012/09/24/about-face-for-bankers-new-lobbyist/?smid=tw-share.

3. Ibid.

4. Ibid.

5. "TR, American Experience," PBS Online, available at: http://www.pbs.org/wgbh/americanexperience/features/transcript/tr-transcript/.

6. Cheyenne Hopkins, "IMF Says Bank Rules Lag on Safety, Too-Big-To Fail Stays," Bloomberg, September 25, 2002, www.bloomberg.com/news/2012–09–25/imf-says-bank-rules-lag-on-safety-too-big-to-fail-stays.html.

7. The Dodd–Frank Wall Street Reform and Consumer Protection Act H.R. 4173 111th Congr. (2010).

8. William Mcgrath, "SEC Chairman Schapiro to Congress: We Cannot Complete Our Duties Under Dodd-Frank Under Existing Budget," Federal Securities Law Blog, http://www.fedseclaw.com/2011/07/articles/sec-news/sec-chairman-schapiro-to-congress-we-cannot-complete-our-duties-under-doddfrank-act-under-existing-budget/#axzz26g0ntix2.

9. Jamila Trindle, "CFTC Approves Key Derivative Rules," *The Wall Street Journal*, July 10, 2012, online.wsj.com/article/SB10001424052702304022004577518613043225518.html.

10. Justin Menza, "Dodd-Frank Won't Prevent Another Crisis," CNBC, September 12, 2012, www.cnbc.com/id/49003944.

11. See Beth Connolly, "SEC Called on Once More to Answer for Favoring Big Banks," September 14, 2012, compliancex.com/sec-favors-big-firms/.

12. Ibid.

13. Report of Investigation, Case No. OIG-505, Failure to Timely Investigate Allegations of Financial Fraud, February 26, 2010.

14. Ibid.

15. Randy Diamond, "Scrum Over $815 Million Grows More Intense," *Pensions & Investments*, June 27, 2011, www.pionline.com/article/20110627/PRINTSUB/306279975.

16. Sarah N. Lynch, "Critics Question Cost As Consultants Nip and Tuck SEC," Reuters, February 9, 2012, www.reuters.com/article/2012/02/29/us-sec-consultants-idUSTRE81S28Q20120229.

17. Ibid.

18. Jean Eaglesham and Telis Demos, "SEC Chief Delayed Rule Over Legacy Concerns," *The Wall Street Journal*, December 2, 2012, http://online.wsj.com/article/SB10001424127887324204540457815369396863404.html

19. Matt Taibbi, "SEC Rocked by Lurid Sex and Corruption Lawsuit," *Rolling Stone*, November 19, 2012, www.rollingstone.com/politics/blogs/taibblog/sec-rocked-by-lurid-sex-and-corruption-lawsuit-20121119 citing Weber v. SEC.

20. Jonathan Karl, "SEC Porn Problem: Officials Surfing Sites During Crisis, Report Finds," ABC News, April 23, 2010, http://abcnews.go.com/GMA/sec-pornography-employees-spent-hours-surfing-porn-sites/story?id=10452544#.UMahw3f4Kkg American investors and taxpayers deserve those possibly thousands of hours back.

21. SEC.GOV, "What We Do," www.sec.gov/about/whatwedo.shtml
22. DealBook, "What Dimon Told Bernanke," *The New York Times*, June 8, 2011, dealbook.nytimes.com/2011/06/08/what-dimon-told-bernanke/.
23. Sabrina R. Pellerin and John R. Walter, "Orderly Liquidation Authority as an Alternative to Bankruptcy," *Federal Reserve Bank of Richmond Economic Quarterly*, 98, no. 1 (First Quarter 2012): 1–31.
24. Title II of the Dodd–Frank Wall Street Reform and Consumer Protection Act H.R. 4173 111th Congr. (2010) sec. 203 (b).
25. Steven J. Lubben, "The Flaws in the New Liquidation Authority," *The New York Times*, April 18, 2012, dealbook.nytimes.com/2012/04/18/the-flaws-in-the-new-liquidation-authority/.
26. "It's All in the Execution: The Dodd–Frank Act Two Years Later," Standard & Poors, www.standardandpoors.com/ratings/articles/en/ap/?articleType=HTML&assetID=1245337429167.
27. Dawn Kopecki, "JP Morgan Erases Stock Drop Fueled By London Whale Loss," *Bloomberg Businessweek*, September 13, 2012, www.businessweek.com/news/2012–09–13/jpmorgan-erases-stock-drop-fueled-by-london-trading-loss.
28. "CFTC and SEC Finalize Key Dodd-Frank Product Definitions, Ushering in Implementation Phase of U.S.," OTC Derivatives Regulatory Reforms, Sidley Austin, August 7, 2012.
29. Silla Brush, "CFTC Approves Swap Definition Triggering Dodd-Frank Rules," Bloomberg, July 11, 2012, www.bloomberg.com/news/2012–07–10/cftc-votes-4–1-to-approve-swap-definition-starting-overhaul-1-.html.
30. Richard Blackden, "JP Morgan Losses Highlight Need for Credit Default Swap Regulation," *Telegraph*, May 21, 2012, www.telegraph.co.uk/finance/newsbysector/banksandfinance/9278330/JPMorgan-losses-highlight-need-for-credit-default-swap-regulation.html.
31. Kopecki.
32. In "Re Lehman Brothers Holdings Inc, Report of Anton R. Valukas," *Examiner*, Volume 3 U.S. Bankruptcy Court, S.D.N.Y. March 11, 2010 at 732.
33. Ibid.
34. Ibid. at 735.
35. "Shadow Banking: Strengthening Oversight and Regulation," Recommendations of Financial Stability Board, October 27, 2011.
36. Crain's Chicago Business, "CME Sees No Need to Revamp Futures Regulation in Post-MF Global Market," www.chicagobusiness.com/article/20120202/NEWS01/120209934/cme-sees-no-need-to-revamp-futures-regulation-in-post-mf-global-market.
37. Duffy Congressional Testimony & Luparello Congressional Testimony, December 8, 2011.
38. Duffy Congressional Testimony, December 8, 2011.

39. Ibid.
40. See Dodd–Frank Section 913.
41. See SEC Study on Investment Advisers and Broker-Dealers, January 2011, www.sec.gov/news/studies/2011/913studyfinal.pdf
42. Carlo V. di Florio, "Speech By SEC Staff: The Role of Compliance and Ethics in Risk Management," www.sec.gov/news/speech/2011/spch 101711cvd.htm
43. Ibid., p. VI.
44. Ibid., p. 116.
45. Ibid., p. 113.
46. Ibid., p. 112.

Chapter 10

The Case for Reintroducing Governance and Morality

T his chapter explores how governance and personal morality and ethics have fallen by the wayside and the essential changes that need to be made to revitalize our global society with virtue.

The Important Demand for Corporate Governance

In the last decades, a plethora of laws, rules, and cases have sought to make companies and other entities and their senior-most executives, especially CFOs, more accountable for the manner in which they manage their organizations.

Indeed, there is universal demand for higher standards of independent corporate governance worldwide. For many institutions, the problems lie in the implementation.

Likewise, in the nonprofit and governmental sectors, illegality concerns at Rupert Murdoch's News Corp, the Red Cross's potential mishandling of the 9/11 funds, the government's abuse of taxpayer funds in various outlandish spending scandals, mismanagement of the relief efforts after Hurricanes Katrina and Rita, and the United Nations' missteps of the Oil for Food Program in Iraq highlight the ubiquity of concerns for governance and transparency and their great impact on the public and private sectors.

Corporate governance is the foundation of rules, "norms," and ethics by which boards of directors meet their fiduciary responsibilities and create accountability, justice, and transparency for shareholders, investors, and other stakeholders in their business and greater community.

While in the private sector some companies have developed sound corporate governance and transparency, many have failed to enact controls that protect against out-of-control vice, fraudulent schemes, and corruption.

The issues are equally important for governments and nonprofits. There must be greater accountability for money spent with public and philanthropic funds. This has simply not occurred in the past decade. Public and philanthropic funds should not be treated as throwaway money.

There must be a renewed sense of responsibility and virtue in handling funds bestowed upon government and nonprofit entities. In fact, these funds are established to produce "good." It is essential that both public and private actors realize their immense responsibility and enact policies of sound governance.

Additionally, for nonprofits, global competition for investment funds means that every organization will be under increased scrutiny for performance at all levels, from governance to service. Investors demand accountability. Funds must be used for a noble purpose and not for waste or excess.

Likewise, governments must demonstrate a commitment to accountability and governance. Since elected officials run democratic governments, these elected persons have the greatest fiduciary responsibilities to their citizens. All too often, it is forgotten that citizens are the true owners of a democracy, and political leaders have a duty to behave in an ethical, virtuous, and prudent manner.

Incentives are raised because of globalization. Governments require foreign investment for funding purposes. At some point, countries that fail to produce tangible results and become saddled with immense debt will see investor funds vanish. This will defeat the many benefits of globalization.

Governments must create solutions to financing woes to reassure private investors and the greater economic market. Operations must be transparent and not opaque.

In the private sector, higher standards for governance and new reform-minded legislation bring increasing responsibility and liability, of which executives must be cognizant. Compliance should not be a "back-office" division, as it is at most every investment bank. Lack of CEO and CFO accountability and marginalization of risk managers are part of the reason governance has become such a concern.

For corporations, attracting financing is integral to day-to-day operations. This makes accountability, sustainability, reputation, and governance that much more important. Corporations throughout the world rely increasingly on global equity financing, rather than on bank loans and retained earnings. This makes risk management and accountability critical.

Additionally, corporations are increasingly subject to pressures from institutional investors that provide key sources of funding. Maintenance of these relationships with institutional investors is of paramount importance. During the credit crisis, the failure of institutions to believe in the reputations, risk managers, and CFOs of major international banks was a prime reason for their destruction.

The Importance of Corporate Responsibility

As a result of the process of globalization, there is increased emphasis on shareholder value through the means of corporate social responsibility.

Some recent developments that have added impetus to the corporate governance movement include globalization itself. Competition for investment funding is higher for all sectors. In transactions that span thousands of miles, trust, transparency, and responsibility are of paramount importance. The need for performance and assessment and improved standards of productivity and service in lead organizations is greater than ever before.

Increasingly, boards of directors, CEOs, and CFOs are adapting to the new cry for corporate social responsibility (CSR). Those who take a lead in setting high standards for themselves are gaining respect and value for their enterprises and organizations.

What is corporate governance supposed to achieve?

The corporation, for profit or nonprofit, is a separate legal entity with a pool of assets that do not belong to any particular constituents. These assets are not the property of those making the decisions. This cannot be overemphasized. Shareholders are owners of the corporation, and directors must pursue policies that are entirely in their best interest.

However, in other countries, particularly in the Euro zone, broader social responsibilities are often imputed to the duties of directors. The notion is that corporations should act not only for profit but also for the overall social good. This idea of social responsibility is a popular governance theme in Europe because there exists pressure for companies to commit to a broader social purpose beyond collecting massive profit.

The dual goals of socially responsible companies are to maximize returns while contributing to social well-being. Also described as sustainable or ethical investing, corporate social responsibility typically champions human rights, social justice, ecological responsibility, and corporate correctness. Different forms of corporate social responsibility have existed for a long time. Investor refusals to invest in tobacco, arms, and alcohol are just some of the historical examples.

More recently, corporate greening and respect for the environment or sustainability have gained attention. Investors have begun to realize the influence they can wield on different organizations, leading them to scrutinize both investment policies and investment vehicles, and to use that influence to change or boycott, accordingly.

Despite pressure from friends "across the pond," the United States has been hesitant to whole-heartedly adopt CSR as an element of our governance framework. Indeed, not everyone is on board with accepting corporate social responsibility as an accepted international governance norm. Aneel Karnani recently wrote in a *Wall Street Journal* editorial that social responsibility is an "illusion, and a potentially dangerous one."[1] Karnani went on to write:

> Very simply, in cases where private profits and public interests are aligned, the idea of corporate social responsibility is irrelevant: Companies that simply do everything they can to boost profits will end up increasing social welfare. In circumstances in which profits and social welfare are in direct opposition, an appeal to corporate social responsibility will almost always be ineffective because executives are unlikely to act voluntarily in the public interest and against shareholder interests.[2]

Karnani's op-ed exemplifies everything that is wrong with our governance assumptions. First, Karnani maintains that CEOs who merely do whatever they can to boost profits will indirectly enhance community standards and social welfare. This is an inaccurate statement.

For example, all that is necessary is to revisit the stock prices of Bear Stearns and Lehman Brothers during the credit crisis bubble. Sure, their respective CEOs were making a boondoggle of profits for their shareholders. Yet, these pursuits of profits were through programs designed to lower social welfare. Social welfare was adversely affected by policies that drove massive foreclosures because of an inability of homeowners to pay back loans that Bear and Lehman knew they could not afford.

It should be the other way around.

Executive-level pursuit of policies that benefit the community through innovation and sustainability create benefit to corporations because they add long-term value. Furthermore, these programs instill trust and confidence among shareholders, investors, and the community at large. Why should shareholder interests be distinct from those of the greater community? They are one in the same. When a company acts responsibility, it boosts its international reputation. Reputation in global markets is essential for any organization that wishes to exist and survive boom and bust economic cycles.

Also, it is highly unlikely that socially responsible programs will ever diminish a company's stock price. How can doing good and pursuing virtuous policies be viewed as negative in the market? Has our corporate culture devolved into a thoughtless vice-ridden environment where rapid profits are celebrated and noble policies of enriching the community are frowned upon?

We think not.

Accordingly, it would be wise for all companies to enact socially responsible programs for the betterment of their shareholders and the community.

The premise that socially responsible policies fail to result in profits is false. Those who comprehend this growing trend around "responsible investing" are no longer early adapters or innovators. The market has caught up. Executives now must understand where it is going over the coming decade. It is a megatrend—too big to miss.

A major source of enforcing governance rules is the legal system itself. The world has witnessed countless lawsuits over the past decade, particularly an explosion in the aftermath of the credit crisis. How helpful is the threat of litigation in ensuring our laws are enforced? Perhaps this is the most powerful deterrent currently in the market.

The Importance of Reputation and Avoiding Long-Term Litigation Costs

Litigation is not only extraordinarily expensive, it erodes away at the very core of a company's livelihood: its reputation. The case of Goldman Sachs is the quintessential example of how litigation can have negative global effects for the company's business.

Goldman has been the subject of various governmental legal investigations, class actions, and other private litigation, mostly over conflicts of interest and mortgage-backed securities. These litigations have spawned popular books, magazine articles, and op-eds in newspapers all over the world. Unfortunately for Goldman, because of the negative investigations, litigation, and news coverage, the company has often become associated with vice.

Popular perception regarding Goldman might be the stuff of fables or it might be true. That is not the point. The point is that because of the governmental investigations, litigation, and news coverage, people believe Goldman Sachs has a negative reputation. Reputation means everything.

In fact, according to the website Brand Index, a quantitative measure of corporate reputation, during the time of the spring 2010 SEC suit against the company, Goldman's reputation score bottomed out at −44.[3]

According to this index, Goldman's reputation score has still not recovered.

As of March 21, 2012, Goldman's reputation score was −36 compared to the score of −4 for its rivals. This means that because of the SEC litigation against them along with other factors, Goldman's reputation was more than 30 points lower than its competition. Litigation against the firm had a profound effect on the firm's global reputation and public perception.

Goldman Sachs is not the only entity to suffer because of damaging litigation. A disturbing number of corporate entities have been the subject of embarrassing and problematic failures, fraud, ethical lapses, and outright scandals that have been exposed by litigation and investigation.

Accordingly, litigation should be the greatest fear of corporate institutions. Especially when government rules and self-governance fail, litigation is a powerful tool to encourage transparency, good governance, and risk management.

Interestingly, the class action is for the most part a uniquely American institution. Prevention of executive misconduct in Europe is accomplished principally by government regulation and criminal sanctions. There are two features that make class actions much more likely to be brought in the United States than in other countries. The first is the widespread practice of bringing such cases on a "contingency" basis.

The second is the fact that the plaintiff's attorney, if he wins the case or achieves a settlement, is entitled to an award of counsel fees based on a substantial percentage of the amount of the recovery. In general, the culture in European countries, including often the United Kingdom, is much less oriented toward litigation and geared more toward governmental regulation.

Vice is not reserved to the United States. It is a worldwide phenomenon. As a result, the Euro zone should consider the class-action
concept as a means for shareholders to appropriately recover. This is
especially critical because European regulators, like their American
counterparts, cannot be universally counted on to enforce governance
and prevent fraud.

To prevent the threat of litigation, corporations and their CEOs
must focus on virtue and ethics. Effective leadership entails knowing
how your corporation will distinguish itself from the pack. A key element of successful leadership involves avoiding the threat of litigation
through good governance. Those CEOs who take a lead in setting high
standards for themselves and their organizations gain respect and value
for their enterprise and from the market at large.

For today's CEOs, presidents, and risk managers, the warning is
clear: Ignore governance, risk, and compliance at your own peril.

Regardless of what side of the governance fence you are on, mea-
suring good governance is synonymous with good performance. It
means, among other things, commitment to effective solutions. These
solutions entail effective best practices, performance reviews, internal
board evaluation of its own performance, forensic audits, and outside
verification and auditing procedures by leading and respected independent authorities.

Bonuses Redux: Corporate Welfare
Reform and Cutting Golden Parachutes

Another source of controversy in the financial community today is
perceived out-of-control compensation for corporate America. A general disgust extends to all sides of the American polity. Take President
Obama, who campaigned against corporate "private jets." Take the
rightist Tea Party movement, which criticized government preserving
the salaries of banks through bailouts. Take a literal walk down Wall
Street in Manhattan and you might see an Occupy Wall Street protester
with a sign deriding executive "greed."

Regardless of political leanings, there is universally precious little
public support today for the so-called Masters of the Universe, be they

Gordon Gekko wannabes or some real-life exotic derivatives traders or oil futures specialists, fitted in expensive suits and suspenders.

Is there something truly out of whack with a private company lavishly compensating an employee? Every January, like clockwork, Fortune 500 companies, banks, retail as well as investment, private equity shops as well as hedge funds, decide the all-critical question of PAY.

These are bonuses *redux*.

Redux is an adjective meaning "brought back, restored" and is from the Latin *reducere*. It exemplifies the essence of the compensation structure in corporate America. Unlike normal salaried workers or even commissioned agents, many executives pay themselves based on anti-quated notions and a scheme called bonuses. These bonuses are typically large, very large, even many times base pay.

The "too big to fail" banks have been singled out for out-of-control bonuses, and sometimes for good reason. During a period of economic recession, many executives accepted bonuses of upwards of $10 million with no logical criteria. These firms were only recently recovering from large losses or bailouts.

Incentive. This is the one-word argument why CEOs should make tens of millions of dollars through bonuses. For example, if X bank doesn't pay me a $10 million bonus, I can become CEO of Y Bank, which will pay me what I am entitled to. The premise is that X Bank must provide me with the incentive to perform my duties, or else I will leave.

When did investment banking become a business wholly dedicated to personal greed, rather than enriching the value of the corporation for the true owners of the corporate modality, the shareholders?

Executives are fiduciaries under the law. This generally means they must act prudently and in the best interest of the owners of the cor-poration, the shareholders. How can meeting one's fiduciary responsi-bilities be equated with taking such gigantic amounts from the owners of the corporation?

In many cases, money funneled to CEOs might not even be in the firm's interest. Take the example of John Thain, Merrill Lynch's former CEO, who, in 2008, lavishly spent company funds to redecorate his office—including an $87,000 rug, curtains for $28,000, and a

"George IV desk" for $18,000.[4] Thain wasted over a million dollars at the onset of the credit crisis, a time when he was letting go of thousands of employees.

Contrary to spending money the Thain way, CEOs must realize that the credit crisis era is one of newfound frugality and hardship. Everyday families all over the nation have had to tighten belts and take massive cuts in nearly every area of life, from the household to the corporation. Likewise, in providing compensation and oversight, boards of directors must look out for the stockholders without being unduly influenced by their friendships and tee times with corporate management.

Most people buy and own stock either directly or indirectly through 401(k) plans. There is no reason why an executive deserves an out-of-control financial incentive of tens of millions of dollars when the true owners of the corporation, the shareholders, are suffering in a depressed economy.

Perhaps, there is another way to do business?

In most other industries compensation experts have come up with ideas like Scanlon plans, profit sharing, gain sharing, or tiered structures such that a ceiling is placed on the top salaries, often a multiple of the average or the lowest salary within the company.

European shareholders have approved and applauded such incentives and voted them in. In the United States, shareholders must aggressively do the same. Business as usual should not include the idea of a bonus redux.

We must emphasize that the private market should still dictate executive pay. However, it must be scaled back from the current unfathomable level.

Let's put a new market-based scheme into place that is both ethical and performance based. Not everyone deserves a bonus or exactly the same amount. If you make money one year and lose it the next, something should plausibly get clawed back. It is only just.

CEO compensation should be tied to incentive. Yet, rather than an incentive to merely make money and receive a huge bonus; an incentive to do well, and to do your absolute best to produce positive returns for your company.

The word *just* may appear foreign when it comes to finance and banks, particularly bonuses. There will undeniably be some pushback. But, like the problem of lack of competition among banks "too big to fail," there must be competition in executive pay through bonuses. The CEO of corporation X that lost 40 percent of the company's value should not be paid the same as the CEO of corporation Y that increased the value of the company by 40 percent.

The current sense of entitlement disgusts America, the world, and the values of competitive capitalism. Executives who believe they are "entitled" to millions of dollars in bonuses regardless of performance offend the corporate modality and do not incentivize any leader to do better.

We do not reject success. We applaud it.

Bonuses are not corporate welfare checks to a handful of executives. They must be justified based on performance reviews and fluctuate based on the affirmative acts of the CEO or CFO in meeting fiduciary responsibilities as charged under the law of most nations.

We do not foreclose the possibility that an executive should be entitled to a lucrative bonus. We say that it is a cornerstone of business ethics and how we characterize ourselves as a meritorious society for executives to earn what their performance dictates.

Anything less sustains a diseased corporate culture of vice as an accepted status quo. Virtuous executives and shareholders must unite to create performance-driven pay. They will have nothing to lose but their commitment to ethics.

The Need to Morally Redefine Ourselves on the Macro Level

Wealth creation is perhaps the most divisive issue in our political and economic discourse today. Top-down, bottom-up, redistribution of income—whatever theory you may prescribe to—it is obvious that there are glaring weaknesses in our financial culture today due to a fundamental lack of responsibility, creativity, and accountability.

Traditionally, there are only three explanations of the origin of prosperity.

1. Wealth is viewed as the product of magic, alchemy, or wizardry, poof!
2. Prosperity is the product of tribal or national conquest. Guess what? You have it and I am taking it!
3. Prosperity is rooted in the value of human creative capacity.

The first two views assume that wealth is preexisting: the third view posits that prosperity can be created by human effort.

America, for the most part, reflects the third way of thinking. This kind of effort and knowledge is not wholly captured by neoclassical economics and its assumption of a completely rational, utility-maximizing, fully informed *homo economicus*. In the past, attention has focused on financial capital and physical capital as static, limited assets to be accumulated and managed.

Strikingly, the source of economic prosperity was taken for granted, largely as an existing condition to be exploited. In this context, economics was modeled more on the basis of resource management, with growth and development coming largely from the management of costs. However, economic growth is not reducible to any mechanical model that can be planned at the macro level. It requires freedom and an inspired effort.

As a point of reference, America's Judeo-Christian inheritance of creative obedience or norms in economic activities is one primary way for adherents to acknowledge and demonstrate faith and personal dignity. America has always exuded "spiritual capital," which is an idea that we are uniquely value-driven persons based on religious and spiritual connection and faith.

Our American heritage illustrates that wealth creation is possible in free markets where integrity, virtue, and moral values are emphasized. However, despite this known tradition, our 300-year-old culture is under assault today from a variety of sources. As a result, we see a progression from governmental bureaucratic centralization to secularism to reductive materialism and ultimately to a social-collectivist conception of human welfare.

These attacks feed the cable news networks' demand for the outrageous. Accordingly, it has now become part of our social fabric to attack traditional values with radicalism and anger. It must be stressed that these perpetual attacks define both the left and the right of politics today.

Unfortunately, in the process, the United States has drifted so far from the decent traditions that have always defined the nation that it has become nearly unrecognizable.

American corporate culture will not survive without a renewal of our established values, ethics, and morals. Free markets rely on the faith of their participants. It is faith and trust that ensure the system is decent and equitable, and that it benefits all for the greater good. We need greater morality among our financial leaders and investors to have the ability to make it work and be successful as it has been for over 300 years.

To effectively defend free markets, greater civic participation is essential. Specifically, this means the importance of personal autonomy, accountability, and responsibility stemming from the dignity of the individual as a person, and the need to support civil association with a robust content-full morality.

Although today's world is chock full of anti-American zealots who also detest capital formation, wealth generation, and the fruits and rewards of competitive free markets, it also gives a voice to persons who believe that fraud and economic vice happen, and that there should be no rules of the game.

If we are to combat such voices that dominate our news and public discourse today, we must revitalize and look back to what made America great—the bedrocks of personal accountability, responsibility, and creativity, along with the values that make up our integrity, or "spiritual capital."

Merely saying, "This is the way the system works and it can't be changed," is not a valid answer. It is incumbent on those of us still able to make a difference to *ring the bell* of our current economic malaise by reinstituting the values that generations of Americans have held dear.

Ring the bell that changed the entire world did as it rang on July 8, 1776. That bell, in Philadelphia, has a quotation inscribed: "Proclaim Liberty throughout the land unto all the inhabitants thereof."

It is incumbent upon all of us, whether shareholder, executive, investor, or other market participants, to accept this liberty as a constant challenge to be ethical, personally responsible, and accountable for our actions.

Rebuilding Our Character

char · ac · ter
noun **\kar-ik-ter**

According to the usually reliable *Webster's Dictionary character* is "the aggregate of features and traits that form the individual nature of some person or thing."[5] Character refers to "one such feature or trait; characteristic."

For most people in the world, universally, regardless of where they live, their sex, religious persuasion, or their economic status, character is a "moral or ethical quality": as in a man or woman of fine, honorable character.

Since time immemorial, when humans started to reason and articulate their thoughts in philosophies and spiritual traditions, a debate has ensued about what exactly are the qualities of character, honesty, courage, or the like integrity. This is true in the Bible and other sacred texts of all religions and spiritual denominations.

The question of the good life or of *virtue* has often been tied to a discussion of that of character. Character, after all, is all about reputation— so a stain on one's character is viewed as negative, whereas a person of good character is highly esteemed and valued by all.

This notion of *good repute* or *good character* may seem old-fashioned or passé in a world where decadence, superficiality, and triviality, not to mention debauchery and coarseness, abound. Nothing could be further from the truth.

Leaders have a definite role in character building. In fact, at Yale in the University Spiritual Capital Initiative, we have conducted extensive research on good companies and highlighted them through case studies. Malloch's book *Doing Virtuous Business* shows how companies can inspire and exhibit virtue on a global level. They are able to recognize virtue and ethics, and praise their worth, often and constantly. This process, which is never ending, is not a quick fix or a fad of the month. When practiced studiously, virtue makes for a highly effective organization.

In the end, you can't force change. Rules and dictates won't do it. But leaders can lead change. People are emotional, physical, and spiritual beings who can be inspired. They are in that sense made to be aspirational. They want to be good. How do you start down this virtuous path?

Build character first.

How to Remedy the Evils in Modern-Day Consumerism

In the long term, an overwhelming desire for more actually creates unhappiness and instability.

Modern-day consumerists, however, have too often turned values of thrift on its head and made desire and want a source of liberation, where having more is the very definition of having arrived.

The historian Christopher Lasch, in *The True and Only Heaven* (using Hawthorne's phrase), traced the story of how since the eighteenth century capitalists have made insatiable desire less and less of a vice and more and more of a virtue. In one view, it is what drives the engine of economic growth and expansion.[6] In consumer societies, former virtues such as thrift and self-denial are perceived as vices because they lead to economic stagnation.

They are called miserly, and such persons are shriveled and unable to enjoy the fruits and pleasures of this life. Thrift in itself does not produce wealth but its opposite—profligacy destroys wealth. The term *spendthrift*, no longer in use, suggests a wasteful polar opposite to thrift.

Notions of restraint are no longer part of modern culture, nor are the shame of an earlier era of too much debt. One could even ask in our world of abundance if thrift has outlived its usefulness. The materialist who lives to consume, more and more, would likely have to answer in the affirmative.

The overheated economy is impeded by such virtues as thrift and thrives precisely on avid consumers who know no limits to their desire. In such a moral universe, desire is the only real absolute. Where nothing is forbidden, it is because nothing is sacred. And nothing is sacred except personal and unlimited desire. The unleashing of unquenchable appetites leads inevitably to corruption and decay, personally and collectively.

Collectively, governments worldwide have fundamentally disregarded thrift. They have spent beyond their means on defense, Cadillac social programs, and economic stimulus programs, all which cannot be afforded.

Governments have plunged into debt because of excessive spending. When international postindustrial nations have less money coming in, it is wholly irresponsible and a breach of their duties as elected officials to continue to spend as if GDP is growing exponentially.

Accepting moral limits and accepting the challenges to our pride and complacency come from taking a sacred moral code seriously. On an individual and collective level, we have ignored any such code of morals or ethics.

For a long period of time, the "American dream" meant a home, a good-paying job, and happy, nuclear family. Only recently has the American dream transformed to mean high consumption, compulsive acquisition, and instant gratification, betraying our own traditional notions of virtue and ethics.

In their book *Affluenza: The All-Consuming Epidemic*, authors John De Graaf and Thomas Naylor describe a "painful, contagious, socially transmitted condition of overload, debt, anxiety, and waste resulting from the dogged pursuit of more."[7]

The traditional notion of the American dream is dead. No longer do people want moderate prosperity and success. The new "dream" is to be outrageously rich and spend until you find yourself in bankruptcy.

The metaphor of awesome consumerism, *Affluenza: The All-Consuming Epidemic* is unfortunately accurate. Consumerism's insatiable urges to acquire things, whether or not they are needed, has reached epidemic proportions. It has caused severe social and cultural dislocations and warped the basic values of American society.

One of the most corrosive impacts of this rampant consumerism is on human relationships. Flourishing in a throwaway culture, a notion of planned obsolescence, the attitudes formed in relation to products eventually get transferred to people, as well. Just as things are discarded after casual use, people are cast off if they lose capacity to participate in the cycle of consumption. In a consumerist culture, therefore, one's status is linked in large part to one's ability to buy.

Virtue and the Moral Life

Counter to consumerism, normative philosophers have long taught that through virtue one achieves genuine happiness. The full flourishing of human beings depends on a moral life. Here, values such as the virtue of thrift are paramount. The great Greek philosopher Aristotle thought that habits of doing "right" always looked at the median as the best course. He considered both the deficiencies and the excesses as vices to be avoided.

His advice, in essence, was to lean toward that extreme to which one is least prone. In thrift, that would mean the ideal is to be generous, avoiding on the one hand cheapness and on the other extravagance.

The mean is a generous life. This implies that a person of thrift does not exclude generosity but embraces it. John M. Templeton Jr., M.D., has written eloquently about the combination in his book, *Thrift and Generosity: The Joy of Giving*.[8]

He recommends, "Thrift is not so much a matter of how much we have, but of how we appreciate, value, and use what we have. Everyone, regardless of income level, has opportunities to exercise the virtue of thrift. We practice thrift by monitoring how we spend our time and money and then by making better decisions."

The age-old parable Jesus told of the talents is indicative of ethical behavior on thrift (see Matthew 25:14–30). That passage begins with a wealthy man going on a long journey who chooses three servants to look after his resources or talents (currencies) in his absence.

While he is gone, each will be judged on proper behavior. He gives the first servant five talents, the second two talents, and the last only one talent. While gone, the first servant puts his master's talents to immediate work. In fact, when the master returns, the servant has turned the five talents into ten. The second servant was as successful, turning two talents into four. The master is pleased with the results of such thrift and stewardship. Each showed themselves true stewards of the assets entrusted to them.

The final servant, who was guided not by stewardship but by fear and lethargy, does not please him. The third servant did nothing with the talent. He simply dug a hole in the ground and buried it for safekeeping. The master punished him by taking the only talent he had and giving it to the servant who had ten talents. The moral of the parable is shockingly clear: Focus on what you have been given. It points unquestioningly to hard work, industry, and the wise use and investment of all resources.

Thrift in this famous and often-quoted passage is not just a better reading of the bottom-line: "Rather, it is part of a spiritual and cultural understanding of how we are to use our time, our talents, and our resources. Creating a culture of thrift means embedding this virtue in a larger framework of personal responsibility, discipline, purpose, and future-mindedness."

The Latin root of the verb thrift is "to thrive." The word comes from Old Norse, thrī fask, "to thrive." This excludes both poverty and excess. The thrifty person, as a thriving person, has a reasonable concern with both the present as well as the future. Thriftiness is not stinginess.

Thrifty persons show a respect for both their own and others' future and financial stability. They are very mindful of the needs of others. They neither hoard nor engage in conspicuous consumption. They do not buy in excess, but they do plan for their financial future.

Faithfulness as demonstrated by wise investing is here not only a part of salvation; it is also worked out in redemptive works of sanctification. There is a cycle of virtue in economic life. It starts with hard work and wealth generation, goes next to thrift and prudent savings, based on wise investing, that allows a degree of generosity, and it ends in the renewal of our culture. We need to get back into that cycle again and stop the casino economics that have prevailed over the past few decades.

The Consequences of Modern Selfishness

In James Collier's book *The Rise of Selfishness*, the blame for terminal decline is assigned to the transition during the last century from a community-oriented citizenry to an overly self-oriented citizenry.[9] This is a book by a confessed liberal who now thinks all of the wonderful "progressive" programs being pushed by government and the media did not really produce progress.

Significantly, he argues that the Victorian ethos—that is, the ideas, attitudes and ideals that characterized Britain and the United States in the latter half of the nineteenth century—have been abandoned to our loss. He writes:

> The Victorians had roots; they had obligations; they had responsibilities. The essence of Victorianism was self-discipline and responsibility. Every man had a responsibility to his wife and children, to his forebears, to his community, to his nation,

to his race, and he was expected to take all of these responsibilities seriously and to put them ahead of his personal self-interest. Having a strong sense of national and racial identity helped a man accept his responsibilities, but self-discipline was necessary too.

Parents raised their children with this in mind, not hesitating to apply external discipline, including corporal punishment, when needed. Thrift was a virtue, and waste a sin. People paid first for what they wanted to buy, not later. There were no credit cards. A man chronically in debt was a man whose honor was in jeopardy. Temperance and self-restraint also were virtues. A man constitutionally unable or unwilling to postpone self-gratification was held in low esteem.[10]

The most dangerous consequence Collier sees in the transition from Victorian virtues to a wholly self-centered population that has taken place in this last century is the utter destruction of the family. He looks at the trends—children growing up without fathers, working mothers putting consumerism ahead of proper parenting—and he warns, "We have seen an abandonment of parental responsibility which is unmatched in human history."[11]

The disregard for law and contempt for authority have sprung from the trend to more selfishness. But the long-term impact is greatest on the essential building block of society—the family. Collier explains:

Increasingly younger people reject marriage, divorce easily, abandon their children, have fewer friends and see less of them . . . How do we explain this? In part it may have to do with the intense involvement with the media, which provide a substitute for human interaction . . . But at bottom, the increasing fragmentation of people is a consequence of the long-term turning inward to the self as the primary concern of life.[12]

Another real consequence of the loss of thrift as a virtue is evidenced in the dilemma of old age. Can one support oneself? What is the role of personal savings, accumulated over a lifetime? Is there a value in not being a burden to others? In the current welfare state mentality, most of this decision making has been passed over to the State.

In that sense, the welfare state has removed actions from consequences. That same mentality has affected the business world with a raft of bailouts, too big to fail, and government socializing the losses.

Modern Theories and Institutions

In modern-day management theory, financial models, and investment strategy, there is little mention of thrift. The term is either used pejoratively or simply excused altogether.

There are a few exceptions. Thomas Stewart, the management guru, suggested in "12 Management Tips for Slow Times" that thrift, "that quaint Calvinist virtue, could be the "first-mover" advantage of the twenty-first century."[13] He advocates thrift. Since profits are down and demand sags, Stewart says, "Companies should turn to austerity." Stewart wrote:

> The future no longer belongs to the irrationally exuberant, but to companies that demonstrate, quarter in and quarter out, the ability to produce and sell more without burning through people, capital, and other resources. The grand strategic challenge, the one real leaders set for themselves, is to use lean times like this to transform a company into an organization that knows in its bones how to do more with less—not just now, but forever.[14]

Here corporate frugality is a means to an end and the vision or a story of what it is, where it is going, and why it's worth the pain to get there.

Another place we encounter thrift today is in the history of savings banks. The concept of savings banks can be traced back to 1810, when a parish minister in a small Scottish town encouraged thrift in his congregation and began to collect more than tithes.

Similar institutions sprang up in Australia, New Zealand, and America, mostly out of a religious impetus. By the 1850s, these thrift banks became involved in an activity that has become one of the most sought after: mortgage finance. Later trends included self-reliance and saving for retirement, education, and, of course, more sophisticated investment advice.

Most of the advancements made in savings over the last two centuries would probably be beyond the comprehension of the early founders of thrift institutions. But the reasons for savings, rooted in the concept of thrift, remain the same—to serve communities, to grow and to help people and families grow, and to preserve their wealth. The twenty-first century of wealth management and complex, diversified portfolios are a long way from rural church-based savings, but its rationale remains virtually the same.

This brings us to the so-called *paradox of thrift*. There is a raging debate in many countries around the world about whether people are saving enough for their own good. The importance of saving is rarely debated. But since it involves the sacrifice of consumption today for the sake of future benefits, it is difficult for a household, a business, or a government to decide on the proper or appropriate rate of saving.

Saving behavior has important national and macroeconomic implications that ultimately affect all citizens beyond the realm of their own domestic financial management. It influences the overall performance of an economy and therefore national prosperity and economic growth.

Adam Smith in *Wealth of Nations* argued the virtue of saving as the key to economic progress. Contrast this with John Maynard Keynes who, in his *General Theory of Employment, Interest, and Money*, saw a high savings rate as far from a virtue, as actually undermining prosperity. His argument became the basis of the celebrated paradox of thrift. Economists have debated for decades about some magic number or formulae for the level of savings in a given country. While there are many sides and positions, most see today's savings rates as too low.

Further, there is general agreement that there are often obstacles in an economy in the way the financial and tax systems function that bias individuals and companies toward consumption and away from saving. Removing these inefficiencies and obstacles is, it is argued, paramount so that people and companies can make clear, rational, and informed choices about what is the appropriate level of savings.

Democratic Morality and Our Current Crisis

Hopefully, this makes it clear that economics cannot be so easily separated from morals and character. "Ordinary integrity," Edmund Burke wrote, "must be secured by the ordinary motives to integrity." Thrift, honesty, and ingenious effort are rewarded in economic life. For Burke, "the vast majority work principally out of self-interest, to benefit themselves and their families.[15] There is nothing wrong with this state of affairs; it is merely a condition of ordinary human nature. Competition puts a premium on industry, thrift, honesty, and ingeniousness, for the slothful, the spendthrift, the known cheats, and the stupid fall behind in the economic contest of free enterprise."[16]

In the end, it is true that more than any specific values or virtues, it is the reluctance to speak the language of morality, and to apply moral ideas to social policies, that separates us from the Victorians.

The Victorian virtues, rooted in the Protestant Reformation—work, thrift, temperance, prudence, respectability—are, as others have suggested, quite modest, even mundane. They rest on no special breeding, status, talent, wisdom, grace, or money. They are, in the ultimate sense, democratic.

The Victorians have too often been condemned as materialist, self-righteous, hypocritical, imperialist, and even, worst of all, earnest. Yet as the latest treatment now shows, these "sturdy, steadfast Britons, confronted the most tumultuous challenges: the incredible rise of industrialism, the rapid spread of railroads, the shift from farm labor to work in mines and mills, the teeming swarm to city living, the soul-wrenching clash of new scientific ideas with ancient religious beliefs, and ultimately, the burden of empire."

The Victorian premium on the self—self-help, self-interest, self-control, self-respect, and self-discipline—allowed for a truly liberal society. It upheld the self, not selfishness, in the context of the family, the other mediating "little platoons," and the State.

That society of middle-class adherents anchored in democratic capitalism believed in and required nothing less than a moral citizenry. All of this ties directly to what we call today *corporate governance*. Don't we need better rules and structures, codes, and frameworks to govern corporate activity?

Notes

1. Aneel Karnani, "The Case Against Corporate Social Responsibility," *The Wall Street Journal*, June 14, 2012, online.wsj.com/article/SB1000142405274 8703338004575230112664504890.html.
2. Ibid.

3. http://www.brandindex.com/article/goldman-sachs-reputation-scores-dive.
4. Charlie Gasparino, "John Thain's $87,000 Rug," *The Daily Beast*, January 22, 2009, www.thedailybeast.com/articles/2009/01/22/john-thains-87000-rug .html.
5. *Webster's Dictionary*, 1st edition, 1828.
6. Christopher Lasch, *The True and Only Heaven: Progress and Its Critics* (New York: W.W. Norton, 1991).
7. John De Graff, David Wann, and Thomas H. Naylor, *Affluenza: The All Consuming Epidemic* (San Francisco: Berrett-Koehler Publishers, 2003).
8. John M. Templeton, *Thrift and Generosity: The Joy of Giving* (West Conshohocken, PA: Templeton Foundation, 2004).
9. James Collier, *The Rise of Selfishness in America* (New York: American Philological Association, 1991).
10. Ibid.
11. Ibid.
12. Ibid.
13. Thomas A. Stewart, "12 Management Tips for Slow Times," *Business 2.0*, February 2002.
14. Ibid.
15. *The Best of Edmund Burke: Selected Writings and Speeches* (Washington, DC: Regnery Publishing, 2000).
16. Ibid.

Chapter 11

The Way Back

We conclude *The End of Ethics* with the way back. It is fundamentally necessary to find the map that leads us out of the vice-ridden maze. Yet, in order to find the way back, we must become uncomfortable with where we are now.

We must not blame others for our current ethical malaise because, on a systemic level, vice has consumed us. Our CEOs, presidents, politicians, celebrities, and sports leaders only exhibit the values that we all have accepted on a global level.

Economic vice is everywhere.

Lambast Gordon Gekko all you want as an out-of-control glutton, yet he has his progeny all over the world. This is accepted. This is now the new normal.

We can no longer look to our governments for virtue and pragmatism. They have uniformly betrayed us. Indeed, nearly every post-industrial nation is battling gigantic black holes of public debt. This massive debt could have been easily avoided through prudential sustainability. Yet, world governments have discharged their immense responsibilities as public stewards.

They have unremorsefully maxed out their own credit cards, which, unfortunately, never had a limit and still do not. Rationalizing out-of-control spending when you do not have the money to pay for such costs, now, or ever, is a heinous betrayal of public duties (not to mention future generations) and a manifestation of the classical seven deadly sins on a grand scale.

Sadly, eventual consequences are never considered. Not enough companies, governments, and individuals consider long-term investment. Credit, debt, and risk for the purpose of short-term prosperity have become a tragic universal maxim.

The cases in the first section of the book demonstrate the manifestation of the seven deadly vices in the corporate environment. These vices, once used as a tool to instruct and understand our own weaknesses and temptations, and to help us become better human beings, are now celebrated as beacons of supposed success.

Being greedy, prideful, gluttonous, wrathful, envious, lazy, and obsessed with lust is no longer frowned upon; it is widely celebrated. Deadly vices are no longer seen as evil outcomes; they are now retained societal norms. In fact, our most successful media (books, TV, movies) and public figures celebrate the human manifestation of the classical seven deadly sins.

Our fascination with lust makes sexy books about topics like "S&M" international bestsellers.

Our fascination with greed and envy makes reality TV shows celebrating money, lust, arrogance, and excess immensely popular. A gluttonous "fabulous life" with unaffordable personal assets is the new American, if not global, dream. Worse, it is accepted that we should commit whatever acts are necessary, regardless of their ethical consequences, to get there.

Why should we expect more from our corporate leaders?

Our CEOs are only citizens, just like you and me, in a global society that has systemically rejected moral fiber and sound governance. Part One of this book shows that we have reached the end of the ethical road.

The solutions recommended in Part Two come with a critical caveat. We cannot rest on our laurels. We cannot expect others to make this society better for us without our active participation. Aggressive civic involvement is essential. Personal responsibility is the starting point.

If we wish for global business and markets to become more ethical and decent, we must look within ourselves. No silver-tongued politician, authentic CEO, or other leader can systemically create change for us. Catchy slogans are fables. Personal accountability is pure necessity.

In today's world, we can accept fraud, corruption, and scandal as established norms and outcomes of our societal fabric; in fact, we already have. Or, we can expect more. We can expect the opposite, a more virtuous and honorable path.

Expecting more does not just mean reforming government legislation and implementing tougher rules that rein in our fallen heroes on Wall Street. Expecting more means knowing that, in many cases, the villain lies within us.

The End of Ethics has arrived. It is up to people everywhere and the institutions they rely on to find the way back.

Appendix

Below is a broad sample corporate governance questionnaire the authors of this book recommend as a means to inspire best practices, ethics, and value for modern corporations. These are questions any board of director or corporate fiduciary should consider when making decisions on the institutional level.

Corporate Objectives

a. Does your company have a tangible plan to create long-term, sustainable shareholder value?
Yes ☐ No ☐

b. Does this plan involve corporate social responsibility components?
Yes ☐ No ☐

c. Is there an established and transparent procedure for making decisions regarding corporate objectives and strategy?
Yes ☐ No ☐

d. Has the corporation retained independent consultants or advisers in the last five years for the purpose of developing long-term corporate strategy?
Yes ☐   No ☐

Composition of Board

a. Are there identifiable internal controls to ensure directors do not engage in self-dealing?
Yes ☐   No ☐

b. Does your board have effective debate around current operations, including weighing all potential risks?
Yes ☐   No ☐

c. Does the board have significant independent leadership?
Yes ☐   No ☐

d. Does the board create and maintain a culture of transparency and openness?
Yes ☐   No ☐

e. Are a diversity of views expressed and encouraged within the board?
Yes ☐   No ☐

f. Are various competences and diversity of perspectives present on the board?
Yes ☐   No ☐

g. Does the nonexecutive element on the board have enough information and knowledge of the business to contribute effectively?
Yes ☐   No ☐

Risk Management

a. Does the board have directors familiar with GAAP rules and procedures?
Yes ☐   No ☐

b. Does the board have transparent procedures in place to measure market risk?
Yes ☐   No ☐

c. Is compliance with these procedures checked daily?
Yes ☐ No ☐

d. Does the board have transparent procedures in place to measure credit risk?
Yes ☐ No ☐

e. Is compliance with these procedures checked daily?
Yes ☐ No ☐

f. Does the board have transparent procedures in place to measure operational risk?
Yes ☐ No ☐

g. Is compliance with these procedures checked daily?
Yes ☐ No ☐

h. Does the corporation have procedures in place to monitor threats to reputational risk?
Yes ☐ No ☐

i. Does the board stress talent and experience among its risk management personnel?
Yes ☐ No ☐

j. Does the board take all concerns, memos, and opinions of risk personnel seriously?
Yes ☐ No ☐

k. Does the board have a procedure in place to resolve disputes between front-office employees and risk management?
Yes ☐ No ☐

l. Does the board have a weekly briefing from risk personnel?
Yes ☐ No ☐

m. Does the board have a monthly briefing from risk personnel?
Yes ☐ No ☐

n. Does the corporation have established risk limits for all business sectors?
Yes ☐ No ☐

o. Does the corporation have procedures for monitoring compliance with such limits on a daily basis?
Yes ☐ No ☐

p. Does the corporation have procedures in place to expediently rectify breach of such limits?
Yes ☐ No ☐

q. Does the board actively oversee the integrity of its internal audit team?
Yes ☐ No ☐

r. Have any recommendations from the internal audit team been implemented in the last year?
Yes ☐ No ☐

s. Does the corporation have procedures in place to encourage potential whistleblowing personnel to come forward?
Yes ☐ No ☐

t. Are independent, neutral personnel involved in assessing the validity of whistleblowing claims?
Yes ☐ No ☐

Sarbanes–Oxley Compliance (Public Companies Only)

a. Does the board have procedures in place to ensure active compliance with Sarbanes–Oxley rules?
Yes ☐ No ☐

b. Is Sarbanes–Oxley compliance reviewed on a quarterly basis through internal audits?
Yes ☐ No ☐

c. Does the board have procedures in place to ensure Sarbanes–Oxley section 401 disclosures are accurate and transparent?
Yes ☐ No ☐

d. Are Sarbanes–Oxley 404 reports computed in accordance with Public Company Accounting Oversight Board recommendations and best practices?
Yes ☐ No ☐

e. Does the board have a committee, division, or another specialized team to effectively manage the firm's Sarbanes–Oxley 404 responsibilities and ensure best practices are followed?
Yes ☐ No ☐

f. If so, is this group of persons independent of the board of directors?
Yes ☐   No ☐

g. Does the corporation have an identifiable set of procedures in place to prevent management override of internal controls?
Yes ☐   No ☐

Board Governance

a. Does the board have a formal and transparent nomination process?
Yes ☐   No ☐

b. Does the board have procedures in place to monitor executive performance?
Yes ☐   No ☐

c. Is there an objective process of self-evaluation and behavior and effectiveness?
Yes ☐   No ☐

d. Does the board have criteria for replacing directors?
Yes ☐   No ☐

e. Is director compensation aligned with performance?
Yes ☐   No ☐

f. Is director compensation based on the salaries of competing positions and industry standard?
Yes ☐   No ☐

g. Does the board have procedures in place to debate and approve the validity of board of director loans?
Yes ☐   No ☐

h. Has the corporation loaned a board member money in the last five years?
Yes ☐   No ☐

i. Does the corporation have a plan to actively monitor and research all board conflicts of interest?
Yes ☐   No ☐

j. Has the corporation identified any conflicts of interest in the last five years?
Yes ☐   No ☐

k. If so, has the conflicted board member been allowed to debate or vote on the matter of conflict?
Yes ☐   No ☐

l. Is full disclosure required of all outside roles and positions any board member participates in?
Yes ☐   No ☐

m. Are there any former corporate employees on the board of directors?
Yes ☐   No ☐

n. Have those directors had a number of years outside the company before joining the board?
Yes ☐   No ☐

o. Does the company disclose to shareholders updates to its active compliance with all mandatory rules of board independence?
Yes ☐   No ☐

p. Does the board have a separate subcommittee for risk management?
Yes ☐   No ☐

q. If the company is an investment bank, does the board have an independent subcommittee on mark-to-market pricing?
Yes ☐   No ☐

r. Does the board have a separate subcommittee for firm ethics?
Yes ☐   No ☐

s. Does the board have a separate subcommittee for internal audit?
Yes ☐   No ☐

t. Does the board have a separate compensation subcommittee?
Yes ☐   No ☐

u. Does the board have a separate subcommittee for director nomination?
Yes ☐   No ☐

v. Do subcommittees report to the board on a monthly basis?
Yes ☐   No ☐

w. Does the board disclose the working procedures of all subcommittees?
Yes ☐   No ☐

The Board Chairman

a. Does the chair make provision for the flow of information to directors?
Yes ☐ No ☐

b. Does the chairman encourage board debate?
Yes ☐ No ☐

c. Does the chair provide, create, and maintain a culture of openness?
Yes ☐ No ☐

d. Is the chair a former CEO?
Yes ☐ No ☐

e. Does the chair participate in executive remuneration plans?
Yes ☐ No ☐

f. Is the chair available to shareholders for questions and or dialogue?
Yes ☐ No ☐

Firm Compensation

a. Is remuneration for all senior managers disclosed?
Yes ☐ No ☐

b. Is executive-level compensation performance based?
Yes ☐ No ☐

c. If so, does the company employ tangible criteria to measure executive-level performance for compensation purposes?
Yes ☐ No ☐

d. Is pay for nonexecutive directors structured?
Yes ☐ No ☐

Corporate Culture

a. Is there an ascertainable company culture that ensures employees engage in appropriate behavior?
Yes ☐ No ☐

b. Does the board have open initiatives to encourage ethics in corporate culture?
Yes ☐ No ☐

c. Does the company have a code of ethics manual? Or similar code of conduct?
Yes ☐ No ☐

d. Does the code of ethics or conduct cover both internal and external stakeholders?
Yes ☐ No ☐

e. Is the code of ethics or conduct integrated into company strategy and operations?
Yes ☐ No ☐

f. If so, does the company have procedures in place to ensure that this code is adhered to across the business?
Yes ☐ No ☐

g. Are yearly ethical audits performed?
Yes ☐ No ☐

h. Is there a chief ethics officer?
Yes ☐ No ☐

i. Does the corporation have an ethical hotline with a neutral third party addressing questions and internal reporting of malfeasance?
Yes ☐ No ☐

j. Is ethics training conducted on a quarterly basis?
Yes ☐ No ☐

Crisis Management

a. Does the corporation have a plan for times of market crisis and black swan scenarios?
Yes ☐ No ☐

b. Does the corporation have long-term sources of financing?
Yes ☐ No ☐

c. Does the corporation maintain capital reserves in excess of Basel, SEC, and other regulatory requirements?
Yes ☐ No ☐

About the Authors

Ted Roosevelt Malloch serves as research professor for the Spiritual Capital Initiative at Yale University and as a senior fellow at Wolfson College, Oxford University. His most recent books concern the nature of virtuous enterprise, the practices of practical wisdom as "virtuous business," the pursuit of happiness, generosity and the virtues of thrift. He is also chairman and chief executive officer of The Roosevelt Group, a leading strategic management and thought leadership company. He has served on the executive board of the World Economic Forum (DAVOS); has held an ambassadorial level position at the United Nations in Geneva, Switzerland; worked in the U.S. State Department and Senate; worked in capital markets at Salomon Brothers on Wall Street; and has sat on a number of corporate, mutual fund, and not-for-profit boards. Ted earned his PhD in international political economy from the University of Toronto and took his BA from Gordon College and an M.Litt. from the University of Aberdeen on a St. Andrews Fellowship. He is frequently on TV and featured as a keynote speaker.

Jordan Mamorsky is an attorney specializing in business regulation, corporate governance, and compliance. He was a postdoctoral fellow at Yale University, where his research focused on the legal, financial, and ethical failures that contribute to financial crisis, corporate illegality, and breach of legal fiduciary duties. Jordan formerly worked at the U.S. Treasury Department, where he received the "special act award" in recognition of his recommendations detailing the dangers of predatory subprime lending in low-income communities. He is a contributor to *Morningstar Advisor*. He is an active practicing attorney and has represented Fortune 500 companies, global investment banks, insurance companies, hedge funds managers, health services corporations, and an international sports league, among other clients.

Index